C000042347

# BICHON FRISE
## AN OWNER'S COMPANION

## Chris Wyatt

The Crowood Press

First published in 1999 by
The Crowood Press Ltd
Ramsbury, Marlborough
Wiltshire SN8 2HR

© Chris Wyatt 1999

All rights reserved. No part of this publication may be reproduced or transmitted in any form or by any means, electronic or mechanical, including photocopying, recording, or any information storage and retrieval system, without permission in writing from the publishers.

**British Library Cataloguing-in-Publication Data**
A catalogue record for this book is available from the British Library.

ISBN 1 86126 196 9

**Dedication**
This book is dedicated to my late Mother Phyllis Munford, who was always very frightened of all dogs until my involvement with the Bichon Frise. After taking in and being totally captivated by Maddy – rescued from a puppy farm in a terrible state – she grew to love the breed as I do, and to play a very active part in everything involving our Bichons. She passed away in July 1994 with her beloved Teide and Emily, her constant companions, at her side. Without the unconditional love, support and complete confidence she always showed me, in anything I did, I would never have presumed I could attempt such a task as writing a book about the dogs that gave her so much pleasure.

**Acknowledgements**
I should like to thank Roy Kelman Jack for putting together such a huge amount of information and allowing me to use it when writing the history of our breed. Roger Dunger has been especially helpful and supportive, both as friend and advisor, at times when confidence was running a little low. I am grateful to my breeder friends, who rose above any egotistic thoughts and took time to share their valuable knowledge and experience. I would also like to thank my vet, Robin Peal, BSc, BVM&S, MRCVS, for his valuable help and advice with the veterinary content; Andrew Brace for his marvellous example of critique writing at its best; Den Thomas for his article on sportsmanship (taken from the first SBFBA year book); and Tamara Dawson, for her contribution on junior handling, and her mother, Val Cumpstey, for her unlimited support.

Finally, many thanks go to all the exhibitors who contributed photographs, and the photographers who allowed them to be reprinted in this book.

**Picture credits**
Pete Adey, page 22; BDM Photography, page 8 (left); David Bull, pages 87, 90; Roger Chambers, page 65; David Dalton, pages 4, 188 (left), 194, 202; John Daniels, 46, 55; Thomas Fall, pages 135, 144; Gerald Foyle, page 117; Dave Freeman, pages 17 (left), 122; John Hartley, pages 17 (right), 60, 70, 73, 185 (right); Heritage Studios, page 146; Steph Holbrook, pages 47, 125; Paddy Holbrook O'Hara, 12 (bottom), 182; Carol Ann Johnson, pages 185 (left), 193; Keeling & Freemantle, page 136; Linda Lindt Photo Studio, page 173; David J. Lindsay, page 131; Diane Pearce, pages 8 (right), 20 (top), 109; Robinson, page 170; Norman Stapely, pages 58, 68, 114, 174, 210 (left); Ernie Steele, page 119; G. Stein, page 138; Michael M. Trafford, pages 196, 221; Alan V. Walker, pages 183, 188 (right), 216; Lionel Young, page 12 (top).

Line-drawings by Annette Findlay.

Edited and designed by OutHouse Publishing Services

Printed and bound in Great Britain by WBC Book Manufacturers, Mid Glamorgan

# Contents

| | | |
|---|---|---|
| 1 | The History of the Breed | 5 |
| 2 | The Breed Standard | 27 |
| 3 | Choosing a Puppy | 48 |
| 4 | Care and Management | 63 |
| 5 | Grooming and Coat Presentation | 80 |
| 6 | Showing | 104 |
| 7 | Judging | 124 |
| 8 | Breeding | 133 |
| 9 | Pregnancy and Whelping | 147 |
| 10 | Ailments and Diseases | 159 |
| 11 | The Bichon Around the World | 169 |
| | Bibliography | 223 |
| | Index | 224 |

*Ch. Fatal Attraction at Pamplona.*

# 1

# The History of the Breed

The origins of the Bichon Frise Tenerife, also sometimes referred to as the Bichon, can be traced back no further than the early 1920s with any real accuracy because records of early litters are very scant. It is a popular notion that through earlier centuries, a white, curly-coated, lap dog, very similar to our Bichon, graced the French court, and there are several great works of art that illustrate this; one such is *Marie Anne Carolus-Duran* (1874), by Emile Carolus-Duran, now in the Fine Arts Museum of San Francisco. The best-known example is the famous painting by Sir Joshua Reynolds (1723–1792), which depicts Miss Nelly O'Brian with a little dog on her lap that is very like our Bichon. However, the painting that in my view contains the finest example is the one entitled *A Bichon*, by the Dutch painter Henriette Ronner Knip (1821–1909). Unfortunately, the work is undated, but is assumed to have been produced during the 1890s.

There is no doubt that the Bichon type has existed for many years, for it is known to have been used as barter by the early sailors who traded around the Mediterranean. This white, curly-coated dog developed into the breeds that form the same Barbichon group: the Maltese, the Havanese, the Bolognese, the Coton de Tulear and, most likely, the Löwchen (or Little Lion Dog). It wasn't until a dedicated group of people in France decided to typify the Bichon type and develop it that it became a breed with its own identity. They purchased many dogs from many different sources and some of these appear in the stud registry in France earlier than 1933. A breeding programme took place and the best offspring were given Belgian registration so that they could be shown in Belgium. When the breed was finally recognized in France, and listed in a separate registry in October 1934, many of these dogs were transferred straight over to the French Register.

In Belgium, the first kennel to establish a Bichon affix was that of M. and Mme A. Bellotte, and their Milton line is easily traced back to their first litter registered on 18 December 1929. The first dog (Pitou, born 23 March 1924) was bought from Mr J. Gillis. Both of Pitou's parents were

5

*Early Bichon, photographed around 1920.*

*The postcard sent to Mademoiselle Serens in 1912.*

unregistered. The Bellotte's breeding programme was to provide the foundation stock for kennels around the world. After a break during the Second World War, breeding resumed and the Bellottes continued to produce Belgian champions. One of them, Youbi of Milton, produced Bellot of Milton who was exported to France to the Valmasque kennels of Madeliene Schlumberger. With him went a son who was exported to Germany in 1954 and helped establish the breed there alongside the first registered Bichon in Germany, Dodine De Steren Vor, a French-born dog. During the early 1960s, three significant Belgian kennels, Villa-Sainval (Mrs Andree Berben), Persaliere (Mrs M. Huvenne), and Chaponay (Mr and Mrs Vansteekiste-Deleu) produced a further fifty Bichons from Milton stock. These kennels developed the lines further within their own breeding programmes and exported dogs abroad. Bichons from these easily recognized kennels were sent to the USA, Canada, France, Holland and Great Britain.

After a further break of three years, the Bellottes started breeding again and produced Karine of Milton, who was sold to the Roi Des Lutins kennels of Mme Janine Naudet in France. This bitch was the grandmother of the two well-known Bichons Lassy of Milton and Lyne of Milton, bought by Gertrude Fournier of the Cali Cols kennel in California in 1962. Lyne's grandson, Am. Ch. Chaminade Mr Beau Monde, was probably the most famous Bichon in the world.

# The First UK Imports

The majority of the Continental Bichons that formed the foundation of the breed in the UK were descended from the Milton kennels and were brought to England via the United States. The Milton kennel produced its last litter in 1970; all three puppies were exported to America.

On 6 February 1974, five puppies were born from a mating of Ra-Va's Regal Valor and Jenny Vive de Carlise. These dogs belonged to Mr and Mrs Sorstein, who had come to the UK from America and brought their Bichons with them. Little was known of the breed at that time and people were only just learning about it. Two – Carlise Cicero of Tresilva and Carlise Circe of Tresilva – were sold to Jackie Ransom, and the remaining three went back to America. From an accidental brother/sister mating, Mrs Ransom's two dogs produced a first Bichon for Eleanor Bothwell (Norcis) and Katrinka of Tresilva for Pauline Block (Twinley). A third puppy, Bianca of Tresilva, was kept.

During 1974, interest in the UK grew and several breeders imported dogs from both the Continent and from America. For a while these imported dogs were described as American type or Continental type. At the time breeders were divided in their preferences, but in retrospect it can be seen that the existence of the two types was of advantage to UK breeders. Early breeding programmes were able to utilize dogs from both sources. It was also fortuitous that a number of dogs came into the UK at around the same time, as this meant that there was a larger gene pool than would have been available had a single breeder struggled to establish a new breed alone.

Mrs Sorstein repeated the mating of Ra Va's Regal Valor and Jenny Vive de Carlise and on 1 March 1975 a second litter was born – two dogs and three bitches. Carlise's Something Else was sold to Mr and Mrs Cormack (Diavolo), Carlise Canny Caprise went to Mrs E. Mirylees (Beaupres), Carlise Columbine went to Chris Coley (Glenfolly), and Carlise Calypso Orion to Vera Goold and Derick Chiverton (Leijazulip).

Eilish Banks already had a dog in quarantine when the first litter was born: Cluneen Javelot De Warnabry was Mrs Sorstein's, imported in 1974 from Madame S. Mazeas Nicholas, who also sent Mrs Banks Cluneen Jesse De Warnabry and Cluneen Jonquille De Warnabry in

Druidswood Belle Ami, born 30 November
1979, owned by Tom Mather.

Austral. Ch. Beau Monde The Dove of
Leander, bred by Rick Beauchamp, and
later sent to Australia.

1975. This mating produced five puppies, one of which started the
well-known Appleacre line for Paddy Holbrook O'Hara.

At this time Wendy Streatfield was importing dogs from America –
an American Champion bitch, C&D's Beau Monde Sunflower, whelped
four puppies on 9 September 1975 while still in quarantine. Of these,
Leander Beau Monde Snow Puff went to Chris Coley, Leander Snow
Carol was owned in partnership with Sally Wheeler, and Leander
Arden went to Madeline Harper (Huntglen). Around the same time
another litter, owned by Pauline Block, was born in quarantine. There
were five puppies: Twinley Tiberius, Twinley Claudius, Twinley Cae-
sar, Twinley Josie Posie, and Twinley Chou Chou. Twinley Claudius
went to Tom Mather (Barklots), and Twinley Josie Posie became Graham Newells' foundation bitch for his Dokham kennel.

In these first couple of years, a total of thirty-three Bichons were
brought into England from the States and the Continent. Many of these
early breeders were experienced dog people whose skills as dog breeders were very important in establishing the Bichon in the show world.
Mr and Mrs Hobart's early Kennel Club registration of their pet dog,
Espor du Kloziers, allowed the breed to be registered immediately in
1974. The first Bichon to be shown in the UK was Eilish Banks's Cluneen
Ledjerdell Tarz Anna, a bitch bred in America by her friends J. and D.
Podell. She was entered and won Best Not Separately Classified class
at Leeds Championship Show and also won at the following WELKS
(West of England Ladies' Kennel Society) show, and Birmingham and
Bath championship shows. In the meantime, Jackie Ransom started

showing her puppy Carlise Cicero at open shows and he soon started accumulating first places. There were no classes for Bichons at this time, but when they were scheduled in October 1974 at South Eastern Toy Dog Society, Cicero won Best of Breed and Best Puppy in Show. He was later sent to Australia where he became a champion.

Even though the kennels that acquired the first dogs bred many litters, demand for this rare breed was very high and outstripped supply. Loyalties were quick to develop, and when I came into the breed only a few years later people were still talking in terms of the Continental Bichon versus the American Bichon. There did seem to be two different types that supposedly had emerged from the different breeding programmes. However, these descriptions diminished by the time the British Bichon had become established and people learned that all Bichons had the same ability to produce both types, sometimes in the same litter. I think, when we recall the early Bichons, some individual dogs stand out as being as good as the dog in the ring today. However, there is now overall a greater depth of quality throughout the breed than there was in the early days.

## Development and Progress

The breed continued to grow but, like anything new that has to be developed to progress properly, direction was needed. The breed could be judged in Rare Breed and Not Separately Classified classes, but it was not until 1980 that Champion status was granted. On 17 April 1976, many prestigious names from the world of dogs came together to hold the first meeting for the founder members of the Bichon Frise Club. Officers were elected. Miss Ferelith Hamilton (now Somerfield), chairman of *Dog World* newspaper, was elected as patron. Mrs Jackie Ransom became president and secretary, and Mr S. Kitrick FTA became treasurer. Vice-presidents were Mrs Eilish Banks, who is still a serving member of the original committee, and Mr Lionel Hamilton Renwick, who was later to have the honour of being the first judge to award Challenge Certificates.

The club was recognized by the Kennel Club in July 1977. Membership grew considerably as many new Bichon fanciers from Britain and abroad joined and boosted membership to around 250. The first Bichon club show was held in the following year on 7 January 1978 at Wembley Park in Middlesex. Seventy-eight dogs were exhibited by forty-two exhibitors. As can be seen from the class results given overleaf, some classes were filled better than others. Some of the imports were shown in the top classes, and Best in Show was Am. Ch. Vogelflight's Choir Boy of Leander, handled and owned by Wendy Streatfield. Best Opposite Sex and Best Puppy in Show was Ann Worth's Glenfolly Silver Lady of Sarabande (by Leander Beau Monde Snow Puff out of Carlise Columbine), bred in quarantine by Chris Coley. The judge that day was Miss L. Graham-Weall MBE.

## Class Results

### MINOR PUPPY DOG
1. Cluneen Jolly Jason
2. Pyrillion Coconut Truffle
3. Twinley Choirmaster of Chitina

4. Barryville Oscar Le Grand
5. Pyrillion Rum Truffle

### MINOR PUPPY BITCH
1. Huntglen Marie-Louise
2. Cluneen Jolly Jennifer
3. Pyrillion Lemon Truffle of Chitina
4. Cluneen Jolly Jemimah
5. Pyrillion Cherry Truffle

### PUPPY DOG
1. Cluneen Jolly Jason

2. Montravia Leander Snow Fox
3. Leander Snow Swept
4. –

5. –

### PUPPY BITCH
1. Glenfolly Silver Lady of Sarabande
2. Huntglen Marie-Louise
3. Leander Snow Show
4. Leijazulip Sabina of Colhamdon
5. Cluneen Jolly Jennifer

### JUNIOR DOG
1. Leijazulip George

2. Tresilva Ariel of Cathay
3. Cluneen Fancy Free

4. Twinley Monsieur Patapouf
5. –

### JUNIOR BITCH
1. Devon's Heavens to Betsy of Leander
2. Leander Snow Show
3. Leijazulip Sabina of Colhamdon
4. Leander Snow Witch
5. Cluneen Jolly Jennifer

### MAIDEN DOG
1. Leijazulip George
2. Twinley Boule de Neige

3. Leander Snow Swept

4. Twinley Monsieur Patapouf
5. –

### MAIDEN BITCH
1. C&D's Milkpunch of Leander
2. Dokham's Esclarmonde of Twinley
3. Cluneen Good Grace at Appleacre
4. Leijazulip The Snowmaiden
5. –

NOVICE DOG
1. Leijazulip The Boyfriend

2. Twinley Boule De Neige
3. Leijazulip George
4. Twinley Tiberius

5. Twinley Boule Neige

NOVICE BITCH
1. Glenfolly Silver Lady of
   Sarabande
2. C&D's Milkpunch of Leander
3. Twinley Josie Posie
4. Dokham's Esclarmonde of
   Twinley
5. Katrinka of Carlise's of
   Twinley

POST GRADUATE DOG
1. Astir de Chaponay of Twinley
2. Beaupres Bouffe

3. Leijazulip The Boyfriend
4. Twinley Claudius

5. Twinley Boule De Neige

POST GRADUATE BITCH
1. Leander Snow Crystal
2. Beaupres Blythe Spirit of
   Bochin
3. Twinley Josie Posie
4. Cluneen Jacinthe De
   Wanarbry
5. –

OPEN DOG
1. Am. Ch. Vogelflight's Choir
   Boy of Leander

2. Astir De Chaponay of Twinley
3. Astor De Villa Sainval of
   Littlecourt
4. Beaupres Bouffe
5. –

OPEN BITCH
1. Leander Beau Monde Snow
   Carol

2. Leander Snow Crystal
3. –

4. –
5. –

As soon as any breed is granted championship status the stakes become higher and the will to win at shows becomes greater. The first champion of any new breed is guaranteed recognition forever in the history books, and so everyone was keen to achieve this particular prize. There were quite a few contenders, and it must have been a very exciting time.Andrew Brace, a well-known breeder, exhibitor, judge and writer, captured the atmosphere of keen competition in that first year:

Few breeds have soared in popularity in the British ring as quickly and with such impact as the Bichon and, just five years after they were first noticed, the Kennel Club decreed that Bichons should be awarded Challenge Certificates at six championship shows.

*Aust. Ch. Astir de Chaponey of Twinley, bred in Belgium by Mme A. Berben and imported to the UK by Pauline Block, was exhibited at the first Bichon Frise Club Show in 1978.*

Virtually since the breed appeared there has been a worrying split within the breed as to what type is correct, and arguments over the Continental versus the American type have been long and heated. The British Kennel Club issued an interim Standard, and later a permanent standard, and it is this latter Standard that all judges should adhere to when judging the Breed in the UK. When I judged the breed at Bath Championship Show last year, I was disturbed at the number of Bichons that struck me as being out of balance, i.e. 'too much length for height', overlong muzzles and heavy bone. This cloddy type of animal did not portray the dainty little toy dog that the Standard conveys to me, and many of the dogs that were unnervingly Poodle-like in many respects also had harsh wiry jackets which are untypical of the breed whose individual coat is so important.

Latterly we have seen several Bichons rise to prominence, and to date the only one to top the toy group in the UK is the Streatfield's USA import Vogelflight Choir

*Cluneen Good Grace at Appleacre.*

12

Boy of Leander. This he did at Bath two years ago. At Bath 1979 I finished with a half-brother and sister as my Best of Sex, and I considered on that day that Gosmore Tresilva Zorba and Gosmore Tresilva Crystal were of the right balance and type, both had superb heads and expressions, and their coats were right. Crystal took Best of Breed as I liked her neck and front better than the dog. Both at the time were owned by the well-known all-rounder Audrey Dallison whose Gosmore kennel has housed many great dogs in a variety of breeds. Zorba was handled by professional handler Geoff Corish, and Crystal by teenager Anthea Colvin. Crystal later passed into Anthea's ownership, and Zorba subsequently went back to his breeder Jackie Ransom, the pioneer of the breed in Britain and the secretary of the breed club. Zorba has remained with Geoff as far as handling goes.

Six shows in 1980 were to have Bichon Challenge Certificates. The first of course was Crufts, held in London, and here the judge was to be Lionel Hamilton Renwick. His Birling kennel has made a great impact in Min Pins [Miniature Pinschers] but his interest in Dobermans and Pharaoh Hounds is also well known. Mr Hamilton-Renwick awards CCs in a variety of breeds and is a much respected all-rounder of international note. The second CC was given at the United Kingdom Toydog Society Show, the only group championship show we have. Here the judge was Terry Thorn. Mr Thorn's original breed was the Saluki, and his Talawi kennel has made up a string of great champions over the years. Since turning his attention to judging Mr Thorn has awarded CCs in various breeds in the hound, working, utility and toy groups and is one of our most celebrated younger judges. The third set of CCs was given to Birmingham National, one of the biggest shows in the world, and I was passed by the Kennel Club to judge at this show.

The Scottish Kennel Club had the fourth set of CCs, and here we saw the breed's first specialist judge in action as Wendy Streatfield was chosen for the job. Wendy's successes in Poodles are legendary, and of course she owned the Kerry Blue that was imported from the States and went Best in Show at Crufts. Since taking on the Bichon, Wendy has built up a very strong kennel which has influenced the breed in various countries. At the Welsh Kennel Club, to whom the fifth set of CCs went, the judge was to be Muriel Lewin, already a great breeder of the Elwin Maltese and a judge of them, of course. She has shown Bichons for some time. The final set of CCs in 1980 will be at Driffield, when Graham Newell officiates. A committee member of the Bichon Club Graham is best known for the world famous Dokham Tibetan Terriers, in which breed he has bred and made up several champions. He awards CCs in various utility breeds.

At Crufts and the UK Toydog Society show, both certificates went to the same dog and bitch: Gosmore Tresilva Zorba, the dog, and Glenfolly Silver Lady of Sarabande, the bitch. The dog took Best of Breed at Crufts and the bitch did so at UK Toydog Society. Silver Lady is owned by a young couple, Ann and Nigel Worth, and is owner-handled. Ann presents her with the help of Paul Williams, a young

Poodle enthusiast who handles and prepares many winning dogs quite brilliantly. He piloted the American-sired Ch. Sablecomb Colomba, a spectacular white Standard Poodle, to Best in Show at Richmond last year under Stanley Dangerfield.

I suppose I had a difficult job in having to award the third set of tickets [Challenge Certificates] as those third tickets could make up two champions. Really, there was no way I could win, for if I put up the same dogs I would be accused of following fashion, and if I did something different I would be accused of trying to be sensational. As it was, I just tried to judge the dogs as I saw them on the day. It was the biggest entry of Bichons seen in the UK to date. The quality was high right through, and it amazes me how the breed had managed to level off in just a year. Most of my winners were well balanced with the right heads and good coats, though they had *all* been barbered far more than the Standard really allows. When it came to my dog Challenge I was torn between two. Zorba had taken the Open dog class, but in Limit I had a youngster who was a complete stranger to me. I thought he was quite breathtaking – beautiful outline, superb movement, and no exaggeration anywhere. Total quality and fabulous ring presence. Zorba's head is classic and that is his really outstanding point. He has a good coat texture, but in the Challenge I felt his front action couldn't match the Limit dog, Leijazulip Kipling of Shamaney, and he didn't have that youthful sparkle and zest. Thus it was I decided on Kipling for the ticket and Zorba the Reserve. I felt for Jackie Ransom, and sporting Geoff Corish, Zorba's handler, as they obviously hoped to make Zorba into the first champion in the UK, but I genuinely felt unable to do it on the day.

*Ch. Leijazulip Kipling of Shamaney.*

14

In bitches, Gosmore Tresilva Crystal won Limit and Silver Lady the Open class. Crystal is exquisite for type and, like Zorba, she has a dreamy head and eyes. She is so feminine and typey all through but her hind action really let her down. Silver Lady is now more finished than she was at Bath when I just gave her a first. And she has a pleasing head, and is very sound on the move. She's a tough bitch to fault and she goes. On the day I felt she deserved the ticket and thus it was that she got her third ticket and consequently her championship. History had been made and I was happy to have played a part in it. For Best of Breed I still couldn't get past Kipling, and he was kept in the final four in the group under Bob Flavell, which pleased me no end.

We now have our first champion, and the breed is going from strength to strength. When I analysed my results, I discovered I had put up both a Continental and American-bred dogs, so it is obvious that both can produce the same type that appeals. I had several youngsters that were in Puppy and Junior that have what it takes to become champions, and in particular the Leander and Montravia kennels have some really stunning youngsters coming along.

I feel sure the breed is now on a more even keel, and if breeders and exhibitors can forget politics and nationalities, the British Bichon will take a Group – of that I am certain.

Andrew was quite right with his prediction: Jo Brown's (now Emerson) Leijazulip Jazz of Zudiki won the Group under judge Nora Down at the Welsh Kennel Club show in 1982. He had just gained his title that day. The breed was judged by Jackie Ransom.

During the early 1980s, the breed continued to grow as more people became captivated by it, not only as a very attractive show dog that can demand attention at any level but also as a pet. Veterinary surgeons became more familiar with the breed and its attributes, and it was not long before they were recommending the breed to many different types of owner. They appeal to young families because of their gentle yet playful and kindly nature, yet they easily adapt to a more sedate life with the elderly. In twenty-four years the numbers of Bichon registered at the Kennel Club has gone from six in 1974 to 2,758 in 1998. They have increased every year, except in 1988 when thirty-four fewer Bichons were registered than in 1987.

By the end of the first year of 1980, when CCs were first on offer, the breed had its first two champions. Zorba was made up at Wales, the judge was Muriel Lewin. The following year, three more champions were made up: Ch. Montravia Persan Make Mine Mink, a bitch, Ch. Montravia Snow Dream, both from the Gibb's Montravia kennel, and Ch. Cluneen Jolly Jason of Hunkidori, the young dog that had won Best Dog Puppy at the first club show.

In 1982 there were a further five sets of CCs, but in spite of this only three more gained their titles: Bernise Perry's Ch. Persan Top Button, Jill Buxton's Ch. Effaldees Angelic Faith, and (the only dog) Jo Brown's Ch. Leijazulip Jazz of Zudiki. The following year many of the existing champions continued to win well, but four Bichons started the year with a single CC already under their belt. A young dog that had been spotted by Andrew Brace back in 1980, Ch. Leijazulip Kipling of Shamaney, joined his illustrious brother Jazz, both boys to make a serious impression on the breed in the future. Chris Belcher and Richard Blackwell made up their first champion, Snarsnoz Dancing Rhythm at Melsel, and shortly afterwards, at LKA (Ladies' Kennel Association) show, Ch. Snarsnoz Show Quest at Melsel, a full brother from a repeat mating, was also crowned. Ch. Rossage Royal Snow Queen at Maybeth gained her title for her owner and breeder Betty Satchell, and a young bitch, Ch. Kynismar Blackeyed Susie, won her third CC, and thus her title, on her second birthday and made history by being the first bitch to win a group as well. Susie was the first of a string of champions for Myra Atkins.

In 1984, more sets of CCs were on offer, which is not surprising considering that some shows were attracting entries of over a hundred dogs. The CCs were being awarded to many different dogs as the judging became more varied. Only five new dogs gained their titles: Ch. Sulyka Snoopy was a first for Sue and Roger Dunger; Marie and George Armstrong got their third at Windsor for Ch. Caywood Little Jack Horner, bred by Sue Baker; Sally Wheeler's Ch. Leander the Sundancer became Top Bichon of the Year and went Reserve Best in Show at UK Toydog Society, and Ch. Si'bon Jasmyn, a young bitch owned and bred by Marion Binder, took her first CC while still a puppy and became a champion at fourteen months.

In 1985 there were sixteen shows offering CCs. A single dog, Ch. Tiopepi Mad Louie of Pamplona, burst on to the scene for Michael Coad and breeder Clare Coxall, known better for her Poodles. Ch. Hunkidori Personality Miss became a second champion for Judy Fender, and this time home bred. Ch. Pengorse Felicity of Tresilva was another champion for Jackie Ransom, bred by Mrs Bendall and usually handled by sister-in-law Marjorie.

We now had a total of twenty-one champions in the breed. Bichons were doing well at all levels. New people were coming into the breed from other breeds while others were totally new to dogs. Entries were really high even by today's standards, and it was not unusual to see twenty minor puppies in a class, especially in bitches. The following year, 1986, saw the battle of the giants. Mad Louie was hugely successful, gaining thirteen of the nineteen available CCs. Myra Atkins introduced young Ch. Kynismar Blackeyed Boogaloo. Ch Rossage Silver Locket and Ch. Bumblerides Overture of Rossage were two more champion bitches for Betty Satchell. Pat Farmer started a super career for her young bitch who had been so successful as a puppy, Ch. Melsel Cracklin' Rosie, who went on to become the breed record holder in bitches with twenty-one CCs.

In 1987, Mad Louie won only eight CCs (they were running out of judges that hadn't already given him a CC). Instead, he won the Group at Crufts, the only Bichon to do it, a record that still stands today. There were now twenty-two sets of CCs available for that breed, and some new people were ready to hit the top spots. My own Ch. Bobander Toot the Flute, and another Snoopy offspring Ch. Emmril Snow Pippit owned by Harry and Jean Frith, both got their titles in Scotland under Ellis Hulme. A Kipling daughter, Ch. Roushka's Song and Dance, was Steven Thompson's first champion. Ch. Edelweiss Ebony Eyes was Eileen Beeson's first, and Ch. Melsel Cracklin' Rose gathered another ten CCs for her collection.

In 1988, Ch. Si'bon Sloane Ranger, owned by Michael Coad and bred by Marion Binder was made up, and Myra Atkins introduced a young Boogaloo son, Ch. Kynismar Boogies Boy. She had also bought back a

*Ch. Kynismar Boogies Boy.*

*Ch. Kynismar Heaven Sent to Roushkas.*

17

bitch, Ch. Kynismar Heaven Sent to Roushka, which she had sold to Den Thomas. Heaven Sent had already gained a CC while she was still a puppy and before she was owned by Myra. This bitch's career was to span four years, and it was she that beat Ch. Melsel Cracklin' Rosie's total of twenty-one CCs by one. Liz Fellow's Ligray kennel had been established in the early days of the Bichon's arrival in Britain, but until now had not made up any champions. In 1988, they made up two, Ch. Ligray Mr Beau Geste and Ch. Ligray Smarty Pants of Ricanna, co-bred with Liz Jones and owned by Ann Stafferton. They were handled by Liz's partner Brian Diaper. In this same year, Linda and Barry Gisborne made up their first champion, Melsel Kiss Me Kate, bred by Chris Belcher.

The Northern and Midland Bichon Frise Club gained championship show status, and the number of CCs swelled to twenty-four. Five dogs were crowned: Ch. Kynismar Billy the Kid, for Myra Atkins; Betty Satchell's dog Ch. Rossage Silver Ghost; Ch. Sulyka Puzzle, a second champion for Sue Dunger; Ch. Orpheus Orion at Atroya (bred by Mrs Bignell), a first champion for Helen Banfield; and Ch. Rusmar Xmas Magic, a first champion for Dawn Russell. Bitches were dominated by Ch. Kynismar Heaven Sent and another one from Michael Coad, Ch. Si'bon Fatal Attraction at Pamplona, who was bought as a junior from Marion Binder.

In 1990, ten years after championship status was granted, there were twenty-six sets of tickets and entries were at an all-time high. At the Bichon Frise Club of Great Britain (B.F.C.G.B.) Show, there were 125 dogs entered. There were five new male champions, but only two females: Denis Diamond's Ch. Ligray Diamond Lil, bred by Liz Fellows and Sally Wheeler, and Wendy Streatfield's Ch. Leander Snow Cat. Michael Coad bred Ch. Pamplona Chances Are for Molly Harris's first champion, and Steve Thompson bred his Ch. Stevos Stand 'n' Deliver. Ch. Melsel Mystic Moses was Linda and Barry Gisborne's second champion from Chris Belcher, and Myra Atkins made up another champion, Kynismar Blackeyed Mr Magoo. Lesley Macleod made up her first champion, Atroya Punchinello of Languilla bred by Helen Banfield, and Michael Coad's Ch. Si'bon Fatal Attraction at Pamplona took most of the bitch tickets, sixteen in all.

There were four new male champions in 1991. Anthea Pleasants (née Colvin) made up her first champion, Vythea Jumpin' Jack Flash, and won the Group at Richmond as well. Jayne Smith's home-bred Ch. Avana Madam I'm Adam won seven of the CCs. Ch. Ligray Desperate to be Dan, owned by Mr and Mrs Lewis and handled by Brian Diaper, gained his title, and Tresilva Toby of Suanalu became a first for Joan

Gadd-Davis, crowned while in the capable hands of Michael Coad and Geoff Corish. In bitches, Claire Kaye's bitch, Ch. Terracita Bossa Nova Baby, handled by Brian Diaper, was impressive and snatched thirteen of the CCs and ended up top Bichon for that year. Although Fatal was still notching up more wins to inflate her total even more, she allowed a litter-mate, Ch. Harene Beatrice Anne at Pamplona, to take six of them and collect her crown in style.

The number of CCs offered for the breed reached its peak in 1992: there were twenty-nine in all. Every show had Bichons classified – even Belfast in Ireland now had CCs. It was certainly a bumper year for champions, and twelve Bichons were crowned. Ch. Sargetta Davilliam of Bylena was a first for his breeder Kathleen Page and his owner-handler, Lena Martindale. Ch. Alareen Precious Sundancer was a first champion out of a litter for Maureen and Alan Miles. I made up my second champion, Bobander Magic in the Air, and another Xmas Magic son, Dawn Russell's Ch. Rusmar Magic Minstrel, got his all-important third. Sue Dunger made up a first champion, Honeylyn Timmy Tiptoes To Sulyka, for breeder Brenda Ellis. Myra Atkins had been fairly quiet the year before so made up for lost ground by making up two this year, Ch. Kynismar Heaven Forbid and Ch. Kynismar Cherished Heaven. Sue Dunger was on a roll and made up a Puzzle daughter for breeder Denise Cleave with her own Ch. Kennichen Sweet Lucinda. Anthea Pleasants, too, followed her success with Jack and brought out his daughter, bred by Mrs Blake, Ch. Snow White Pipah at Vythea, proving that as well as breeding good dogs she could also spot them in others' litters! Joan Gadd Davis campaigned another Tresilva-bred Bichon, Ch. Tresilva Minuette of Honeylyn, and Linda and Barry Gisborne bred their own Ch. Lynelba Kiss Me Freely, who also won the Group in Scotland the day of her first CC. Ch. Eithlynn Unforgettable was a first English champion for young Linda Robinson, not long over from Ireland and already successful over there.

In 1993 there were another twenty-nine sets, and three more of each sex gained their titles: Dawn Russell's Ch Rusmar Magic Rainbow, destined to become so famous abroad and at home; Michael Coad's and Geoff Corish's Ch. Pamplona Latest Attraction gained his title at Leeds; and the Vythea and Melsel kennels joined forces to produce Ch. Vythea Jack's the Lad at Melsel. In bitches, Joan Gadd-Davis gathered the three CCs required to crown Tresilva Little Madam at Suanalu. Louise Stafford from Wales made up her first home-bred champion Louisiana Highland Fling, while Marilyn and Terry Holgate's made up a first champion with their home-bred bitch, Clanmarret Gemini

*Ch. Pamplona Latest Attraction.*

Moon. Highland Fling and Gemini Moon were to take a major portion of the bitch tickets in 1993.

In 1994 there were another twelve titles, two of which were mine I'm delighted to record. Ch. Bobander What Ho Bertie and Ch. Bobander Spring in the Air, both Magic in the Air offspring, together with a third gaining a single CC, made me top breeder that year. There was another champion for Joan Gadd-Davis, this time a dog, Ch. Tresilva Snowdon at Suanalu. Hilary Stapely made up her boy, Ch Fougere Winging Willie, a Puzzle son, after a monumental career as a puppy.

*Ch. Bobander What Ho Bertie.*

Newcomers, Colin and Cynthia Caspall, bought a dog from breeder Lyn Webster and promptly made him up – Ch. Pomlyn Fancy Man at Colynthia. A son of Ch. Tiopepi Mad Louie of Pamplona, Ch. Hylacer Northern Topic, broke new ground for Les and Brenda Dickinson, and Ann and Lawrence Lee saw their future change with the crowning of their first champion, Warmingham Hobson's Choice. Making her first English champion was a new experience for Irish breeder Marie Renahan; Ch. Spelga Sweet Heaven was also a first in England for breeder Pat Keery, although she did part-own Ch. Alareen Precious Sundancer. From Cornwall, Peter and Sylvia Cole would experience their first big win with home-bred champion Penwyvern Silk Collection, and Sue Dunger would make up another Bichon bred by Brenda Ellis, Honeylyn Step in Style to Sulyka.

Ch. Rusmar Magic Flame was Dawn Russell's fourth champion, and Margaret Hoad's patience paid off when she made up her home-bred Ch. Mahendi Miss Bliss with tickets to spare. Another exhibitor new to us all, Linda Clarke, showed her bitch, Ch. Eithlynn Vanessa, two years running at Leeds and got the CC each time. She showed her rarely, but turned up at Crufts and took her third CC and Best of Breed as well.

In 1995 there were five dog and seven bitch new champions. Myra Atkins started the ball rolling with Ch. Kynismar Feels Like Heaven, making up her ninth champion, all home bred. Ch. Fougere Baggy Britches was a successful repeat mating for Hilary Stapely, and Dawn Russell bought in Ch. Rusmar Divine Rainbow, a divine little dog that was all her own breeding from Ian Watts in Scotland. Ch. Ridgegrove White Idol was a dream come true for new exhibitor June Wilson: this was her first Bichon. It had been a while since Eileen Beeston had made up a champion, but she returned to the top spot at speed with Fionavar Billy Whizzes about Asilene, bred by Maureen and John Reynolds. Sid and Mary Hicks crowned their first boy Ch. Hicker Luke Who's Here. The Mileses went to early breeder Judy Fender for a Puzzle daughter and made Ch. Hunkidori Miss Serendipity of Alareen into a champion. A first champion for Doreen Harvey was named Ch. Frendors Georgeous Gabby. Nick Skeets made up Ch. Leading Lady from Riordan, with a little help from Michael Coad and Geoff Corish. Margaret Moss bought a puppy from Lena Martindale, Ch. Bylena Me and My Girl, who was also crowned that year. Diane Story took just enough time off from her valuable work rescuing Bichons to gain a crown for her Ch. Strydonia Precious Angel. And a very youthful Tamara Dawson ran from winning the international Junior Handling title into the ring at Crufts, where she started an illustrious career for her Ch. Tamalva Keep

*Ch. & NZ Grand Ch. Rusmar Magic Rainbow.*

the Faith for Mistama by winning her first CC and Best of Breed, followed by fourth in Group. Ch. Warmingham Crack of Dawn was crowned by me in my capacity as judge at LKA, the last show of the year. She was the breed's one hundredth champion.

In 1996, Ch. Appleacres Any Dream Will Do was a first in Bichons for Paddy Holbrook O'Hara; this was certainly a dream come true for Paddy. Ch. Lynelba Per Se was another champion for Linda and Barry Gisborne; this boy had taken his first CC as a puppy. There was a new champion dog for Betty and Roy Kelman-Jack, Ch. Shoolters What's is Name – an unlikely name for a dog belonging to the two people who have just about every fact and figure concerning the breed at their fingertips. My own Ch. Bobander Secret in the Air gained her crown, giving my Ch. Bobander Magic in the Air his third champion offspring.

Another young bitch to emerge as quite a star was Warmingham Scarlet O'Hara, another champion for Ann and Lawrence Lee, who were continuing to come up trumps each time they used Dawn Russell's dog, Ch. Rusmar Magic Rainbow. Before 1997 was out, yet another two champions were added to this total. One of them owned by Dawn herself, Ch. Warmington Reflections, won CCs when the Lees left Scarlet at home – and sometimes when they didn't. Ch. Atroya Christmas Gift delighted his owners, the Caspalls and his breeder,

Helen Banfield, by winning the Group at Windsor. Eng. & Irish Ch. Spelga Solitaire was a second champion for Irish breeder, Pat Keery.

The next year, 1997, started with a bang for two exhibitors, both of whom made up their dogs at Crufts, which is the start of the season for most of us since the number of CCs was cut to twenty-six. Ch. Fionavar Miss Kitty was the first owner-bred champion for John and Maureen Reynolds. Another first was Terry Burgess' Ch. Dobrugh Zig, who was four years old before he got his magic third ticket. Doreen Harvey's first bitch champion had a son, Ch. Frendors Spitting Image, who was certainly well named. Ch. Riordon The Beach Boy at Canengis was made up through the team efforts of owner Nick Skeet, and handler Michael Coad. Ch. Ronamars Freddy Farns Barns was Jean and Tony Youe's first taste of success; as a groomer, Jean already had a head start and Freddy is always presented to perfection.

Peter and Sylvia Cole's Ch. Penwyvern White Diamond, sired by local dog Ch. Riordon Beach Boy at Canengis, and previously Top Puppy in the breed, won Best of Breed at Crufts in 1996. Ch. Akwasulis Chuckles Charlie, bred by Sylvia Thomas, was campaigned by the sire's breeders, Maureen and Alan Miles, for Mr and Mrs Neil Baxter. The year concluded at LKA with Sue Dunger making up her fifth champion, Ch. Sulyka Happy Hurbert.

No doubt some of the breeders and exhibitors will fall by the wayside and others will go from strength to strength. Some will achieve all they have set out to do and others will not. The last two years have been good for the breed. The number of Bichons appearing in the ring seems to have diminished, but I am convinced this is a result of the costs involved in travelling to and from shows rather than a symptom of problems relating directly to the breed itself. Some of the big breeders and exhibitors have almost disappeared owing to ill health or advancement in years, and most of the big names are no longer seen in the champions' lists. Their legacy, however, lives on in our dogs – proof of their success in developing our breed.

# Breed Clubs

The first Bichon club was founded just a few years after the breed was introduced. Its formation was essential if the breed was to be accepted and provisions made for its development. As the breed increased in numbers individuals started new clubs in new areas, each functioning alongside the parent club. The Kennel Club is the governing body for all canine affairs in Great Britain, but it will approach an individual club on matters regarding the specific breed, its welfare and general business.

It is generally considered that the people who run these clubs are in some position of power, and to some extent they are. The club's committee lays down rules concerning qualifications when judging, and it is also responsible for the approval of new judges. The organization of club shows and the choice of judges can be quite a responsibility, for committee approval of a judge is taken into account when the Kennel Club considers whether that individual should award CCs. In view of the importance of such decisions, it follows that club-committee members should be experienced people in the breed; it is not enough merely to be willing to serve.

It is also the responsibility of a club to educate its members and keep them informed about anything that is of interest; to this end, clubs publish a newsletter a couple of times a year. In addition to organizing shows, clubs provide many other opportunities – at educational events, Christmas parties, Easter parades – for members to meet each other with their dogs. This means that there are plenty of events for those who do not show their dogs but just enjoy Bichon ownership. In this breed there is the added responsibility of providing grooming workshops in different areas of the country for those who wish to learn for themselves the correct way to groom and trim their dog. Each club will provide a rescue service, and keep a puppy register and a list of professional groomers in every area. The clubs are involved with everything that may affect the welfare of the Bichon Frise.

Each of the regional clubs has its own character and each club's strengths are dictated by the type of people who work on its committees. A brief history of each of the regional clubs is outlined here.

The inaugural meeting of the Northern and Midland Bichon Frise Club was held in Eccleston in October 1979. Mrs Dorothy Garlick was elected as chairman, Tom Mather as treasurer, Liz Fellows as secretary and Paddy Holbrook O'Hara as assistant secretary. The original committee members were Val Blore, Jayne Broadhurst, Chris Coley, Pat Farmer, Eileen Spavin, Sally Wheeler and Les Dickinson. The club was granted recognition on 9 March 1982, by which time Paddy had taken over the reins as secretary.

There had already been two informal gatherings but permission was needed to hold a show. Pamela Cross-Stern judged at the first official show, which was held at Baginton in Coventry on 17 October 1982. The club was soon awarded championship show status and held its first championship show in October 1986; again Mrs Pamela Cross-Stern was the judge. There were 115 entries. The Dog CC went to went to Myra Atkins's Ch. Kynismar Blackeyed Boogaloo and the Reserve CC to my Bobander the Muffin Man. The Bitch CC went to Sally Wheeler's Ch. Leander the Sundancer, the Reserve CC to Ch. Melsel Cracklin' Rosie. Best in show was Boogaloo, and Best Puppy in Show was Maggie Message's Barnaby The Sundancer.

The Mid-Eastern Counties Bichon Frise Club was set up primarily through the efforts of Liz Fellows and her partner Brian Diaper, both of whom were very experienced in the breed and had already been responsible for establishing and running the successful Lincoln Toydog Society. The club's inaugural meeting was held on 21 November 1986, with Les Dickinson as chairman, Brian as vice-chairman, Liz as secretary, and Roger Richardson as treasurer. The patron is Joyce Mann. The committee included Brenda Dickinson, Judy Lloyd, Miss Godsell, Mrs Richards, and Brenda and Gordon Ellis.

The club's first show was held at Kegworth Village Hall in Leicestershire on 18 September and attracted 117 entries. Joyce Mitchell judged the dogs, and Betty Kelman Jack judged the bitches. Best Dog and Best in Show was Eileen Beeston's Ch. Edelweiss Ebony Eyes; Best Bitch and Reserve Best in Show was a junior bitch, Clanmarrett Crazy Moon, owned and bred by Terry and Marilyn Holgate; Best Puppy in Show was Brenda and Gordon Ellis's Sulyka Sasha of Honeylyn from the puppy bitch class. This club was soon awarded championship show status, and its particularly lovely show, held in summer in excellent surroundings, continues to be one of the highlights of the Bichon exhibitor's calendar.

The Southern Bichon Frise Breeders Association is a bit different from the other clubs in that the purpose of its formation was not to run shows. It was the brainchild of Helen Banfield, who felt there was a need for an organization that concentrated on educating Bichon owners, especially those who were not particularly interested in the showing side. These people had very little opportunity to learn about the breed and, especially, little or no instruction in the art of trimming. (In theory the purpose of this club did not differ from that of the others, but in practice, financial considerations meant that a club's profit-making events, such as championship shows, tend to take priority.) Helen and Alan Banfield and Sue and Roger Dunger met with other friends who wanted to pursue the idea, and the new club was formed in 1986.

The first committee was headed by Roger Dunger as chairman, Helen Banfield as secretary, Andre Etienne as treasurer, Mark Hutchings as president, and Peter Bedford as vice-president. Jackie Ransom became patron and Sue Dunger had the special role of activities co-ordinator – an important job, considering the main purpose of the club. The committee consisted of Andre's wife, Angela, Den Thomas, Steven Thompson, and Alan Banfield. This club implemented a rather unusual, two-tiered membership system: full membership is given to established breeders and exhibitors; and associate membership is reserved for people who have very little interest in the breeding and exhibiting side of the Bichon world and yet would benefit from the activities enjoyed by all the members.

In keeping with the club's philosophy, the club's first major event was not a show but an extremely ambitious seminar, which was held at the Ramada Hotel in Reading. The speakers were Rick Beauchamp, Peter Bedford (vice-president and distinguished vet), and Dr Roger Mugford (familiar to most people as an expert on dog behaviour). The day was an enormous success and extremely well-attended. However, in time the club came under increasing pressure to run shows. Finally, the committee capitulated and held its first open show in 1988, although it was organized with education in mind. The aim was to give quite new judges the opportunity to judge a club show while at the same time providing a relaxed atmosphere in which associate members might have a go at exhibiting their dogs, many for the first time. When still more pressure was applied, and the more serious financial advantages of running a championship show considered, championship show status was achieved. However, after only two years the club lost its allocation of CCs – not through any fault of its own, but as a result of the CC cuts made by the Kennel Club. The cuts affected all breeds and all the major championship shows.

## The Super Match

Over the last few years a different event has emerged, and drawn attention from others outside the breed. The Northern and Midland Club worked alongside the Southern Breeders Association to host a Super Match at which a single dog would be proclaimed 'Bichon of the Year'. To qualify, a dog must have been awarded a Reserve CC during the previous year. These dogs are judged in pairs on a knock-out basis by one of three championship show judges until a winner is declared. A similar competition is run for Best Puppy. The Parade of Champions at the end is a highlight, especially for the dogs that may not be being actively campaigned any more. If anyone harbours any doubts about whether dogs enjoy showing, this event will dispel them: the excitement of some of the older dogs, as they are brought out to be seen again, is obvious.

# 2

# The Breed Standard

A breed standard describes the features of a particular breed. The picture created by the standard is the ideal, by which any specimen of that breed should be judged, and towards the attainment of which any breeder strives. However, each individual will inevitably interpret a standard slightly differently from the next, or place slightly more importance on one characteristic than another. This is why it is impossible to guarantee which dog any one judge might consider to be superior to all the others. The matter is made more complicated by the fact that the wording of the standard is not always as clear as one might wish. For this reason it is worth familiarizing oneself with the Bichon standards produced by both the American and UK kennel clubs, as well as the first Standard, produced by the Societé Centrale in France, in 1933. All three are reproduced here.

## The UK Breed Standard
(Reproduced by kind permission of the Kennel Club.)

### General Appearance

Well balanced dog of smart appearance, closely coated with handsome plume carried over the back. Natural white coat curling loosely. Head carriage proud and high.

### Characteristics

Gay, happy, lively little dog.

### Temperament

Friendly and outgoing.

## Head and Skull

Ratio of muzzle length to skull length 3:5. On a head of the correct width and length, lines drawn between the outer corners of the eyes and nose will create a near equilateral triangle. Whole head in balance with body. Muzzle not thick, nor heavy, nor snipey. Cheeks flat, not very strongly muscled. Stop moderate but definite, hollow between eyebrows just visible. Skull slightly rounded, not coarse, with hair accentuating rounded appearance. Nose large, round, black, soft and shiny.

## Eyes

Dark, round with black eye rims, surrounded by dark haloes, consisting of well-pigmented skin. Forward-looking, fairly large but not almond shaped, neither obliquely set nor protruding. Showing no white when looking forward. Alert, full of expression.

## Ears

Hanging close to head, well covered with flowing hair longer than leathers, set on slightly higher than eye level and rather forward on skull. Carried forward when dog alert, forward edge touching skull. Leather reaching approximately half-way along muzzle.

## Mouth

Jaws strong with a perfect, regular and complete scissor bite, i.e. the upper teeth closely overlapping the lower teeth and set square to the jaw. Full dentition desirable. Lips fine, fairly tight and completely black.

## Neck

Arched neck fairly long, about one-third the length of the body. Carried high and proudly. Round and slim near head, gradually broadening to fit smoothly into shoulders.

## Forequarters

Shoulders oblique, not prominent, equal in length to upper arm. Upper arm fits close to body. Legs straight, perpendicular, when seen from front; not too finely boned. Pasterns short and straight viewed from front, very slightly sloping viewed from side.

## Body

Forechest well developed, deep brisket. Ribs well sprung, floating ribs not terminating abruptly. Loin broad, well muscled, slightly arched and well tucked up. Pelvis broad, croup slightly rounded. Length from withers to tailset should equal the height from withers to ground.

## Hindquarters

Thighs broad and well rounded. Stifles well bent; hocks well angulated and metatarsals perpendicular.

## Feet

Tight, rounded and well knuckled up. Pads black. Nails preferably black.

## Tail

Normally carried raised and curved gracefully over the back but not tightly curled. Never docked. Carried in line with backbone, only hair touching the back; tail itself not in contact. Set on level with topline neither too high nor too low. Corkscrew tail undesirable.

## Gait/Movement

Balanced and effortless with an easy reach and drive, maintaining a steady and level topline. Legs moving straight along line of travel, with hind pads showing.

## Coat

Fine, silky, with soft corkscrew curls. Neither flat nor corded, and measuring 7–10cms (3–4in) in length. The dog may be presented untrimmed or have muzzle and feet slightly tidied up.

## Colour

White, but cream or apricot markings acceptable up to 18 months. Under white coat, dark pigment is desirable. Black–blue or beige markings often found on the skin.

## Size

Ideal height 23–28cm (9–11in) at withers.

## Faults

Any departure from the foregoing points should be considered a fault, and the seriousness with which the fault should be regarded should be in exact proportion to its degree.

**Note** Male animals should have two apparently normal testicles fully descended into the scrotum.

# The American Breed Standard
(Reproduced by kind permission of the American Kennel Club.)

## General Appearance

The Bichon Frise is a small, sturdy, white powder-puff of a dog whose merry temperament is evidenced by his plumed tail carried jauntily over the back and his dark-eyed inquisitive expression. This is a breed that has no gross or incapacitating exaggerations, and therefore there is no inherent reason for lack of balance or unsound movement.

Any deviation from the ideal described in the Standard should be penalized to the extent of the deviation. Structural faults common to all breeds are as undesirable in the Bichon Frise as in any other breed, even though such faults may not be specifically mentioned in the Standard.

## Size, Proportion, Substance

**Size** Dogs and bitches 9½ inches to 11½ inches to be given primary preference. Only where the comparative superiority of a specimen outside this range clearly justifies it, should greater latitude be taken. In no case, however, should this latitude ever extend over 12 inches or under 9 inches. The minimum limits do not apply to puppies. **Proportion** The body, from the forward-most point of the chest to the point of the rump, is a quarter longer than the height at the withers. The body from the withers to the lowest point of the chest represents half the distance from withers to the ground. **Substance** Compact and of medium bone throughout: neither coarse nor fine.

## Head

**Expression** Soft, dark-eyed, inquisitive, alert. Eyes are round, black or dark brown and are set in the skull to look directly forward. An overly large or bulging eye is a fault, as is an almond-shaped, obliquely set eye. Halos, the black or very dark skin surrounding the eye, are necessary as they accentuate the eye and enhance the expression. The eye rims themselves must be black. Broken pigment, or total absence of pigment on the eye rims produce a blank and staring expression, which is a definite fault. Eyes of any color other than black or dark brown are a very serious fault and must be severely penalized. **Ears** are drop and covered with long flowing hair. When extended towards the nose, the leathers reach approximately half-way along the muzzle. They are set on slightly higher than eye level and rather forward on the skull, so that when the dog is alert they serve to frame the face. The **skull** is slightly rounded, allowing for a round and forward-looking eye. The **stop** is slightly accentuated. **Muzzle** A properly balanced head is three parts muzzle to five parts skull, measured from the nose to the stop and from the stop to the occiput. A line drawn between the outside corners of the eyes and the nose will create a near equilateral triangle. There is a slight degree of chiseling under the eyes, but not so much as to result in a weak or snipey foreface. The lower jaw is strong. The **nose** is prominent and always black. Lips are black, fine, never drooping. **Bite** is scissors. A bite which is undershot or overshot should be severely penalized. A crooked or out of line tooth is permissible, however. Missing teeth are to be severely faulted.

## Neck, Topline and Body

The arched **neck** is long and carried proudly behind an erect head. It blends smoothly into the shoulders. The length of neck from occiput to withers is approximately one third the distance from forechest to buttocks. The **topline** is level except for a slight muscular arch over the loin. **Body** The chest is well developed and wide enough to allow free and unrestricted movement of the front legs. The lowest point of the chest extends at least to the elbow. The ribcage is moderately sprung and extends back to a short and muscular loin. The forechest is well pronounced and protrudes slightly forward at the point of the shoulder. The underline has a moderate tuck-up. **Tail** is well plumed, set on level with the topline and curved gracefully over the back so that the hair of the tail rests on the back. When the tail is extended towards the head it reaches at least half-way to the withers. A low tail set, a tail carried perpendicularly to the back, or a tail which droops behind is to be severely penalized. A corkscrew tail is a very serious fault.

## Forequarters

**Shoulders** The shoulder blade, upper arm and forearm are approximately equal in length. The shoulders are laid back to somewhat near a forty-five degree angle. The upper arm extends well back so the elbow is placed directly below the withers when viewed from the side. **Legs** are of medium bone; straight, with no bow or curve in the forearm or wrist. The elbows are held close to the body. The **pasterns** slope slightly from the vertical. The dewclaws may be removed. The **feet** are tight and round, resembling those of a cat, and point forward, turning neither in nor out. **Pads** are black. **Nails** are kept short.

## Hindquarters

The hindquarters are of medium bone, well regulated with muscular thighs and spaced moderately wide. The upper and lower thigh are nearly equal in length, meeting at a well-bent stifle joint. The leg from hock joint to foot pad is perpendicular to the ground. Dewclaws may be removed. Paws are tight and round with black pads.

## Coat

The texture of the coat is of utmost importance. The undercoat is soft and dense, the outercoat of a coarser and curlier texture. The combination of the two gives a soft but substantial feel to the touch, which is similar to plush or velvet, and when patted it springs back. When bathed and brushed, it stands off the body, creating an overall powder-puff appearance. A wiry coat is not desirable. A limp, silky coat, a coat that lies down, or a lack of undercoat are very serious faults. **Trimming** The coat is trimmed to reveal the natural outline of the body. It is rounded off from any direction and never cut so short as to create an overly trimmed or squared-off appearance. The furnishings of the head, beard, moustache, ears and tail are left longer. The longer head hair is trimmed to create an overall rounded impression. The topline is trimmed to appear level. The coat is long enough to maintain the powder-puff look which is characteristic of the breed.

## Color

**Color** is white, may have shadings of buff, cream or apricot on the ears or on the body. Any color in excess of 10 per cent of the entire coat of a mature specimen is a fault and should be penalized, but color of the accepted shadings should not be faulted in puppies.

## Gait

Movement at a trot is free, precise and effortless. In profile the forelegs and hind legs extend equally with an easy reach and drive that maintain a steady topline. When moving, the head and neck remain somewhat erect and as speed increases there is a very slight convergence of legs towards the centre line. Moving away, the hindquarters travel with moderate width between them and the footpads can be seen. Coming and going, his movement is precise and true.

## Temperament

Gentle mannered, sensitive, playful and affectionate. A cheerful attitude is the hallmark of the breed and one should settle for nothing less.

# The First Breed Standard

This Standard was adopted by the Societé Centrale in France in March 1933.

## General Appearance

A little dog, gay and joyful, with a medium-sized muzzle and long hair curling loosely. Dark eyes are bright and expressive. Viewed from the side, gives a slightly roached appearance.

# Head

The cranium is larger than the nose and will measure from approximately 2 inches to 3½ inches. The nose is rounded, definitely black, smooth and glossy. **Lips** Fine, somewhat dry but less so than the Schipperke, never drooping or heavy. They are normally pigmented black. The lower lip should not be heavy or noticeable but should not be soft and should not let the mucous membrane show when the mouth is closed. **Mouth** Normal; the foreteeth of the lower jaw should be against and behind the upper teeth. **Muzzle** Should not be thick and heavy, but not pinched. The cheeks are flat and not muscular, the stop accentuated slightly. **Eyes** Dark, as much as possible surrounded by black. Rather round and not almond shaped. They should not be placed at an oblique angle. Lively, not too large, not showing any white when looking forward. They should not be too big and prominent like the Pekingese. The eye socket should not sag and the eye globe should not bulge in an exaggerated manner. **Cranium** Rather flat to the touch although the fur gives a round appearance. **Ears** Drooping, well covered with long wavy hair, carried forward when at attention. The length of the cartilage cannot reach the truffle, as the French Poodle, but only half-way the length of the muzzle. In fact they are not as large, and they are finer, than those of the Poodle.

# Crest (Neck)

Rather long. Carried highly and proudly, it is round and fine close to the cranium, widening gradually to meet the withers. Its length is approximately one third the length of the body (proportion being about 4½ inches to 13½ inches for a subject for a subject 11 inches high).

# Withers

Rather oblique, not prominent, giving the appearance of being as long as the forearm, approximately 4 inches. Forearm should not be spread out from the body and the elbow, in particular, should not point outward.

# Legs

Straight when looking from the front, of good standing, of fine bones, the pastern short and straight when viewed from the front, very slightly oblique from the profile view. The toenails should be black by preference but it is difficult to obtain.

## Chest

Well-developed, the sternum is pronounced, the lower ribs rather round and not ending abruptly, the chest being horizontally rather deep. The flanks are close to the belly, the skin is fine and not floating.

## Loin

Large and muscular. The hock is more elbowed than the Poodle.

## Tail

Normally carried upwards and gracefully curved over the dorsal spine. The hair of the tail is long and will lie on the back.

## Pigmentation

Under the white hair the skin is preferably dark. The sexual organs are also pigmented black, bluish or beige, as the spots are often found on the body.

## Colour

Preferably all white, sometimes with tan or grey on the ears and body.

## Hair

Fine, silky and loosely curled, its length being approximately 2.5 to 4 inches. Unlike the Maltese, the Bichon Frise also has an undercoat.

## Size

The height at the withers cannot be more than 12 inches, the smaller dog being the element of success.

**Reasons for disqualification:**
Over or undershot, inferior prognathism; pink nose; flesh-coloured lips; pale eyes; tail curled in a corkscrew manner; black spots in the fur.

# Understanding the Standards

On studying the standards it can be seen that the UK Standard appears a little vague when compared with the American one. However, it could be argued that precise descriptions might sometimes be counterproductive when using it to assess the degree of quality in any living being. If someone were to suggest drawing up a breed standard for the human race, we would immediately see the flaws in such an idea, quite apart from the distastefulness of it. One only has to watch a group of runners in a marathon to see how we are all so different and yet the same. They too would fit into a blueprint with slight variations in build, colour and degrees of soundness and yet, like the runners, able to function extremely well in spite of them. I have often watched athletes running and wondered at their ability to perform so well, even though there is always a variety of some extremely bad movement which, if observed in a dog, would be totally unacceptable to an experienced judge.

We have to wonder, then, why we set such standards for our dogs. The main reason is to maintain each breed's individuality so that it will be easily recognized by anyone, just by observing the dog's head alone. It is also worth remembering that most dogs were originally developed to fulfil a purpose: they were bred to do a specific job, and the breed standard would ensure that future dogs were bred with the necessary attributes. As a toy dog, the Bichon has only to bring joy to his owner as a companion, and be a pleasure to look upon. In the Bichon's case, the Breed Standard lays down the characteristics that have endeared them to their enthusiasts, and ensures that the breed

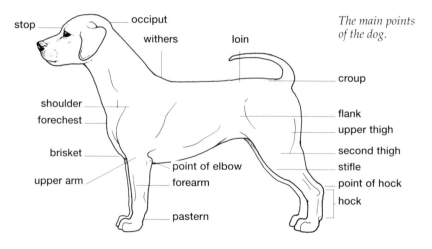

The main points of the dog.

retains the temperament and appearance that enables them to fulfil this particular purpose.

Anyone reading a breed standard for the first time will notice and understand parts of it, but a complete grasp of all the details is possible only as familiarity with the standard is gained. As your knowledge and experience increases, read the Standard again and again: over a time a picture will develop in your mind, and this will be used as your own blueprint for the breed. Most people will have in their minds a picture of a favourite dog – usually a successful champion – and will use this as a reference.

Although the Bichon breed standards all describe the same breed of dog, there are some differences. The most obvious difference is in the permitted size range, which varies from country to country. It will also be noticed that the subject of presentation is referred to in detail only in the American Standard. Other, more minor differences between dogs are primarily the result of individual interpretation. Everyone has a different way of seeing things according to what a particular word or description means to them. If you were to ask a number of people to define 'coarse' or 'medium', you could expect as many answers as people you asked. Some would consider that as the Standard is only a guideline then the slight variations in type that we see is not only to be expected but to be considered an advantage. If the Standard was more precise than it is now, and judges adhered to it rigidly, the range of dogs achieving success in the show ring would be greatly reduced. Would that be healthy for the breed? I think not. Of course, there will always be those people who do not judge exactly to the Breed Standard, but I am not convinced that they would stick to it better even if it was clearer and more detailed.

Size seems to present a problem in the UK. It would be unfair to say that judges are unconcerned with size, but it would appear that many judges do not place the overall height of a dog very high on the list when assessing the overall qualities of a dog. The range of size allowed for in the Standard is quite considerable (nine to eleven inches), especially when you take into account other details in the Standard: the forequarters must not be too finely boned, and the frame must be substantial enough to support a broad loin, pelvis and thighs, and a well-developed chest; from this description it would not be unrealistic for someone to be looking for a dog that is quite sturdy; but others would allow for more refinement ('not too finely boned' is not the same as 'not finely boned'), and such a dog would show much less substance. A dog only nine inches tall at the withers and finely boned, even if he should be quite well

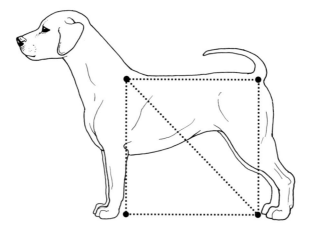

*Basic outline of the Bichon, illustrating the appearance of a square when a line is drawn between the withers and the tail-set, and the withers and the ground.*

covered, could quite realistically be only half the overall size and weight of an eleven-inch dog, and yet both dogs could appear in the same class. Although the breed was considered uniform enough in type to allow the original phrase 'smallness being highly desirable' to be dropped, it might have been wiser to retain it as it encouraged greater consistency.

## Head and Skull

This section of the Standard is self-explanatory, with the exception that many people have some difficulty with the requirement for there to be a near-equilateral triangle between the outer corners of the eyes and nose.

*The outline of the dog, seen beneath the outline of the coat.*

The Standard fails to state whether it is the very tip of the nose that is the point of reference or the point at which the nose begins.

**Eyes**
Another area of confusion is the precise definition of 'dark'. How dark should 'dark' be, and compared to what? However, while the

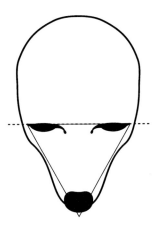

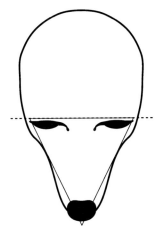

*Diagram showing the correct equilateral triangle on the head, which has the correct ratio of 3:5 and a forward-facing eye.*

*Here the width of the skull is correct but the muzzle is long; the whole balance of the head is lost.*

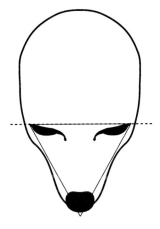

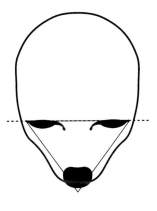

*The triangle is equal and the ratio of 3:5 is maintained; but the skull is narrow, causing the eye placement to become oblique.*

*The correct width is maintained but the muzzle is too short; this may appear attractive but it is just as incorrect as the muzzle that is too long.*

interpretation of this allows for a colour range from black to mid-brown, it is nonetheless sensible to allow for some diversity of colour. Only when the eye colour is sufficiently light to detract from the dog's expression should it be considered as not within the Standard. The dark pigment that is called for around the eye rims is generally accepted as being unbroken, although this is not entirely clear in the Standard. The haloes, however, are pigmented in a way that very often fades in the winter months; a dog whose haloes hold their pigment all the year round is fortunate.

## Neck

The neck must be one third the body length. This is straightforward and not difficult to assess. Rarely does a Bichon have too much neck, and if he did he would rarely be penalized for it. Shortage of neck is much more common and more serious in that it can completely alter the whole balance of a Bichon. Remember, when assessing length of neck, that it should be one third of the whole body length, and not one third of the back length, which of course is a lot shorter.

## Body

This area is described in depth in the standards and should eradicate any confusion that anyone may still have regarding any similarity between a Bichon and a Poodle. The Bichon has substance, and is well rounded, with a deep chest; this depth and substance is relative throughout the

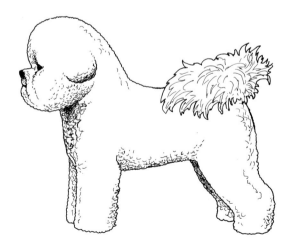

*This dog is too short in neck.*

whole dog. 'Not too finely boned' suggests that we should be looking for a dog that although quite fine in stature and features, should have a well-rounded and substantial feel to him. The requirement that the distance between withers and tail-set should equal that between the withers and the ground, makes more sense if you view your dog as if he had no coat. If you take into consideration correct front assembly, with a well-pronounced chest, and a well-rounded, broad thigh and well-placed tail-set, your Bichon will look longer overall than he may appear in the show ring in full coat.

Stifles must be well bent and hocks well angulated to provide the free and effortless movement that is so characteristic of the breed. The

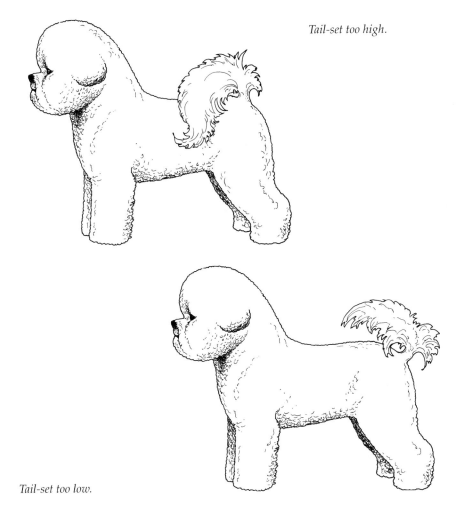

*Tail-set too high.*

*Tail-set too low.*

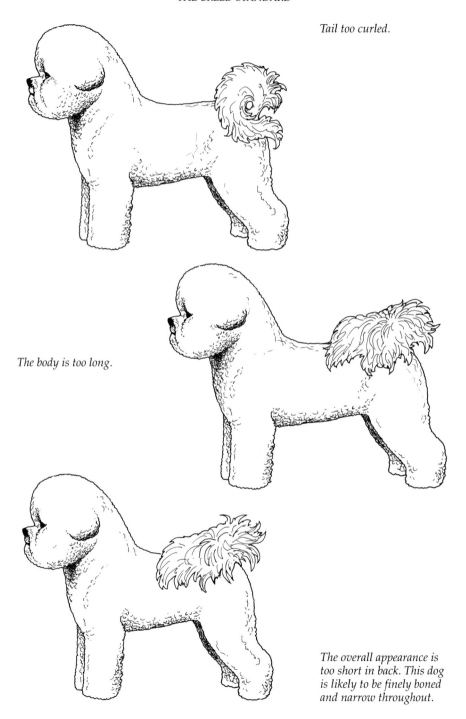

*Tail too curled.*

*The body is too long.*

*The overall appearance is too short in back. This dog is likely to be finely boned and narrow throughout.*

42

hindquarters require the same level of angulation as the shoulder does in the front. Without a sufficient angulation (of approximately 45 degrees) the correct reach and drive will be impossible to attain and the dog will appear to shuffle.

## Gait and Movement

The importance of understanding how a Bichon should move will be everything to some people and of no apparent significance at all to others. 'Legs moving straight along the line of travel' should be easy to understand: one has only to watch a small number of dogs in turn to assess which ones demonstrate what is required in the Standard. However, an understanding of the way dogs move can be extremely useful in that a dog's gait can convey to the experienced eye everything that is right or wrong about the basic conformation of a dog. It will also convey much about the dog's general attitude and temperament, which are very important characteristics of the breed.

## Coat

'Fine, silky, with soft corkscrew curls, neither flat nor corded, and measuring 7–10cm in length. The dog may be presented untrimmed or have the muzzle and feet slightly tidied up.' Here we have quite a problem because all exhibitors in the UK disregard the description. The coat remains fine and silky but the curls are deliberately blow-dried out and

*Poor angulation of the rear may be disguised by profuse hair. A thorough judge will always feel the angulation and not rely just on how it appears.*

the length cut to less than half an inch in places. This practice has been in operation since the breed came to the UK and has become more and more sophisticated as the years have passed. Only in the American Standard is there any mention of a trimming style, but then the practice was developed in the USA and partly responsible for popularizing the breed. It is widely accepted that Bichons are shown trimmed, and many references to the dog's needing better trimming have been made on occasions. Trimming should enhance an already correctly balanced dog, and few judges are fooled completely by clever scissor work. The powder-puff appearance is, unfortunately, easier to achieve if the coat is a little coarser than it should be. However, a correct coat is important to maintain and should be preserved. Judges that have an in-depth knowledge of the breed will look for these features of the coat.

## Colour

The coat must be white, although apricot or cream markings are allowed in young dogs of less than eighteen months. Black, blue or beige markings on the skin are acceptable. In the UK, the dying or bleaching of the coat is illegal. If a Bichon is stained at all – for instance, by eye discharge – the overall attractiveness of the dog is compromised. Most such staining can be avoided by good management. Frequent use of chemical preparations to remove staining will eventually damage the coat.

## Size

Although the size range is generous, I think it is fair to say that a nine-inch mature dog is quite rare and an eleven-inch one is quite common. This is partly because of the popular belief that a flashy eleven-inch dog will attract far more attention in the ring than a nine-inch one. There should be no difference in size between a dog and a bitch, unlike many other breeds where the dog is expected to be a little bigger.

## Temperament

'Friendly and outgoing' is quite self-explanatory. However, it is worthy of comment because although this is so important to the true Bichon character, many breeders pay insufficient regard to it when considering which dog they will campaign. You can have the most physically perfect Bichon in the world, but if his temperament is unsound he is of little use. Bad temperament will be passed on to his progeny as surely as his beautiful head and thick coat. Even if you are able to explain his behaviour as something that someone else has inflicted upon him – and therefore not his fault or yours – you have to accept that some dogs cope with adversity better than others. A truly friendly and outgoing personality will cope far better than the more timid, less typical type. There is nothing more frustrating for an exhibitor than to prepare a Bichon for the ring, pay out entry fees, and travel many miles to a show, only to find that the dog will not keep his tail up or backs away from the judge in the ring. It can be just as frustrating for the judge as well, especially if the dog is clearly the physically superior specimen in that class.

## Faults

'Any departure from the foregoing points should be considered a fault and the seriousness with which the fault should be regarded should be in exact proportion to its degree.'

The way in which anyone regards a fault and its impact on the dog as a whole is to a great extent a personal matter that develops with experience of the breed. It is important to decide which faults you are prepared to accept, all else being equal, and which you consider to be unforgivable. In the earlier standards, an undershot or overshot mouth was a disqualification, as was a wry or open bite, pink nose and lips, light eyes, corkscrew tail, and black spots in the fur. No dog with any of these faults would have been shown. Since the Standard was reworded such dogs can be shown, but generally the severity with which these faults were considered has stayed with most of us. Nowadays, it is not uncommon to see a dog being shown with a slightly faded nose – not pink in the true sense, but not black either. I personally find it easy to decide whether a nose is faded enough to consider it a serious fault: if the paleness does not alter the expression of the dog I will let it pass; if the pigment is also poor around the haloes, giving the dog a bland expression, I will not. Eye colour works in the same way. It seems foolish to put eye colour so high on the list of priorities that a dog with very dark eyes but a dreadful head should be considered superior to one with a lovely head but a slightly lighter eye (providing everything else is pretty equal). The head qualities must be considered to be more important than eye colour.

Faults can be divided into two main categories: in the first are those points that are essential in maintaining breed type, such as the coat, dark pigment, eye size and colour, overall shape and size, and the character and temperament of the dog; in the second category fall faults that apply to all dogs, like construction, dentition, movement, overall presentation, general condition and performance.

It used to be said that breed specialist judges would generally concern themselves with breed points, while an all-rounder would be less likely to penalize a dog for any breed-specific faults and more inclined to value good conformation and stylish movement, even if this manifested itself in a dog that was two inches over the measure and had a head like a Poodle.

Understanding the nature of faults will develop as you experience each one in your dogs. Some faults are easily accepted and forgotten, such as a patchy pad or a crooked tooth. Others, like a light eye or an

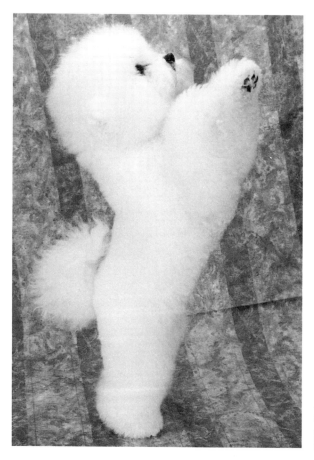

*A typical Bichon trick,
illustrating the first line
of the Standard: 'A gay,
lively, happy little dog'.*

off nose, are there for all to see and detract more easily from the overall picture of the dog.

Faults in soundness and construction are more likely to be overlooked through ignorance than intention. Understanding good movement and recognizing a well-constructed dog does not come naturally to some people and never will.

The final note at the end of the Breed Standard demands that 'male animals should have two apparently normal testicles fully descended into the scrotum'. A dog that does not fulfil this requirement is no longer subject to disqualification but, since the Standard also says that any fault should be considered according to its severity, there is some confusion about how such a dog should be regarded. In our breed, and probably others, there is a condition that causes the two testicles to lie in tandem, that is one in front of the other, rather than in the normal side by side position. This occurs when the second testicle hasn't reached the scrotum and lies just outside, easily felt but not descended. Usually the cord attached to the testes is short. The male cannot be considered monorchid (having only one testicle) because two are present, but it is a fault and should be assessed in the same way as a missing tooth or a coarse coat.

# 3

# Choosing a Puppy

We can assume that for a variety of reasons you and your family have decided that a Bichon Frise is the only dog for you. You will be familiar with the breed, you will have fallen totally for its many charms, and you will have decided that the prospect of becoming a budding worker of miracles with the comb and scissors does not worry you in the least. You may already have one Bichon and have decided to give him a canine companion. Some people make the mistake of buying a Bichon because it is still a relatively new breed and, as such, has a lot of novelty value. This is a mistake: the ownership of any dog entails a lot of responsibility, but a Bichon is especially demanding.

Whatever the reason for your choice, you must next decide where you will buy your puppy. The choices are many, ranging from the country's most successful and respectable, specialist breeders to the dealers who may offer a large number of breeds.

A litter from a respectable breeder will have been bred in order to produce a puppy for exhibition and future breeding programmes, so the standard must be high to ensure an acceptable measure of success. The breeder will usually retain one or two puppies from the litter with the intention of exhibiting them. (This is called 'running on'.) Other puppies in the litter can then be sold as companions; or as potential show puppies, perhaps to novice exhibitors. The purchasers will usually have been on a waiting list for some time.

At the other end of the spectrum are the large kennels and breeders who have a large selection of different breeds on offer, and who usually place classified advertisements for their stock. Any prospective purchaser must beware of such places. While I am sure that many of them do not deserve the awful reputation that puppy farms have acquired over the years, even the very best of them are unable by their very nature to provide the care and specialized rearing necessary for every breed of dog. Such puppies are usually bred for financial profit alone, so the overall quality of the dog is not a major consideration; its breed points, temperament and soundness must be minor considerations. Aside from these factors, with cost being the primary consideration, quality food, warm bedding, and clean and comfortable surroundings are a rarity. Little wonder that the mortality rate is so high and that the puppies' health is usually so poor. Virtually no care is taken in the breeding of such puppies. The bitches are selected arbitrarily, and are often the products of similar litters. They are bred time after time until they are exhausted. The sires that are used are rarely any better in quality, and it is clear to experienced breeders that no thought can possibly be given to inherited disease and abnormalities. Many of the basic rules to be observed when buying a puppy are impossible when buying from such a place: the opportunity to see the mother, and the conditions in which the puppies are being reared, is often denied to the purchaser. Unscrupulous dealers survive only because once on the premises dog lovers can rarely bear to leave the ill-fated puppies behind: if they are in a pitiful state there seems all the more reason to take them home and care for them.

You really must accept the importance of finding a caring and responsible breeder, even if it takes more time and involves more travelling. Contact the Kennel Club or find the address of your local breed club, who will give you the names and addresses of breeders who are well thought of among their contemporaries. Club telephone numbers can often be found in dog magazines. A puppy from one of the breeders who exhibit their dogs is far more likely to be well bred and carefully reared. The aim of the caring breeder/exhibitor is to produce Bichons that conform as closely to the Standard as possible, and their puppies will therefore have a far better future than a puppy bred for profit alone.

It is occasionally possible to find an acceptable puppy from what you may hear described as a pet litter. There are quite a few people who are unable or unwilling to show their dogs, but who nevertheless breed good, sound dogs. Quite often they work closely with a successful, more widely known breeder, who may have provided the stud-dog and is therefore able to reassure you of the overall quality of the puppies. These puppies are often raised particularly well, often in a family environment, and they certainly receive much attention and all-important socialization.

If you are looking for a puppy for the show ring then it makes good sense to attend a number of shows first. Breed club open shows are the best place to start. Exhibitors are usually relaxed and have time to chat, unlike those at the Championship shows where the atmosphere can be a little tense at times. We have many good breeders who are only too happy to give advice, providing they are not just about to go into the ring. Even if you have to wait a long time for your puppy from a favoured breeder, it will be to your advantage in the long term. Most exhibitors start with a Bichon bought as a pet, and then become captivated by the show scene. As precious as their pet is, they often discover that it is necessary to buy another Bichon with better show potential before any serious campaigning can begin. You are going to have your Bichon for up to fifteen, perhaps more, years. Far better to wait a few more months in the hope of a better one.

Let us assume you have found a breeder with some puppies for sale. A good breeder will have asked you lots of questions to satisfy herself that you can offer your puppy the right kind of home. Make sure that you visit the breeder before you commit yourself. You will need to see the puppies with their mother before deciding. It is worth remembering that the dam will not be looking her best at this time, but her temperament can be judged quite reasonably. She may be a little cautious – she has a litter to be concerned about – but she should not be timid and definitely not aggressive.

The area where the puppies are kept, usually a good-sized pen, should be clean, comfortable and free from any offensive smell, as should the puppies. Well-looked-after puppies should not have to be specially cleaned up for visitors, so the way they themselves smell is an indication of general hygiene. Basic cleanliness reflects an attitude of genuine care. If the puppies' area is disappointing and they look a bit grubby or, worse still, they are stained around their feet, you would be well advised to look elsewhere. The pups should be clean and obviously well nourished and, providing your visit has not just woken them, they should be ready to play.

Don't expect to take your puppy home before he is nine weeks old. These early weeks spent with his dam and siblings are very important to his healthy development. A puppy taken away too early is likely to be anxious and to have difficulty settling down in his new home. In any case, to pick a puppy for show from a quality litter before nine weeks would be foolhardy; after nine weeks it is much easier to assess the puppies' conformation and temperament. Quite aside from anything else, it will be comforting to know that, in taking a little extra care by buying your puppy from a knowledgeable breeder and waiting a little longer for him, you will have a source of help and support after you have taken the puppy home. A commercial establishment is unlikely to provide 'after sales' service, even if it has the experience to do so (which is unlikely).

# Rescue

Any breed that develops at the speed that ours has will produce its casualties. When the breed was introduced to the UK some saw it as a money-spinner and bred quite indiscriminately. Of course, irresponsible breeding is not the only reason that a Bichon might find himself in the care of a rescue society. As breeders we like to think that we will remain ultimately responsible for all the puppies we produce and that we will always take back an unwanted dog. In an ideal world this would be so, but there are occasions when even the most dedicated amongst us are unable to introduce what is now a strange dog back into our households. In the event of the need to rehome a dog, breeders should at least attempt to deal with the problem themselves and leave those people who spend an enormous part of their lives coming to the aid of unwanted dogs free to deal with the emergencies.

There is no way to dress the situation up: every dog that goes through rescue is unwanted for one reason or another, and we have all heard of most of them. Probably the main reason that folk give up on their pet is that he has a definite problem. For example, some Bichons are not the most reliable dogs when it comes to house-training. This is not because they have fewer brain cells than other breeds (in fact the reverse is probably true); more often it is down to attention seeking, or even the dog's way of 'punishing' his owner. How often do we go out, leaving our pet alone for a few hours, and then return to find that he has soiled the carpet, even though you know he went out shortly before you left? Some people believe they actually feel disgruntled; others that they are anxious at being abandoned. Either way the result is the same. It must be said that even the most well-behaved dog will have an accident from time to time, but some people are unable to cope with this. Such owners were probably unwise to have had a dog at all: occasionally people do buy a dog without realizing what is involved in dog ownership.

There are always some genuine reasons for rehoming, and probably the saddest occasion is the death of the owner. It is very traumatic for the dog, for not only must he contend with the loss of his owner, but he must cope with the upheaval of moving to a new home. It is so important to make provision in your will for the care of your Bichon by a relative or friend. Your pet's welfare is more important than your material things: his needs will have to be attended to without delay, and it is always better that your Bichon goes to someone he already knows and trusts.

There are occasionally horror stories of abuse and shameful neglect. And some Bichons are too badly traumatized to be rehomed with anyone other than the most experienced people. Badly bred Bichons also throw up an assortment of problems, especially those bred by people whose only concern is the number of puppies in a litter and how many litters the poor mother can have.

I think that the people who organize Bichon rescue will agree that, unlike some larger breeds, Bichons are quite easy to rehome. They have such adaptable natures and such winning ways that there are often waiting lists of people prepared to offer a home to a Bichon in need.

As breed numbers increase, demand on rescue services increases accordingly. When a Bichon is taken on by the rescue society, he is bathed, trimmed and checked over by a vet. He is then offered to the home that is considered most suitable. Prospective new homes are assessed, and only homes that are deemed to be ideal are selected. This is no way to obtain a Bichon on the cheap; in fact, many people who offer to take a Bichon are rejected. It is never worth the risk of making a mistake with a rehoming: these Bichons are already unsettled and it would be unkind to risk their being rejected a second time.

The Kennel Club holds a register of those splendid people who have taken on the enormously difficult task of rehoming dogs. Each organization has its own breed club's approval and support, and it is always wise to approach a breed club rescue society, rather than a general rescue organization, if you are looking either to acquire a Bichon or to find a home for one. The general organizations are excellent, but they are under considerable pressure and do not have the breed-specific expertise to give full advice to Bichon owners. Occasionally, rehoming can be avoided if you seek help from such a society when you are first experiencing a problem with your dog. Many problems are solvable, and if your breeder is unable to help, your local club will.

## Assessing the Puppies

If you are choosing a puppy for the show ring, the breeder will point out any that she considers to be promising. If you are seeking a puppy for a lively young family then it would be a mistake to buy a tiny quiet puppy that is a little timid. This puppy would be better suited to an elderly couple whose family are grown. You will already be familiar with the breed points, even more so if it is your intention to breed. There is much to look for and, although every Bichon puppy is a joy to behold, you must have a clear idea of the type of puppy you want. In any case you will want a puppy that is healthy and, if you intend to start showing, the one that conforms most closely to the Standard.

## General Appearance

The coat should be clean and white, giving a round and fluffy appearance. You need not be too concerned by beige or apricot patches, especially on the head. These are common but usually disappear by the time the puppy is eighteen months old. The overall impression should be of a small white bundle with black eyes and nose.

The puppy should be playful and outgoing with an alert expression. When a puppy is nervous, shy or unhappy – perhaps through lack of confidence, or even illness – the tail will hang down rather than adopt its normal position over the back.

The head is the main feature of the adult Bichon, and this is no less the case in the immature puppy. Some will still be decidedly prettier than others, usually the ones with the slightly larger eyes and the equilateral triangle that is so essential if the head is correct. If the nose is too long at this age it will never improve – noses usually become longer; heads do broaden across the skull but rarely sufficiently to produce the triangle.

The pigment should be black on the nose and pads. All other pigment should be as dark as possible. The eye-rims should be well defined and the haloes clearly visible. Any pigment missing from around the eyes is

*At ten and a half weeks, all the quality should be there to see: this one became another Kynismar champion.*

53

not good at all; even if you are assured that it will improve, which it might, it will be the first pigment to fade in the winter or at times of stress or illness. The pigment around the lips should be black and unbroken.

More difficult for the untrained eye to assess is the general conformation of the puppy. At this young age, puppies are going through a great period of change, and I have been known to change my mind daily regarding which puppy to keep and which to let go! It is possible to assess the balance between neck and back length, but even then there can be no guarantees and breeders that give them do so at their peril.

## Temperament

The major consideration for any buyer has got to be temperament. A puppy that will develop into a happy, easy to live with well-adjusted family pet may not be easy to recognize if he is carried in from a room 'out the back' by the breeder. You need time to observe the puppy at play and with people around. If the breeder doesn't own the stud-dog, and you are therefore unable to see him, it is important to ask questions about him. His temperament is just as important as the dam's. You will always want to see the dam. Be concerned if the breeder refuses to allow you to meet her, or hastily removes her as soon as you arrive. My bitches are normally delighted to be made a fuss of and usually find a lap to sit on. Most breeders are similarly happy to demonstrate the attributes of the mother, especially if her nature is as good as her physical conformation.

## Hereditary Defects

There are relatively few defects that are detectable in a young puppy. As a rule, Bichons have very few problems compared to other breeds. Any problems that do crop up are usually breed points that will determine the ultimate success of a Bichon in the show ring rather than affect the health or well-being of a family pet. However, such defects are of importance to the serious breeder and exhibitor. The presence of just one of these faults would at one time have meant disqualification from exhibition; nowadays they are tolerated, although they will adversely affect a dog's success in the show ring.

### Teeth
The correct bite for a Bichon is called a scissor bite: the top row of six incisors fit neatly in front of the bottom six. The incisors should be in

*A scissor bite. Note also the complete lip and nose pigment.*

a neat line, both top and bottom. A puppy's deciduous (milk or 'baby') teeth are sometimes evident as early as four weeks, but in some lines teeth can be slow to emerge and may not be completely through the gums at eight or even nine weeks. An undershot bite is a serious fault and will give the puppy's jaw an appearance similar to a Bulldog's: the positions of the teeth are reversed and the bottom incisors will overlap the front of the top teeth (although the canine teeth may still be in the right position). An undershot bite present in a nine-week-old puppy will rarely improve with maturity. Teeth that are crowded because the lower jaw is narrow may improve as the puppy grows, and missing milk teeth may be replaced by the correct number of adult teeth. However, unless the puppy is outstanding I would prefer a potential show puppy to have correct dentition at nine weeks. The adult teeth are less likely to be disappointing when the Bichon matures.

## Tail
The tail should be a good length and straight. Feel it gently along its length: there should be no bumps or kinks in it as these indicate that the adult tail will be kinked. In a pet Bichon, a kinked tail is of no real consequence, but in a show dog it is a fault.

## Black Hair
Bichon coats are white, with soft corkscrew curls. The coat should never have black coarse hair in it. There are a few theories about, the

main one being that black-Poodle genes may exist in the Bichon but nothing has ever been substantiated or is ever likely to be until DNA testing becomes more widespread.

## Monorchid and Cryptorchid Males

At nine weeks one should be able to detect a male Bichon's testicles. They will feel like two peas lying in or around the scrotal sac. Sometimes only one can be felt, and this may indicate that the Bichon is 'monorchid' (having only one testicle descended into the scrotum). Occasionally, you may find that the other one is present but located in the groin. It may descend later, but if there is a history of monorchidism in the line I would be inclined to wait before purchasing such a Bichon for exhibition.

In the cryptorchid male, neither testicle descends into the scrotum. Again, this may correct itself, but in many cases it does not. Dogs whose testicles are slow to position themselves in the scrotum will inevitably produce similar offspring so dogs with this condition should not be bred from. It is absolutely necessary for a dog to have two normal testicles fully descended in the scrotum if he is to have any success in the show ring.

## Poor Pigment

This is a problem that probably causes more grief than any other fault. Many breeders expect a puppy to be fully pigmented at nine weeks, with the hope that intensity at this age will indicate a lasting depth of pigment that will stay with the dog throughout his life. Unfortunately, this is rarely the case. Pigment seems to be affected by so many things, from the weather and the time of year, to what may be present in or missing from your dog's diet. The one thing you may be sure of is that if pigment is generally weak at nine weeks, it is most likely to stay weak. One can only hope to maintain that which is present in the nine-week-old puppy.

There will be exceptions – there always are – and the area that can take a while to develop the black pigment is the pads. If the pads are uniformly grey to black, they are likely to improve with age, but if they are black and bright pink, with the patches well defined, they are likely to stay that way. Pigment missing from the eye-rim is likely to remain poor. Complete pigment on the eye-rims and the nose is absolutely essential as unpigmented eye-rims detrimentally affect a dog's expression.

Pigment is giving Bichon breeders much cause for concern – nose pigment in particular. It is proving very difficult to determine the real reason why nose pigment appears to come and go as it does, and as usual there are many theories. The way forward must include selective line-breeding with only well-pigmented dogs and bitches. If you intend to breed, you must be careful to look for missing pigment in your prospective purchase. Look carefully at the dam: remember that a bitch nursing a litter in the summer will probably be at her best as far as pigment is concerned. However, a bitch nursing in winter will be at her worst, pigment wise, so if such a bitch has a black nose it is a good indication that she has good pigment generally. The intensity of the sire's pigment must also be considered. Ask the breeder about her choice of dog and particularly his nose pigment. If at all possible check this for yourself: again, it is especially helpful if you can check it during the winter months.

# Terms and Arrangements

Buying a puppy these days is not as simple as it used to be for one main reason: lack of control over the way many people are allowed to operate. There have always been kennels with dubious reputations throughout the history of dog breeding and showing. Fear of disapproval from one's peers, and the general overseeing of behaviour by the Kennel Club, is of consequence only to responsible breeders. The others, who have no respect for any authority, any more than they have for the dogs in their care, have no interest in the judgement of others and are a cause of concern to all reputable breeders. Some years ago, UK farmers were actively encouraged by European Community officials to take up dog breeding as a way of supplementing reduced incomes. These breeders produce dogs, often in large quantities and usually in poor conditions, with little consideration given to soundness and breed type. There seems to be little anyone is able or willing to do about it. The one action any single breeder can take is to be particularly careful where she sells her puppies.

## *Endorsements*

A good breeder will make every effort to ensure that her puppies go to good homes and do not end up as overused breeding stock in disreputable kennels. To assist the breeder in this, the Kennel Club provides a system of endorsements that can be used when registering a new puppy. One of these enables a breeder to disqualify a new owner from

*Ch. Shoolters What's is Name at seven months.*

registering any puppies that the dog may produce. This is often deterrent enough to the would-be breeder or dealer. A further endorsement prevents a dog being sold overseas and an export certificate being issued, and this is a deterrent to the puppy dealer who might otherwise hope to make a profit by selling the puppy abroad. As with everything, there are always loopholes in such regulations, but when they are substantiated by a carefully worded contract signed by the purchaser, the vendor does have the option of bringing a civil suit against the purchaser if the circumstances demand it.

The genuine pet purchaser will have no qualms about entering into such agreements. In fact, in my experience, purchasers are reassured of the integrity of a breeder whose motives are clearly the protection and welfare of the puppy. I appreciate that if all breeders were to place such restrictions, it would have a considerable effect on the quality of the dogs available to the genuine would-be breeder, so compromise is necessary. Any of my puppies that go to purchasers that are not personally known to me are sold with breeding endorsements, but these can be lifted later if circumstances justify it. To those purchasers who express an interest in breeding, I suggest waiting until the puppy has matured before deciding whether the dog is of sufficient quality for breeding. By that time, I will have got to know the purchaser well enough to make a more informed judgement, and if the dog in question has developed into a good breeding prospect I will lift any endorsement on the registration.

It can be appreciated from all this that endorsements are made to protect both the individual puppy and the breed as a whole. Any good breeder will be happy to discuss the endorsements and explain them to you.

## Breeding Terms

These were used quite often in the past and seemed to vary from daylight robbery to quite an amicable arrangement for a purchaser with limited resources. I have known whole litters to be handed over to the brood-bitch's original breeder in exchange for legal ownership of the bitch. Usually sums involved are reasonable and the prospect of having a puppy back at a later date from a bitch puppy that you are unable, for a variety of reasons, to keep yourself, can be quite attractive. It has to be quite an effective method of remaining in control over what happens to your puppies. However, unless you are experienced in breeding, this is not usually an option that would be open to you.

## Registration

All puppies should be registered with the Kennel Club. At birth or very soon after, the breeder submits to the Kennel Club all the relevant information about the litter. Providing both parents are already registered very few litters are rejected. Registration will be refused if the bitch is eight years old, or older, or has previously whelped six litters or more. When this restriction was introduced to protect bitches from being over used, the numbers of puppies born to individual litters increased. Many suspect that puppies from bitches that would no longer be accepted because of their age or previous history had their puppies' names added to other bitch's litters for the purpose of registration. Thus fraud is added to the list of such breeders' misdemeanours.

At registration, the breeder suggests a suitable name for the puppy and adds it to her affix. An affix is a name that identifies a breeder and is attached to any dog that she is closely associated with. It usually appears in front of the name if she has actually bred the puppy, after it if she owns the dog but did not breed it. You will see that every dog that I have bred will have a name beginning with my affix, Bobander. Anyone can apply to register an affix at the Kennel Club but, since there is a fee to maintain it, it is best left until you are sure you can use it. Most new exhibitors are happy to own a dog that carries an affix from a prestigious and successful kennel. I can remember clearly being told by a very successful breeder that owning and exhibiting a dog from her could only be compared to driving a Rolls-Royce instead of a Mini.

# Naming Your Dog

Choice of name is a very personal thing, but there are practical considerations. A name should be easily recognizable and different from any other dog you have already. If you are choosing a name that will be registered with the Kennel Club, the whole name (including the affix) cannot have more than twenty-four letters. Many breeders are fond of adopting a theme for each litter of puppies (flowers, characters from a particular storybook, musical instruments, and so on). Others like to include a particular name or word in the names of all puppies by a particular sire. For example, I used 'In the Air' for one sire's offspring, but it is easy for people less familiar with the individuals and their pet names to become confused, so it is unwise to do this for long. Try to avoid names from other pedigrees: you may think you are paying a compliment to someone else by naming your puppy after his champion, but it is rarely appreciated and it can cause confusion. All dogs have pet names, so the registered name need not be the one by which the dog will be known outside the show ring but it is always useful to choose a name that includes a pet name, such as Bobander What Ho *Bertie*.

Naming a puppy can be great fun and may be the first thing you are keen to do once you know that a puppy is on the way. If you have chosen early, or already have a favourite family name for your dog, let the breeder know what it is as soon as you can. If the registration has not been applied for already it may be possible to use it in the Kennel Club registered name.

*Ch. Bobander Magic in the Air.*

# Paperwork

When a puppy is purchased from anywhere, there is always some essential paperwork. At the very least you can expect a correctly completed three-generation pedigree listing the names of your puppy's parents, grandparents and great-grandparents. Some pedigrees will show five generations. Insist on a sales receipt, and make sure that the purchase price and any other important details are stated on it. The Kennel Club registration document should also be available, but make sure the vendor has signed it otherwise the puppy cannot be transferred into your name by the Kennel Club.

If your puppy has already been given one vaccination, make sure that you are given the vaccination certificate, which should indicate the type of vaccination given and the date when the next part of the course is due. You should take the certificate with you to your vet. Every responsible breeder is meticulous about worming the puppies, so ask for a worming record. This information can then be passed on to your vet who will then devise future worming programmes. A diet sheet is another essential item. This will tell you what, when and how much to feed your puppy, and it is very important that you take notice of all these instructions and any other nutritional advice that the breeder may give you: sudden changes in diet can cause problems, especially in a vulnerable young puppy who is already stressed from the abrupt change in his environment and the absence of his dam and litter mates. Some breeders will also supply

*Ch. Si'bon Jasmyn, the breed's youngest champion.*

you with an insurance certificate, although cover will usually last only for the first few weeks. After that it is up to you to renew the policy or investigate alternative ones – either way it is well worth keeping your dog insured.

Finally, you may be asked to sign a contract stating that you accept the terms of sale. Terms might reinforce any 'endorsements' that may have been placed on the puppy at the time of his registration with the Kennel Club – such as one that prevents you from using the puppy for breeding purposes. Such terms and conditions may seem excessive, but the breeder who insists on them is concerned primarily with the welfare of her dogs, and that in itself is reassuring to potential purchasers.

# Taking your Puppy Home

Before taking your puppy home you should be well prepared for the little whirlwind that has entered your life! Everything should be made ready in advance: there should be a bed in a quiet corner, feeding utensils, toys and, if possible, a supply of the food that the breeder has recommended. Place the bed in an area that can be sectioned off so that the puppy doesn't have too much space in which to wander at night. I find the thick plastic beds are the best as they can be chewed quite safely (unlike a wicker basket or cardboard box). Ask the breeder for a piece of bedding that has the scent of the other puppies on it, and maybe a familiar toy – anything that will make his new surroundings more welcoming. Your garden must be secure, not only to prevent your puppy from getting out but to protect him from being stolen. For this reason alone you should never consider leaving a Bichon unattended in a garden when you go out: no garden is impenetrable when a thief knows he will not be disturbed. Finally, check each room for inviting bits of wiring and sharp corners, in the same way you would for a toddler. Prevention is always better than cure.

When you collect your puppy, you are well-advised to have someone with you. Your helper can then look after the puppy on the home journey. It is worth covering the car seat with plastic and then with a blanket: especially if the journey is a long one, little accidents are quite possible. Some people have a travelling cage for transporting the new puppy, but most will prefer to hold the puppy on their laps, offering the puppy warmth and comfort at what is for him a traumatic time.

# 4

# Care and Management

Many years ago I trained as a student psychiatric nurse. I mention this because one essential part of that training can be considered relevant to animal care. The reason that taking care of psychiatric patients can be so difficult is that communication is frequently limited. Patients may have lost the ability, or the will, to inform the nurse of their needs, so in addition to the usual skills involved in nursing the sick, the psychiatric nurse needs to be able to determine by other means where the pain is or whether the patient is cold or hungry.

To demonstrate to students how debilitating it is to be unable to speak or hear, or sometimes both, each nurse was asked to assume the role of the patient and to try to express her needs while being unable to speak or communicate in any normal way. It was an extremely effective exercise in that it not only gave us some idea of the extent to which patients depend on their carers, but made us think about the various ways in which we might try to understand and respond to the patient. It is difficult to imagine what it feels like to be very thirsty but unable to ask for a drink, or to have a pain and yet be unable to tell anyone about it.

Animals have no choice but to hope that you as their owner will guess what they need and provide it. Your dog may have his way of telling you that his water bowl is dry, or he may bark at his lead when it is time for his walk. But he cannot always let you know if he is ill, or that he has a pain. You may not notice that he has a flea that is driving him mad, or that his corner in the kitchen where you have put his crate is particularly draughty some nights. How can you know? He cannot tell you. It is necessary for you to watch your dog and get to know his individual habits so that you can judge his condition from slight changes in his behaviour. Most dog owners are very quick to notice if their dogs are behaving differently, or are off their food or drinking more water. We share our homes and our lives with our dogs, so the observant owner will notice very quickly if something is not quite right. If you suspect something is amiss, it is always worth a trip to the vet. The vet may be able to find a physical cause for it

Problems may occur for a variety of reasons, but the most obvious is the increase in the number of Bichons kept for showing and breeding. The number of dogs you keep must be determined by the facilities you have available and the amount of time you have to spend on each individual's care. The majority of people are sensible and keep only as many dogs as they can cope with. There is no better life for a Bichon than that of being one of a small family group. I am not for one moment suggesting that a Bichon kept as one of a sizeable group, by a breeder, does not have a good life. There are disadvantages, of course, but lack of care cannot be allowed to be one of them. The breeder must work hard to ensure that her Bichons have the contact and attention that is so essential if she is to be sympathetic to all needs. This cannot be done if dogs are kept in cages for long periods of time and denied the attention that we know is a particular must for a Bichon.

# Vaccinations

Your veterinary surgeon will vaccinate your puppy against four major diseases: infectious canine hepatitis, distemper, leptospirosis and parvovirus. In puppies, these diseases are often fatal; even in adults there can be no guarantee of survival. In any case the symptoms are very distressing, and it is your responsibility to ensure that your dog is properly protected from them.

Puppies will have received much of their early immunity via the placenta and, after birth, from the mother's milk (especially the colostrum). This is one of the reasons that routine vaccination of brood bitches is so important. However, the puppies' acquired immunity wanes in the weeks after birth, and by the age of about seven or eight weeks it will have reduced to such an extent that vaccination is necessary to ensure continued protection. The vaccines are usually given in a combined form (DHLPP), and administered in two doses – the first at nine weeks, the second at twelve.

Since my puppies go to their new homes at nine weeks of age, I usually recommend allowing the puppy to settle for a few days before taking him to the vet for his first vaccination and a general check-up. If you collect your puppy after nine weeks of age, the breeder will give you a vaccination certificate. This will contain details of the type of vaccine used and the date is was given, and it should be taken to your vet when the next part of the vaccination is due. Some vets use a vaccine that requires a further dose to be given at the age of five months, but this is unusual.

As a rule, I cannot consider a puppy to be covered until two weeks after the last vaccination in the course. Only then should you take your puppy into public places. However, the disease resistance provided by vaccination is not lifelong. Your vet will advise you on how often your puppy will need to return for 'boosters' – usually once a year.

# Choosing a Vet

If you have not had a pet before you will need to find a local veterinary practice and register your puppy. Ask other dog owners, who may be able to recommend one; otherwise you will have to take pot luck. Over the years I have had a number of experiences with different vets: as in all professions some are very competent, others are less so. Do not feel that once you have registered with a vet you have to stay with him. He provides a service and receives a fee, so if you are not satisfied with the way you or your pet are treated you are quite at liberty to go to another, although it is of course courteous to let him know that you are doing this. Location must be a consideration when choosing a vet. Can you get to your surgery quickly in an emergency? Or do you have to drive through a busy shopping centre? Will you be able to park your car outside or will you have a long walk, perhaps carrying your dog? There are many things to consider and quite often other dog owners or a local pet shop can point you in the right direction.

It may not be the major consideration in your life now but, believe me, when your little puppy is clearly off colour and your imagination

*Ch. Kynismar Blackeyed Susie.*

moves into top gear, you will want to see the very best vet that ever graduated from veterinary college, and you will want him to be sympathetic and understanding. So it is worth taking a little extra care when you decide which vet to register with.

# Diet

## Feeding your Puppy

The majority of breeders will send a puppy to his new home with at least a week's supply of food. It makes little sense to alter the pup's diet at a time when everything else around him is changing. It is very hard for a new owner to accept that an incredibly boring-looking bag of apparently unappetizing dry food can possibly be good for their new precious little baby: they would far rather feed him a little roast chicken or steak mince. There is nothing wrong with fresh meat providing that it is what he is used to, but if it's not then you could find that your puppy is not only unsettled and unhappy because everything is so strange but has an upset tummy as well.

Keep to the diet recommended by the breeder for as long as you can: your puppy is used to it and has thrived on it. So much research goes into making sure that modern foods contain everything for a growing puppy that it is difficult to go wrong with them.

If you find that the food your puppy has been used to is not available in your area, contact the breeder for the name of another product that is similar enough to change to. However, it is important to remember that any change in diet must be made gradually. The puppy's system is extremely sensitive to dietary change, so the new diet should be introduced over a period of a few days – at each meal reducing the quantity of the usual foodstuff and increasing the quantity of the new one – until the change is complete.

Do not be concerned if, in the first couple of days, your puppy seems uninterested in his food. Many puppies are reluctant to eat at first because of the upheaval and the lack of competition from his siblings. For many weeks he has had other puppies around the food bowl all in a hurry to eat their share; now there is no hurry at all. It is at this point that the over-anxious mum starts to bring out the 'goodies'. This is a mistake: the way you behave now can set the pattern for a very long time, and if you start feeding succulent pieces of steak your puppy will be even less inclined to eat his normal food. Give the puppy thirty minutes to eat, then

*NZ Grand Ch. Kynismar Hidden Destiny.*

remove any leftover food. If he knows that he cannot keep returning to the bowl, he will be more inclined to eat at the next mealtime.

If you are unable to accept the concept of feeding a complete dry diet, and you want to feed your puppy on fresh or tinned food, there are a few things to know. The quality of tinned meat is reflected in the price, and the main ingredient is water. Once you have opened the tin the food becomes less palatable and great care must be taken to use the remainder quickly. Always buy puppy food: ordinary food is not high enough in protein for the growing puppy. If the tinned food is not 'complete', i.e. the instructions tell you to add biscuit to it, it is advisable to add a vitamin supplement. Fresh meat is preferable to tinned, and those people who know me well will recall my days as an amateur butcher. I couldn't possibly feed my dogs with anything other than lamb's tongues or, in times of unavailability, lamb's hearts. I would buy in bulk (as much as 60kg/120lb at a time) from a meat wholesaler and, because the meat was supplied in a frozen block, spend all day chipping it into 4½lb (2kg) pieces, squeezing it into bags, and storing it in many freezers that were accumulated for the job. My kitchen resembled the set for a horror film, but my dogs would be in doggy heaven as they darted around the kitchen licking up bits of iced blood. Each bag of frozen meat would be thawed, cooked, chopped in the food processor (more finely for puppies), added to a small-bite mixer, and fed. My puppies were weaned quickly and easily, and my dogs adored their food without exception. I was delighted with their overall condition – thick coats,

*Rusmar Magic Quest.*

healthy skin and good pigment – the only real disadvantage beside all the work was that many of my dogs became fat!

Unless you are happy to put in the work involved in feeding a fresh-meat diet, and are prepared to ensure that the meals are properly balanced, you are better advised to stick with a complete dry food. The fussy puppy can be tempted by adding a little gravy or tinned fish to the dry food, but it is worth bearing in mind that dogs do not need variety in their diet; it is we humans who need to feel satisfied that they are happy.

Most information about feeding a puppy will advise up to four meals a day. However, I have found that by twelve weeks of age the average Bichon puppy is satisfied with only three meals a day; by sixteen weeks he should be happy with two meals and, by six months, one meal. On this regime my puppies eat readily, are full of energy and are well bodied. I use a complete dry food that is easily available for the new puppy owner, and I am a great believer in giving raw vegetables, especially carrot, to chew on rather than biscuits. Hide chews are generally not recommended, especially for puppies, who can easily choke on them once they are reduced in size.

## Feeding the Adult Dog

As a general rule, Bichons are not fussy eaters and a well-exercised, happy dog will eat most things. If he has become fussy it is usually your fault. There are many dog foods on the market, and most of them are so good that it would be difficult to go wrong when it comes to providing a balanced diet. Before the production of dog food, the provision of a well-balanced diet was considered to be quite an art amongst the well-respected breeders. They all had their favoured foodstuffs, mainly fresh meat and biscuit with a careful blend of additives – all essential for that extra glossy coat or firm condition. These days the only art involved is picking your way through the choice on the pet-food shelves. With surprising regularity, the manufacturers bring out new foods in newer varieties, and present them in new ways. However, I do not know a Bichon yet that would not be perfectly happy to eat exactly what you give him, especially if it's still on your plate!

The main rules for feeding apply to all dogs. Most of the advice on puppy feeding is relevant for adults, with the main exceptions that only one main meal a day is necessary (although some people prefer to feed two small ones), and you will provide a diet formulated for adults rather than puppies. If you decide to feed your adult Bichon twice a day, make sure that each meal is equivalent to half a daily ration, otherwise your dog will grow fat. There is a wide range of adult-food products available, and nowadays most manufacturers produce more than one type of adult diet. Amongst these you are likely to find a diet formulated for the highly active or working dog, one for the older dog, one for the dog that needs to lose weight, one for the dog that is allergic to wheat and, of course, a bare 'maintenance' diet for the dog that doesn't fit into any of the above categories. This standard diet will suit most pet dogs.

I have to confess that I did resist feeding these complete dry foods for a very long time. They looked so awful, so very unappetizing – my dogs couldn't possibly like them. However, I was experiencing some difficulty in purchasing fresh meat so I weakened and took another look at dry food. I had already started feeding my puppies on one of the most popular puppy foods, and they were certainly doing well on it. The bitches were not averse to stealing it from their babies either, so I gave it another go. To begin with, I added tasty bits and pieces to it, just to dress it up and make it more palatable. This achieved nothing, for really all I was doing was making it more attractive to me, not to my dogs. It was not only an unnecessary thing to do, it was extremely unwise because by adding any kind of protein I was upsetting the balance of the complete food. This I now know can cause troubles in later life, including kidney problems. As we have already seen, the different ages and stages of the dog's life are catered for in a variety of different diets. Everything is calculated and balanced. Dog food manufacturers spend millions of pounds in nutrition research, so who are we to consider that our own home recipes are bound to be better.

Try to avoid changing your Bichon's diet. If his weight is stable and his condition is good, there is no reason to try something different. If you do find it necessary to change, follow the advice given in the puppy-feeding section, and remember that if he does suffer from an upset tummy it is most likely to be the change and not the actual food that is to blame. With Bichons I believe it is wise to avoid red meat and foods that are made of beef and pork. Lamb is preferable, but I find that Bichons do better on a blander diet of poultry and rice. (This is yet another type of diet produced by the food manufacturers.) Poultry and rice diets are especially good for Bichons who suffer from 'hot spots' and itchy skin.

My vet considers that the majority of problems in the dogs that visit his surgery are diet related; obesity is very high on the list. Bichons tend to put on weight easily, and every fellow Bichonist who knows me and my dogs well will now be enjoying a snigger at my expense, for it is a well-known fact that if I owned a Whippet it would be well covered. I have changed! I have seen my dogs, who have been pampered for years with all kinds of gourmet-food offerings, tuck into the most boring-looking complete food as if it were a rump steak. It doesn't matter to

*Bobander I Do Declare.*

them what I feed them; they are unconcerned with the colour, shape or texture. It is food, and if they are hungry they will eat it. As a result they are leaner, in excellent condition, and full of energy. Mealtimes are considerably easier too.

## Fussy Eaters

Owning a faddy Bichon can be a nightmare. Bichons are very clever and will exploit any anxieties you may have. However, it is never too late to change bad habits. When he is older and suffers from all the ailments that are related to bad diet – the diet provided by you – you will have only yourself to blame.

Changing your dog's diet to a healthier one may mean a difficult few days ahead, but make the change now. It is unfair to continue feeding an unhealthy diet, even if you think it looks good enough for you to eat. Remember to make the change over a period of days, as described earlier. If you introduce the new diet gradually, he may never notice the difference. If he leaves his food, pick it up and throw it away. Be determined, and do not weaken. Remember that you are doing this for him and his health. When he is hungry he will eat.

# Training

Every dog requires some degree of training. In common with other small breeds, Bichons do not require the advanced training that is necessary with the large breeds; but they must nevertheless be taught basic standards of behaviour. The first of these is house-training. As your puppy grows older, he will need to accept a collar and lead, and to respond to some basic commands. If you intend to show your Bichon, you will also need to teach him to stand correctly in the show ring; and any Bichon must learn to accept grooming (*see* Chapter 5).

## House-Training

From the age of around three weeks, puppies develop an instinct to relieve themselves away from the area in which they sleep and eat. When you first take your new puppy home, he will feel confused and unsure of himself in his new environment. Your first priority is to help him adapt to life without his siblings and mother; house-training should be left until he has settled down a bit.

71

Decide where you will want your puppy to relive himself. For most people, this is in the garden. Take your puppy to that area as regularly as possible so that the puppy gradually learns what the place is for. He will catch on sooner if you take him out at the time when you know he will need to go; otherwise you can spend a lot of time making fruitless trips, the purpose of which he will not associate with the business of relieving himself. A puppy will need to be taken out as soon as he has eaten and as soon as he wakes up after a nap. It is at these times that you are almost guaranteed a result. At other times you need to be vigilant and will have to judge the right moment from his behaviour: he will usually start to sniff the ground and/or move in a small circle. At the first sign, pick him up and take him out. Puppies do not spend much time in these preliminaries, so you have to be quick. When he performs in the right place, praise him lavishly. This is very important if he is eventually to understand what is required of him.

Dogs do like to urinate in the same place as before, and they will distinguish this place by its smell, so it is important to remove the scent from anywhere you do not wish the puppy to use again. There are many cleaning products that claim to remove pet odour from your floors and carpets, but I still consider soda water to be the most effective. When your puppy has accidents – and he will have quite a few to start with – it is important to remain calm and composed. You cannot expect your puppy to stop what he is doing if you suddenly start to shriek at him, and the very worse thing you can do is punish him for doing what is perfectly natural for him. The ancient practice of rubbing the puppy's nose in his own excrement is not only barbaric but completely futile.

Rather than punish your puppy make a mental note of the circumstances and time of the accident and resolve to take evasive action next time. As you get to know your puppy better, you will be able to predict his behaviour more accurately. As a result, the puppy will have fewer accidents and will settle into the habit of using the right place. Puppies learn most quickly through praise, not through bullying or punishment. Dogs have a natural desire to please you, and this is what you must utilize. Consistency is the key, which is one of the important reasons for not leaving a puppy alone while you go off to work for hours at a time. Quite aside from anything else, a puppy does not have the bladder and bowel control that the adult dog has, and you cannot expect him to wait until you come home.

Some dogs will become very uncomfortable about relieving themselves within the boundaries of the family home, including the garden. This can cause some inconvenience, so make sure there is a corner of

*Ch. & Austral. Ch. Charnel Born to be Wild about Roxara, handled by Marita Rodgers.*

the garden that he can consider his own. He is less likely to feel this way if house-training has been conducted calmly; if it is made into a battle he will feel inhibited about it thereafter.

Puppy training pads or newspaper have their uses for during the night or at times when he has to be left. Don't be in too much of a hurry to change the pad as soon as it has been used, for your puppy is more likely to use it a second time if he can easily identify it as the place that he went last.

Please always remember that you are responsible for clearing up after your pet, and in public places always carry a plastic bag for this purpose. Remember that in most areas it is no longer acceptable or safe to allow your pet to use the gutter.

## The Collar and Lead

We are all advised to keep a collar on our dogs, preferably with a name tag attached, and this is good advice. However, if you are showing your Bichon you will naturally be concerned about preserving the coat around the dog's neck. You will be unable to leave any collar on your

73

dog without damaging the coat in some way. For the show dog, you will need to find an alternative.

For the pet Bichon, any fine, light collar made of a soft, pliable material will do, as long as it is comfortable and removed during grooming sessions. When I take my dogs for a walk I use a show lead, which is a combined collar and lead made of soft knitted material. The part that goes around the dog's neck is adjusted for size with a simple clip that slides up and down and makes removal and adjustment very easy. This type of lead should be used only by experienced adults, and only if you are confident that your dog is unlikely to escape. No dog's overall security should be compromised in the interests of preserving a little neck coat.

Start your puppy off with a little cat collar until he is used to the feel of something around his neck. When he is used to this, attach the lead and allow him to play indoors or in the garden, but do not leave him unattended. Watch him to make sure that he does not become caught up on anything. When he seems comfortable with wearing the collar and lead, pick up and hold the lead. Be very gentle at all times. Without exerting pressure, encourage him to follow you. Never drag a puppy along by his lead for he will learn to hate it. Make it fun and comfortable, and he will soon enjoy his walks with you.

If you find that he snorts and chokes on his collar it may be necessary to use a halter. This will interfere with the coat even more than a collar, but will give the handler more control. If you have problems, try taking your puppy to your local obedience class; they will advise you on how to use the lead and control your pet.

A common occurrence in the show ring is the problem of 'soft palate'. One of the causes is the handler exerting so much pressure on the throat, by pulling too hard on the lead, that the dog is made to snort (*see* Chapter 10). It is quite distressing and incapacitating for the dog. Most exhibitors have overcome this problem by using a lead whose cross-section has a very wide piece that goes around the throat. This extra width spreads any pressure over a wider area. The dog finds this more comfortable and the spasm is avoided.

## Training Classes

Bichons are like all dogs in that they are naturally subservient to a pack leader, which should be you. When problems with dogs occur, they are quite often the result of an insufficiently defined owner-dog relationship. Problems may manifest themselves in blatant disobedience, aggression, nervousness, or in any number of deviant behaviours –

even finicky eating habits – most of which can be solved, or at least improved, by the owner's reaffirming his position as pack leader. This does not mean that you should adopt an overbearing manner or treat your dog unkindly in any way; rather it means ensuring that the guidelines you set down are clear and reasonable and, essentially, that you are consistent in your responses and in your judgement of what is and what is not acceptable behaviour.

Responsible dog ownership demands that you teach your dog to obey simple commands, such as 'Come', 'Sit', 'Stay' and 'No', if he is not to cause a nuisance to other people. Although the Bichon is a small, inoffensive dog that we might never expect anyone to fear, there are some who have an aversion to being approached by any dog, no matter how casually; so it is better to avoid any kind of confrontation, however innocently it might arise, by ensuring that you can control your dog.

It is very easy to allow your little darling to rule you completely, to answer to his every whim and allow him complete freedom in all he does. But it should be remembered that it is the dog that will have to face the rejection that unruly behaviour will elicit from people who do not find it as endearing as you might. There is also a safety aspect: if your dog is unable to respond to simple commands you will have little hope of averting disaster if he should one day slip his lead and run into the road. And the consequences may affect not only your dog, but anyone else that may become involved. Bichons are a naturally friendly and exuberant breed, so it makes sense to control them properly when they come into contact with the general public.

Basic control skills may be learnt at any one of the many training classes that are available, and since obedience training is absolutely essential for the larger breeds there is usually more than one training club to choose from. Some training clubs and societies offer separate classes for smaller dogs that might be intimidated by the larger breeds, and specific classes for puppies. Quite aside from the benefit that both you and your dog will derive from your learning specific training skills, it is well worth joining a club for the opportunity it gives you to meet like-minded people and for your dog to learn the all-important socialization skills that will enable him to mix happily with his own kind as well as with people.

In attending classes some people discover that they have natural training ability, and they enjoy the experience so much that they decide to take their Bichons into obedience competition. Others, who are already competing in obedience, may decide to try their skills with a new breed. Jacquie MacKenzie was one such: many years ago, she came to me and bought a dog called Bobander Captain Charisma. She and her

*Swed. Ch. Chonfri's
Ghostbuster.*

husband had been involved in obedience work with Border Collies, as I had, but then became taken with the idea of showing a more glamorous Bichon. She had quite a bit of success with Captain in the show ring, and the rest of us in the breed admired the way the dog moved out so well and stood so steadily. Jacquie had clearly utilized her skills as a trainer in teaching her Bichon to show, and it was not long before Captain was working competitively in obedience. He did very well; as did her second Bichon, Lynelba Jack the Lad. Her work with these dogs resulted in their being used in television and both dogs appeared in a play with Julie Walters and Robert Lindsay. Jacquie had to train them to do a number of different things for the cameras, and this in turn led to work in advertising. The dogs apparently enjoy every minute of it.

Whatever your ultimate aims, it is very satisfying to be in basic control of your dog, for it is control that ultimately allows your dog freedom. A dog that can be controlled may be permitted the luxury of running along a deserted beach or, on occasions, in the park – a joy that must be denied to the dog that is not reliably responsive to his owner's commands. Having said this, it should be remembered that there are always risks involved in letting your dog roam off the lead, and common sense should be used when deciding whether to do it. It should certainly not be attempted until you are absolutely confident that your control is such that you know your Bichon will return to your side the instant you call him.

# Exercise

Bichons are very adaptable: they can be just as happy curled up on someone's lap for the day as they are walking for miles. However, if you have already decided on a Bichon because you feel he will suit your lifestyle, which might be quite sedentary, do not be tempted to think that as a toy breed the Bichon needs no exercise. When you have many dogs it becomes obvious how much energy they do have, and they use it by playing constantly with each other. All dogs need some exercise: it is necessary to stimulate the circulation and to keep the muscles in good condition; it improves appetite and enhances the feeling of well-being. Bichons are sturdy little dogs and are very game: they love to chase a ball or toy, and will happily run around even if it is only in your sitting room. If your own health or lifestyle prevents long walks, it is still not impossible to engage your dog in some physical activity. If exercise is very limited then it is common sense to alter his diet. There are 'light' diets available in most ranges of complete dry food; but be careful not to supplement these with titbits, which will defeat their object. However, regular exercise remains the best form of weight control.

Dogs who live without other dogs will look to you as a playmate. Young dogs and puppies will play together for many hours. Their games are easily identified, and mine have a particular game of chase that is easy to follow. They play it anywhere with any dog, young or old, who is willing to join in, and they will very happily spend all day at it, especially if they are out in the garden. If your Bichon is alone, you will have to provide the stimulation that he will otherwise miss.

*Cluneen Good Grace at Appleacre.*

Play with your dog, vary his walks, allow him the opportunity to come into contact with other owners and their dogs, but if you allow him off the lead do be particularly careful not to let him wander too far away from you. It is not unknown for Bichons to come under attack from larger working breeds, so you must keep him close enough for you to be able to intervene if an aggressive dog should appear on the scene.

# Identification

This is becoming quite a big issue, and more and more people are having to consider using a more permanent form of identification than that provided by a name tag attached to your dog's collar. At the moment there are two main options: microchipping and tattooing.

Microchipping involves inserting a small microchip (about the size of a grain of rice) under the skin of the dog, usually in the neck region. The procedure is supposed to be completely painless and safe, although there are bound to be exceptions. The microchip bears a number which can be 'read' by a special machine when it is passed over the region containing the chip. Each chip's number is listed on a national register and identifies the animal's owner. While microchipping is in itself very efficient, its effectiveness depends on whether the person finding the dog has access to the equipment necessary for reading.

Tattooing also makes use of a national register, but this time the number is indelibly printed into the skin pigment, usually on the underside of the ear flap. The tattooing procedure cannot be described as comfortable but one can at least be sure that there is no pain at all after that. Tattooing has another advantage in that the number is detectable without the use of any special equipment. The tattooing system has been in successful operation on the Continent for many years, and of the two forms of identification it is the one that I would favour. When DNA testing or genetic 'fingerprinting' becomes cheaper and more widely accessible, it may provide an even more effective identification method that is not at all invasive or painful.

# The Elderly Bichon

As a rule, small dogs live longer than their bigger cousins. A very famous Bichon called Jazz died recently at the age of sixteen years and ten months. He had remained remarkably well during his last months, although he was fortunate to have had knowledgeable and experienced owners.

Your Bichon's advancing years do not mean that you should allow him to become inactive; nor should it be used to justify giving him too many food treats as this will cause excess weight which will place strain on his joints and organs. Although a twelve-year-old dog may not want to chase after a ball, he will (and should) continue to enjoy regular, if more gentle, exercise. His diet will require less protein, but this adjustment is easy to make as most good manufacturers produce low-protein diets especially balanced to suit the needs of the elderly dog. He will also become more susceptible to age-related illnesses, such as arthritis and aching joints, so he will probably need more care from the vet. However, given a good diet and a considerate owner, most Bichons will live to enjoy a long and healthy old age.

Eventually, of course, your pet's quality of life will diminish, and there will come a time when you know that however unbearable it seems, you must let him go. The decision to put a dog down is rarely an easy one to make, but the loving owner will make it knowing that it is the kindest and least selfish thing to do. You may find yourself hoping that someone – perhaps your vet – will make the decision for you. But with rare exceptions, the owner is the only person in the position to know when life has become too difficult for a dog. Euthanasia is a kind and dignified end for a much-loved pet. Ask your vet about what is involved and, when the time comes, try to take another member of your family with you. If your dog has always feared going to the vet and you suspect that he may be unco-operative, let your vet know in advance: he may prescribe a sedative first. For your dog's sake, you must try to be the one holding him at the end, for no one else will be able to reassure him as you can. However difficult this may seem, you will later be able to take some comfort from knowing that you did everything you could for your Bichon.

You may have a spot in the garden where he can go, but if for any reason you are unable to bury him your vet will have details about cremation. In some areas there are pet cemeteries where your dog can be buried with others. Grieving for your dog is a natural process that you will have to go through. The intensity of your grief will lessen in time, although it may be years before you are able to talk of him without a lump in your throat. You may also feel for a while that you will never be able to go through the pain of losing a dog ever again, and so cannot possibly contemplate owning another. But there is no greater testament to the special nature of your relationship with your Bichon than wanting to repeat it with another one.

# 5

# Grooming and Coat Presentation

The Bichon coat is one of the defining characteristics of the breed, but it is also the feature that causes the greatest problem for the average pet owner. I am sure that the prospect of maintaining the coat is the single most common reason that some reject the breed. However, many new owners delight in the grooming, and keeping their dog looking good gives them much satisfaction.

I encourage new owners to take on the responsibility of trimming their dogs themselves. Most people can learn the skills involved, although it is also true that not everyone will be able to reach the standards required in the show ring. For those who do not feel confident enough to trim the coat, help will be needed from the local grooming parlour, although professional trimming does not absolve the owner from the responsibility for day-to-day care. The biggest nightmare for the professional groomer is a very matted dog. It is extremely unfair to your Bichon to allow him to become matted: apart from the discomfort and unhealthiness of living with a matted coat, there is the shock of having the entire coat shaved to the skin, which is the only humane option that a groomer has for dealing with it. It takes a little time every day to keep your Bichon looking good. If you are not prepared to accept responsibility for the coat, this breed is not for you.

When grooming is carried out daily, your Bichon will soon accept it as part of life's routine. He will learn to stand still as he discovers that grooming is much quicker and easier if he is co-operative. For basic, day-to-day care, no artistic skill is required. The coat should first be brushed properly and thoroughly, the procedure completed by combing. This combing is important – you will be surprised how many knots are left in the coat after it has been brushed. If you do come across a matted area, prise it apart with your fingers. A little neat conditioner may help. Avoid tugging at the coat with a comb: we know ourselves that having hair pulled can be most painful, and when subjected to it your Bichon will

80

start to dislike his grooming time. It is worth spending a little extra time to ensure that the grooming experience is never unpleasant.

Grooming is more difficult when the coat is long or dirty. Regular bathing and trimming are necessary. As a rule, bathing should be carried out every two weeks, trimming every four to six weeks depending on the rate of growth. If you learn to bath and trim your Bichon yourself you will not only save a considerable amount of money over the years, but you will be able to have your dog looking particularly good when you want, and not just when the groomer can fit you in.

# Daily Routine

Besides the brushing and combing, you should check your Bichon's eyes. The eyes secrete a mucous substance that stains the crease that runs from the inner corner of the eye and down the side of the muzzle. Most dog's eyes do this, but it is particularly noticeable in a Bichon because of his white coat. There are many products available that claim to prevent or remove staining, but few are effective. The only reliable means of reducing staining is the regular use of a cleansing agent that is safe near the eyes. It can be an advantage, especially if you intend to show your Bichon, to apply a small amount of paste to the crease. The paste can be made up from equal amounts of boric acid powder, or white Fuller's Earth or kaolin, and cornflour, mixed together with water. The paste will absorb the discharge and help to protect the hair underneath.

Check your dog every day for any abrasions or cuts. His pads can gather all kinds of debris and so should be checked. It is important to check your dog regularly for anything unusual: a spot or an abrasion, or even a parasite can go unnoticed in a thick coat; and the longer they are ignored, the more difficult they are to deal with.

# Bathing

The most essential advice I can give you is to gather all that you are likely to need before you start. There is nothing worse than trying to keep a wet Houdini in the bath while you set off to find a towel. The essential items are:

- Good quality shampoo.
- Conditioner.

- Shower attachment.
- Towels.
- Rubber mat.
- Hair-dryer (one with a hands-free stand is ideal).
- Slicker-brush.
- Comb.

Check that there is sufficient warm water in the system and that your hair-dryer works before you make the dog wet. And be prepared to ignore the telephone once you have the dog in the bath or on the grooming table. There is a golden rule that must be applied at all times: *never leave a dog on a grooming table unattended*. I hope the reason for this is obvious but you would be amazed at the number of occasions that dogs have been left, just for a moment, and disaster has occurred. If the table is the correct height for your comfort, the chances are that it will be dangerously high for a Bichon

Up to the age of twelve weeks, bath your puppy in a sink. After twelve weeks you will need to use the bath. Bear in mind that, to a Bichon, a bath is a strange and frightening place until he has become accustomed to it and confident that it will do him no harm. So it is essential to make sure that his first encounter with the bath is not unnecessarily terrifying. For the dog, one of the most disconcerting aspects of the bathing experience is his inability to stand securely on the slippery surface, so make sure that he is not allowed to slide all over the place. A rubber mat placed in the bottom of the bath can be very useful, but in any case hold him gently and firmly so that he begins to gain confidence. Talk to him all the time. Constant reassurance is essential if bath day is not to become a difficult time for you both.

Wash your dog thoroughly with a quality shampoo, paying particular attention to any areas that tend to pick up the most dirt. Rinse off and apply the conditioner. Conditioner is quite important as it helps to prevent knots forming in the hair, but it is essential to ensure that you rinse the dog thoroughly. Keep rinsing until the water runs clear, making a last check between the legs and around the abdomen to be sure that no soap or conditioner has escaped the shower. Squeeze out the excess water and transfer your dog to the towel. Towel dry, and then carry your dog to the grooming table.

Arrange the dryer so that it is directed on the coat while leaving both hands free. If you don't have a dryer stand, it is a good idea to enlist someone's assistance. Blow-dry him gently but thoroughly. It is necessary for that typical powder-puff appearance for the coat to be brushed while being blow-dried, but if you find this awkward to begin with, it will be sufficient to give him a good brush halfway through and then return to drying him properly. Do check periodically that the dryer nozzle is not so close to the dog that it begins to burn him.

With practice, both you and your Bichon will gain confidence. Your use of the slicker-brush and the comb will become more adept, and by the time your puppy has a full adult coat you will be ready to cope with it. A slicker-brush is the ideal equipment to use but can be quite uncomfortable if used incorrectly or unsympathetically. Be careful that you don't work on one small area until it is dry (a method that is so often recommended). Move the brush frequently so that you do not make him sore. Direct the dryer nozzle so that the warm air parts the coat. Brush in the direction that the hair is flowing from the parting, working from the base of the hair to the ends. Make sure that you brush the hair, not the dog's skin, and that at each stroke the brush leaves the hair completely, and does not carry the ends back to the roots on the next stroke, otherwise you will create tangles. If your dog is wriggling about and trying to get away, do not immediately assume that he is just being difficult: you may be hurting him. Remember, he has no way of telling you this other than by trying to move, so check that the dryer is not burning him, that the metal prongs of the slicker-brush have not become hot, and that you are not scraping the skin with the brush.

*Am. & Can. Ch. Craigdale Yoannewyn El Toro.*

83

Determining how often your Bichon needs to be bathed depends entirely upon your lifestyle. Mud picked up during a walk will quite often brush out once it has dried naturally, leaving the coat quite clean, so it is never necessary to bath a dog daily. However, if you intend to show your dog, you may have to accept that more regular bathing is necessary. Always bath your Bichon before you show him or attend ringcraft classes. Regular bathing will help prevent any staining of the feet during the months when there are few shows. Aim to bath your show Bichon weekly for the duration of your showing campaign.

Bathing and drying your Bichon may seem an awkward and difficult chore to begin with, but it will become progressively easier as you gain experience, so try not to despair if you feel that you've not made a good job of your first attempt. Everyone feels like that at first; try instead to enjoy this special time with your dog and make it a pleasurable experience for both of you.

Anyone starting in the breed these days has the opportunity to attend grooming workshops, which are held at various venues by each of the breed clubs. Your breeder will be able to tell you more about them and which one is nearest to you. Workshops are extremely useful, for there is no real substitute for practical demonstration.

# Trimming

Whether or not you feel confident enough to trim your Bichon yourself, you should attempt some level of scissor work, even if it is only to clear the hair from around the eyes and mouth.

The Breed Standard makes only one reference to the way that your Bichon should be presented. It states that, 'The dog may be presented untrimmed or have the muzzle and feet slightly tidied up.' There is no reference at all to any type of trimming or how it should be performed. When the breed first became popular in the United States, its success was directly attributed to the style of presentation, which was deliberately designed to make the dog more appealing. It certainly worked, although it should be remembered that it was in any case necessary to do something with the Bichon's coat because it is really quite unmanageable when left in its natural state. Some will say that it can be no more difficult than, for example, a Tibetan Terrier's or an Old English Sheepdog's. This might be true, but then these dogs also have problems with their immense coats, and so often, especially in pet homes, it is necessary to trim them very short (or even clip them off altogether) because the owners have been unable to cope with the grooming.

The Americans are quite often accused of over-presentation, and in some cases of primping to the extent that a breed is made to look very different from its counterparts elsewhere in the world. Soft-coated Wheaten Terriers and Briards are examples that spring to mind; and I imagine that in the early days of these breeds' appearance in the American show ring the reaction to their presentation was similar to that of some of the early breeders on the Continent when they first saw how the Bichon trim was developed. Considering the resistance from France to allow any Bichon to be exhibited in a show trim, I should imagine the response was far from favourable.

In the UK, we deliberately ignore the Breed Standard's call for the white coat to fall naturally in loose curls. When preparing our dogs for the show ring, we aim for a powder-puff appearance, which can only be achieved by blow-drying absolutely straight. Nothing in fact will create more panic in the average Bichon exhibitor than the threat of rain at a dog show and the chance that a freshly prepared Bichon might become even slightly damp, for even high levels of humidity – let alone rain – will render a powder-puff coat a mass of corkscrew curls. It is almost impossible to trim such curls into the desired shape while at the same time achieving the crispness that is so coveted.

The style of trimming has changed over the past fifteen years, and in a relatively short space of time some major changes in presentation practices have developed. A little more than a decade ago, the Breed Standard was followed a little more closely, especially with respect to the length of the coat. A 'full coat' – that of the mature dog presented in upper show classes such as Limit and Open – would be not only dense but a good two or three inches (5–7cm) thick on the body and legs, with long, flowing furnishings. The coat has always been dense with a soft undercoat; but while we still value a silky feel, the Americans consider a silky coat to be a fault. One thing that became increasingly evident was that it is easier to create a lovely finish in a coat that is technically incorrect because it is coarse. And so many dogs that looked good because of this did a lot of winning. It would be wrong to infer from this that the possession of this type of coat was the only reason for winning, but it is an example of how the desire for more impressive presentation in a breed can result in subtle changes.

The very long furnishings fell out of favour with exhibitors for several reasons: they were very difficult to maintain – and they had to be wrapped and kept clean and oiled (the ears as well as the beard and

*The furnishings used to be left long.*

moustache); they also gave the dog a different expression, which could be described as 'hangdog' and heavy. We were starting to look for a Bichon with a stylish and more lively demeanour, the 'show pony' attributes favoured by the American fraternity. Even the best dogs in the UK didn't seem to fit the bill, appearing heavy and old fashioned compared to the type of Bichon that was to become more popular and more successful at group level.

The first dog to break any real ground in this area was Eng. and Ir. Ch. Tiopepi Mad Louie of Pamplona, usually handled by Geoff Corish who is probably one of the best trimmers I know. He presented Louie in a way that enhanced not only the individual good points but the overall balance of the dog. This new style of trimming accentuated the roundness of the head: in effect he changed the outline of the head from a bottom-heavy triangle to a sphere. Other exhibitors were quick to reproduce this outline in their dogs, and when this was combined with cutting the coat away from the upper chest and streamlining the sides of the neck the effect was quite dramatic and very eye-catching.

The main conclusion that can be drawn from Geoff Corish's successful experiment is that there are no rules. Trim your dog in a way that suits him: if he lacks neck then shape him in a way that will accentuate the neck that he has; if he is a little low on leg, then subtly trimming a shade more from his undercarriage will enhance him. These tactics do not alter a dog's real shape – and any judge worth going under will know this – but it is your job to make your dog look the best he can. It would be nice to think that presentation is not the be all and end all, but a beautifully presented coat, that is very white and expertly trimmed – making the most of every aspect of the dog's outline – is one of the most important features of your dog and certainly the most influential when it comes to impressing a judge. Whether or not this is a good thing is open to question, but it is the case and must be taken into account by the exhibitor.

It is unfortunate that the first dog most novice trimmers have to contend with is a puppy. Puppies are always more difficult to trim than their adult counterparts for they rarely have the courtesy to stand still for very long; how much more of a challenge they are to the budding trimmer who, ideally, needs a dog to stand like a statue while the skills of the task are mastered. Far more fortunate – and there are many who come into this category – are those people who already have a family pet and then purchase a puppy with the intention of showing him; they have in their adult pet a patient model on which to practise.

*The rounder style became more popular.*

Before you can attempt to trim your Bichon yourself it is important to obtain the necessary equipment. In addition to the brush and comb listed in the bathing section of this chapter, you will need a pair of good-quality, sharp hairdressing scissors. This is important because it is impossible to achieve adequate results with normal household scissors, or any that have been used for another purpose. Buy the best you can afford. Avoid the very short-bladed scissors favoured by hair stylists: they may seem easier to handle but the techniques employed in trimming a Bichon's coat are very different to those used on human hair, and you will find that the longer blades will enable you to obtain the desired results far more easily. It is also sensible to buy a pair of good, round-nosed scissors. These will be used for trimming the face until you are skilled enough to be able to use the normal trimming scissors in this area.

You will also need a sturdy table. If its surface is slippery, place a rubber mat on it, for it is very difficult (not to mention dangerous) to trim a dog whose feet are sliding about. For some people – especially those who have more than one dog to trim – it is worth investing in a grooming arm, which prevents the dog from moving so far away from you that he risks falling off the table. It looks something like a small scaffold, the base of which is fixed to the table; the suspended section, to which a collar and lead or chain is attached, is positioned above the dog. The grooming arm is a useful piece of equipment as long as it is used properly: the collar should fit the dog, and the lead or chain must be adjusted so that the dog is able to stand naturally – it should certainly not be so short that the dog is standing on 'tiptoe', nor so long that the dog can still reach the edge of the table.

The other essential item is a large photograph of a well-trimmed dog. When I first started trimming we did not have the benefit of good descriptive books, and nor did we have the demonstrations and grooming workshops that are available today. So in those days, the novice trimmer would either have to seek the help of a sympathetic exhibitor (who sometimes knew only a little more than the novice), or spend a great amount of time studying the dogs whose exhibitors were the experts. They didn't all appreciate the attention and, for fear that you might learn a little too much, would tell you in no uncertain terms to go away. My best aid was my large photograph. It was a full-page advertisement of Ch. Snarsnoz Dancing Rythym at Melsel, advertising her gaining her title. Chris Belcher, her co-owner with Richard Blackwell, was standing behind the dog and wearing a dark top, against which the dog was silhouetted. It was the most stunning outline I had ever seen, and I fixed the photograph to my wall so that I could refer to it whenever I trimmed my dog. I collected other photographs of different dogs presented from all angles, and it was not long before reference to this picture library was necessary only to reassure myself that my dog looked just as good.

Sooner or later the day will come when you will be standing with your freshly washed dog in front of you, all fluffed up by the slicker-brush and hair-dryer, scissors ready, wondering where to start. There are always a few rules, and since most of them concern the safety of your dog it is wise to remember them:

1. Never, when lifting the hair with the comb, trim underneath the comb: if the comb catches on a knot the comb will lift the skin up towards the scissors and you may cut it.
2. Don't leave your dog unattended on the table, especially if the dog is secured to a grooming arm.
3. Always keep your scissors completely parallel with whichever part of the dog you are trimming. It is safer, and although it may feel awkward at first it will result in your making fewer mistakes.
4. If possible, stand your dog against a dark background. This will clarify the outline of your dog and help you to judge distances when deciding at what depth to trim.
5. Never use your scissors as a prod to adjust the position of a leg or to move any part of your dog. It is a dangerous practice and in any case suggests a lack of respect for the dog.
6. Never attempt to trim a dog that is dirty or matted.
7. Take a break if you or the dog starts to tire, and remember that if you have just bathed and blow-dried your dog he may need a drink or to go outside before you start trimming.

## Balance

Balance in a Bichon may be difficult to assess, and for the experienced onlooker easier to recognize than it is to describe, but it is the essential factor to be taken into account when trimming a dog. Overall balance is achieved when a dog has the correct length of back and leg, just the right amount of neck, and a correct head carriage, which together makes for an aesthetically pleasing whole. Too little neck, an undeveloped chest, or a long back are some of the reasons a dog may appear to be unbalanced. In smooth-coated breeds, such as the Great Dane or the Miniature Pinscher, these problems are the result of poor conformation.

*Ch. Appleacre's Any Dream Will Do.*

But in the Bichon, they can just as easily be the result of poor trimming: under that profuse coat there may be a conformationally sound, well-balanced dog, but so badly styled that he appears to be wrongly put together. The whole shape can be influenced by scissoring, especially if the coat is particularly thick. Judges can be fooled, but I will always maintain that more good dogs are disguised by bad trimming than poor specimens by clever trimming. The most common reason for this happening is the trimmer's overcompensating for minor failings in a dog's conformation. The overall shape of the dog is sacrificed in the eagerness to rectify one or two small faults. The whole dog is thrown out of balance and the overall results far worse than they would have been had the trimmer actually ignored the original fault.

It is worth remembering that our own perception of our dogs will lead an observant judge straight to a dog's failings. We see it all the time in the ring: the imperfect tail-set being held in place by the nervous exhibitor; the skin showing through the hair on a dog whose front and rump have been scalped (the trimmer's attempt to reduce the apparent length of his exhibit); lots of hair left on top of the head combined with a huge mane of hair down the back of the neck ending at a point half-way along the back (another attempt to increase length of neck and shorten the back). These exaggerated tactics serve merely to draw the eye towards the problem, rather than to disguise it. An uncertain trimmer will always cut too much off the hocks, causing the dog to appear

*This dog is a little short of neck. Overcompensating can have a knock-on effect. Too much cut from underneath will cause too much undercarriage to be revealed. If you try to lengthen the neck by taking the mane further past the point of the withers, the whole balance is lost.*

*This dog may be a little long in back but the trimmer's attempt to overcompensate results in a bizarre looking dog, with the body shape of a sausage.*

poorly angulated and straight in stifle. Too much coat over the chest and shoulders will make the dog appear to be short in neck, while too much coat on the undercarriage will make the dog appear short in leg.

Expert trimming will enhance a good dog, and it can disguise minor faults, but it is important to remember that no amount of expert trimming will turn bad conformation good. To achieve balance, your dog

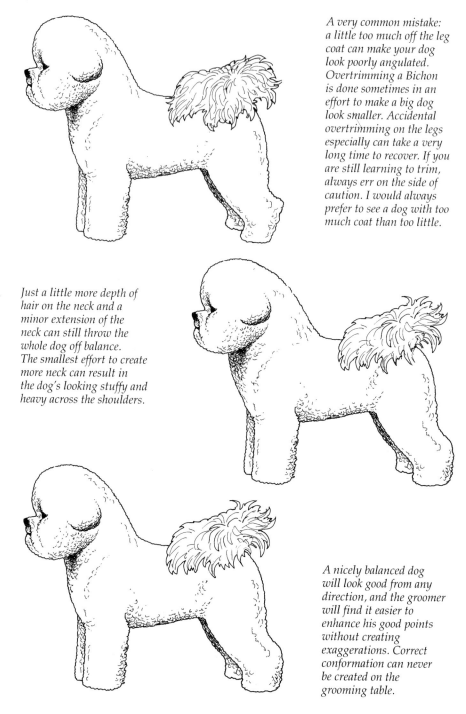

*A very common mistake: a little too much off the leg coat can make your dog look poorly angulated. Overtrimming a Bichon is done sometimes in an effort to make a big dog look smaller. Accidental overtrimming on the legs especially can take a very long time to recover. If you are still learning to trim, always err on the side of caution. I would always prefer to see a dog with too much coat than too little.*

*Just a little more depth of hair on the neck and a minor extension of the neck can still throw the whole dog off balance. The smallest effort to create more neck can result in the dog's looking stuffy and heavy across the shoulders.*

*A nicely balanced dog will look good from any direction, and the groomer will find it easier to enhance his good points without creating exaggerations. Correct conformation can never be created on the grooming table.*

must be of basically sound conformation; and it is balance that must be the ultimate aim. Be sure that in the quest for perfection in every small detail you do not sacrifice it.

## Creating a Shape

Most other references to the trimming of the Bichon Frise usually set out a certain shape that is aesthetically pleasing to the author and then you will be expected to apply this to your own dog. However, this approach never seems to work well in practice, for every dog is different and every curve and straight line that is appropriate for the dog in the demonstration will not necessarily suit your dog. I trim all my dogs differently: some are easy to trim in that they need no exaggeration to enhance specific areas and I can merely follow their basic shape; others, like a bitch that has put on weight or a puppy with an undeveloped chest, require more effort if I am to enhance the good points and minimize the weaker ones. Aim to find a reference of a dog whose outline is similar in type to your own – perhaps his sire, or your own dog on a day when his trim is just right. You can follow this pattern and make small adjustments as you become more confident.

Start by forming the basic shape. Keep your scissors parallel to the part you are trimming and keep the outline that you want to achieve in your mind. Err on the side of caution: you can always trim off a little more if the coat is too long. When looking at the dog side on, support his head with your left hand under his chin. Trim from his tail-set

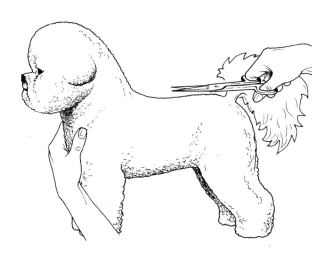

*Hold your dog firmly with your left hand and follow the line of his back, keeping your scissors parallel at all times.*

93

to his withers, following the shape of his body. This is not a flat line, there should be a slight rise over the loin and the coat should start to slope up the neck at the point of the withers. Follow this line from tail to withers in one, smooth movement, i.e. do not lift the scissors away from the coat when you open the blades for the next cut.

If you turn the dog round, or move so that you are now facing his tail, you can round off the body, the shoulders and the outer thighs. When you take your scissors over the rump and down the outside of the legs, never let them point towards the dog. At regular intervals, lift the coat with the comb – you'll be amazed how much your scissors will be flattening the coat as they go.

Follow the line over the shoulder and straight down the outside of the leg, but do not be tempted to cut in under the arm to create shaping between the elbow and the undercarriage as this has to be done very carefully at the end, as does the head. Facing the dog, trim up the sides of the neck, remembering that the natural line of the neck widens into the shoulders and tapers towards the head. It should resemble the neck of a horse, but with a slightly wider mane. Looking side on again, and with the tail in your left hand, take the excess hair from around the tail and around the anus. The hair between the anus and the testicles or the vulva can be taken very short for obvious reasons. However, do take tremendous care when doing these parts; a dog will never

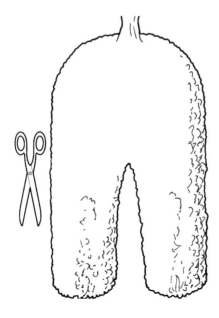

*This is the correct view of the rear. If you have kept your scissors parallel you will make fewer mistakes.*

94

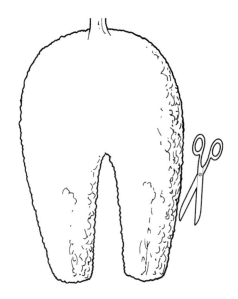

*If your scissors point in towards the dog you not only risk making contact with his skin but will probably produce the wrong shape.*

forget an accident in this area and I remember painfully how my first dog 'Blue' would resist being examined on the judge's table after I nicked a testicle with my scissors while preparing him for the ring. It didn't even draw blood, but he never forgot it. He's fourteen years old now and still resents having his back end examined!

Follow the line down the back of the leg, but stop before you reach the hock and do not cut in towards the dog. Try to follow the line of the dog's natural shape until you reach the top of the hock; here you need to leave the hair long. If you keep the hair short down the back of the leg this will emphasize your dog's rear angulation; if it is left long here the dog can appear straight. When scissoring down the front of the hind leg you need to create a line that will not only enhance a good stifle but have a direct influence on the overall appearance. Try to trim the front of the back leg so that the line meets the line that comes down from the back of the neck. If you take too much coat from the front of the back leg and from the back of the front leg it can make your dog look longer in body, so great care must be taken: you can always take a little more off if necessary, but the hair on the legs seems to take a long time to recover from a bad trim.

When trimming the chest and the front legs it is tempting to follow a straight line from the chin, over the chest, and down in front of the legs. But if you do this, you will probably create the most common mistake seen in the show ring. The breed's pronounced sternum, well-

95

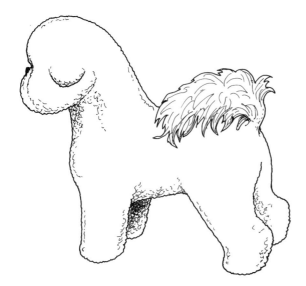

*The line down the front of the dog, over his chest and down the front of his leg is not a straight line, and you must avoid trimming it as such. Follow the gentle curve of your dog as it is, and avoid trying to exaggerate any point. The same applies to the line over the rump and down the back of the leg. Be especially careful when trimming the hocks. You should be aiming for the front and hind legs to be equal in width.*

laid-back shoulders and well-arched neck creates an elegance that is easily lost if it is trimmed out. I am aware that those who usually complain that our breed's exhibition has become a trimming competition usually feel that a heavily trimmed dog has an advantage. I firmly believe the opposite is true for I have seen quite well-constructed dogs whose good points have been obscured by over-enthusiastic trimming. The coat should be short down the front of the neck, but don't attempt this without holding the head and its furnishings right up, out of the way of your scissors. When you reach the chest, allow the line to curve out so that the chest remains pronounced. Still looking side on, follow this line down the front of the legs, remembering that a Bichon's body 'sits over' the front legs; trim the hair so that there is definition down the front side of the leg. The leg does not go from shoulder to foot in a straight line; the shoulder should slope slightly towards the leg, so be careful not to trim it out. If extra hair is left on the front leg, you lose emphasis on the chest and the gentle sloping of the front leg.

By standing in front of your dog and keeping his chin and furnishings still cupped in your left hand, you can now blend in the parts that you have already trimmed. Keep referring to your picture as you go, but resist the temptation to work on one spot until you feel it is perfect. It never will be until you see it in relation to the shape of the whole dog, which will gradually become clear over a period of time. Each front leg should resemble a cylinder, and I am unable to find a better description than that, but leave the coat longer at the point of the elbow. Don't be tempted to lift the leg up and trim around under the arm 'just to tidy it up', as this will create a hole that will take ages to recover. The back legs have almost taken care of themselves, by trimming down just past the bottom, and following the line over the back and straight down each side of the leg. You can neaten off the front of the back leg down the stifle but, as with the front leg, this part can make a tremendous difference to the finished picture. If you trim too much off and make the leg look thinner then the distance between the front and back legs is increased and the dog will look longer. If you leave too much on the back leg all round then he will appear to move close behind.

The part of the body where the upper thigh joins the body is quite a stumbling block for most people. If you've left a good length of coat on the body, just follow the line round, gently sloping it into the upper thigh. This is the area where some feel they can create a little more leg: by

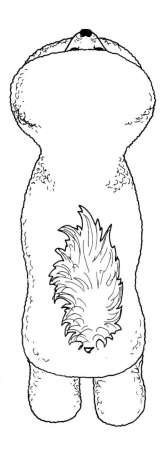

*When viewing from above, the correctly trimmed Bichon will be quite curvaceous. The neck should have a distinct tapering towards the head, widening at the shoulders; the width at the shoulders will then become more streamlined along the loin. There will be a little fullness over the hips that will be maintained down the legs.*

scalping the undercarriage and trimming high into the groin, they feel they create a longer leg or, rather, the illusion that the leg is longer. But this doesn't work. Instead, the penis is totally exposed, completely altering the outline of the dog (unfavourably in my opinion). Aside from this, the tactic is apparent to the onlooker in the ring, who will conclude that the groomer feels the dog is lacking leg. In any case, these adjustments tend to have a knock-on effect and result in a very bizarre-looking dog.

The area where the head joins the neck may seem difficult because there are so many different lengths of hair in this area, but if you have trimmed the back and the chest in the way described, the line of the head and neck should suggest itself. If you are very unsure of yourself, the face and head should be attempted only with round-nosed scissors. Remove any long hair from the corners of the eyes. (This should not be too difficult as you should have had plenty of practice in doing this from the pup's very early days.) If this basic grooming is neglected, then besides obstructing the puppy's vision the risk of tear staining is greatly increased. The hair over the forehead is shaped into a characteristic bulge that comes out beyond the line of the eye and sweeps up over the head in a ball shape. The line of the hair over the crown, rounded over the ears and connecting up with the hair from the beard, creates the complete circle that really does give a powder-puff appearance. Be careful that in your efforts to create this shape you do not keep tipping away at the hair until the head resembles a grapefruit

*How to trim your Bichon's head is a matter of personal choice, but aim to range somewhere between these two particular styles. I find the most pleasing shape is the one where the triangle, created by black eyes and nose sits in the centre of the realm of coat. The shorter style will enhance a shapely neckline and can be easier to maintain. However, it is of little value to the overall appearance of your dog if his long ear and face furnishings are not white.*

rather than a football. The shape can be difficult to achieve and requires practice. Use your favourite head study for reference, and keep referring to it throughout the process.

Remove any stained hair from around the mouth and on the lips. This staining cannot be helped in any way by daily cleansing or by applying lotions and creams, for they are too easily ingested. I consider that where there is a choice between leaving darkly stained hair and leaving no hair at all, it is better to remove the hair and reveal the skin pigment underneath (providing it is black).

The back feet are always a source of amusement to me. Exhibitors spend a long time trimming their dogs, but many of them fail to pay any real attention to the back feet. The back leg is allowed to taper off past the hock in no definite shape at all and, so often, great strands of hair can be seen flapping about, resembling those on the foot of a Shire horse. Whatever the reason for doing this, it does seem a shame to spoil the whole picture for the want of a final little bit of shaping. The worst and most common mistake that occurs is the total removal of the hair off the point of the hock, rendering the unfortunate dog the appearance of having no rear angulation at all. Longer hair in this area accentuates angulation, but it needs to be softly rounded to give it density. This is important because it will affect the way the dog appears to move. Too much, strangely shaped hair can make a dog appear to move too close behind; if your dog naturally moves a little close behind, you can lessen the apparent fault by trimming off a little more hair from the inside of the hocks.

## *Finishing Off*

I try to round the feet off just a little. While the leg should be cylindrical, a neater finish will be achieved if you avoid giving the feet the sharp angle associated with the bottom of a cylinder. However, be careful not to exaggerate this – a common mistake in many grooming parlours. You should not be able to see the nails unless you lift the coat up. Another area to be forgotten is the tail. I was told many years ago never to use the slicker-brush on the tail, presumably because the brush is too harsh and will cause tail hair to be lost. I have found this to be good advice and have tried to heed it. A beautiful, full tail plume really makes such a difference to the overall picture that a dog presents that it should be taken care of. Lost tail hair takes a long time to grow back, and any adult dog with a damaged tail never looks right. Use a no-rinse conditioner on the tail, and then a comb for grooming.

For most purposes, it is not necessary to achieve a professional, sculptured finish to the trimmed dog. However, while a neat outline will suffice, it is surprising how much more stray hair can come off at this point and how much longer your Bichon will stay looking good if you spend a little extra time on the final touches. If you are preparing your dog the day before a show you may want to leave him with a good outline and do the finishing at the show the next day. Some exhibitors will even leave a major trim until they get to a show, but I find that this is not only too distracting but unfair to other exhibitors who have to suffer the hair flying around. In any case, the time between the major trim and the final finishing can be used to give your dog a little break, and to enable you to have a look at him running around in the garden. You can assess what you have achieved already and make a note of what you might do a little differently next time.

Before you pick up your scissors again it is essential to run the comb right through the coat again. You will see lots of bits of hair start to stick out beyond the outline that you have so carefully formed. Keeping your scissors absolutely flat, and moving them slowly, take these ends off. As you do this, you can make minor adjustments to the shape here and there, as necessary.

## Ears and Feet

### Ears

If you lift the ear flap, you will probably find a number of fine hairs protruding from the ear passage. These must be removed regularly, otherwise they will begin to trap debris and wax. First dust the hairs with a little ear-dusting powder. Then, using your finger and thumb, grasp a few hairs and tug them towards you.

### Pads

Pads will be checked in the show ring to ensure that they are black. Apart from this there is nothing you need to do to the pads, except to clear away the hair and to check for any grass seeds or other debris that may have become caught between them. This is very important, for matted hair and foreign bodies can cause irritation and, ultimately, infection.

# Nails

Your dog's nails will need to be trimmed back if your dog is not regularly exercised by pavement walking. Even if his nails do wear down naturally and evenly, it may still be necessary to clip his dew-claws. The dew-claws are the canine equivalent of the human thumb. Their position on the inside of the leg, above the foot, means that they do not come into contact with the ground and therefore do not wear down. Many breeders have the dew-claws removed shortly after birth, but many vets are reluctant to perform any procedure that may be regarded as unnecessary mutilation, especially when no anaesthetic is used. If your dog still has his dew-claws, you must be sure to check them regularly. Untrimmed dew-claws will curl round until eventually the claw tip penetrates the digit, causing discomfort and possibly infection. You must also be careful to avoid catching them with the comb during grooming. If someone else is grooming your dog, you should draw his attention to any retained dew-claws.

*NZ Ch. Tamalva Union Jack.*

101

Your vet, or a professional groomer, will trim your Bichon's nails for you, but it is a simple task that is well worth learning to do yourself. Nail-clipping is automatically covered at grooming workshops, but otherwise your breeder or groomer can show you how to do it. First buy some good nail-clippers. Buy the guillotine type that is available from pet shops and trade stands at shows; do not attempt to trim your dog's nails with your own manicure scissors or clippers.

The main thing to remember when clipping nails is that there is a 'vein' or quick that you must avoid cutting into. In a translucent or white nail, the quick is easily visible: cut off the tip of the nail a couple of millimetres below the end of the quick. Black nails are more difficult because you cannot see the quick: cut only the very tip.

# Teeth

I did not pay a lot of attention to my early Bichons' teeth. Having had only Border Collies in the past I had not considered that dogs could actually have a problem with their teeth. Unfortunately toy dogs do not enjoy the benefit of naturally strong teeth, so we do have to make a special effort. Keeping them clean is quite easy, and there are doggy toothpastes and special brushes available for this purpose. Feeding 'harder', or at least less sloppy, foods should help the teeth, but even if your Bichon has a perfect scissor bite and a mouthful of lovely, even teeth you will probably find that they are covered in tartar by the time he is eighteen months old. It is amazing that some breeders do not consider this to be important, but dental decay, which is the inevitable result of tooth neglect, is painful. Eventually a dog will lose his teeth, and not always with the aid of an anaesthetic.

Clean the teeth every time you bath your dog, and in-between as well if you can. Include tooth care in your regular coat-brushing routine, and make sure that you at least polish the teeth with a piece of lint or linen material. The dogs really don't seem to mind. Fresh tartar can often be removed with your thumbnail, otherwise you can use the same instrument that your dentist uses, but it is worth asking someone to demonstrate its use because it is very sharp and can cause damage. If you are skilled enough to use a scraper, you will need to polish the teeth afterwards. A metal scraper can easily score the surface of the tooth, making it even easier for new tartar to attach itself; polishing will help. In any case, do not be tempted to leave tartar. If you cannot deal with it yourself, you must ask your vet to do it for you. If you notice that decay has taken hold, deal with it quickly. It is possible for the vet to fill an offending tooth, thereby saving it, but not if the decay is not caught in the early stages. If your dog has an irregular bite or crooked teeth it will be harder to maintain the teeth, but it is not impossible. A crowded mouth, that is one with irregular, overlapping teeth in a narrow lower jaw will lose teeth early because the roots do not seem to be so well established. A misaligned mouth will have to be checked for soreness, and sometimes it is kinder to have particularly crowded teeth removed.

# The Pet Bichon

If you have any ambition to show your dog, it is of course essential that you learn to achieve a high standard in coat presentation. Otherwise, it makes good sense to remember that, like babies, as long as your dog is comfortable, well fed and in no doubt that you love him, he won't care less what he looks like. Providing your dog has no tight knots and is reasonably groomed and cared for, the matter of whether you have taken too much coat off the neck is not really important to your dog's welfare. Your ability as a trimmer must be kept in proportion: talent with scissors is an advantage, but it is not essential. Some owners prefer their Bichons to have a very short coat because it is so much easier to manage: it is far easier to bath and dry a coat that is shorter than usual, and it is certainly easier to follow the dog's outline with the scissors. As long as you leave the head coat quite full and round and the tail in the characteristic plume, few people will confuse your Bichon with a poodle. However, if you are going to keep your dog in a very short style it may be wise to consider using a dog coat or some kind of protection against the elements in winter, especially if his coat is thin or he is elderly.

A major reason for our breed's popularity is his non-shedding coat, but this does not mean that the coat does not suffer loss at all. The difference between the Bichon and most other breeds is that lost hair remains within the coat. During the autumn and spring, your Bichon will shed his hair, and this will be apparent in the coat's tendency to mat more than usual at these times. All this said, the fact that the Bichon does not shed his white hair everywhere as other dogs do makes him an excellent choice for many asthma sufferers. It is still necessary for an asthma sufferer to wear a mask when trimming, but it is a small price to pay if you are then able to enjoy owning a Bichon.

# 6

# Showing

---

Before you decide to show your Bichon, think very carefully. Dog showing means entering a world that will affect the way you live, and quite possibly change your life completely. It is not a decision to be taken lightly. If someone had told me what an impact owning and showing my Bichons would make on my life I would never have believed them. Don't think that these changes happen only to those who keep a great number of dogs, for most of the effects that I experienced occurred in the first five years of my taking up the hobby. So, take heed: it will make a difference to you in some way or another.

When you first start out, it helps if you have a caring breeder to guide you along the way. If you haven't anyone to turn to for advice then the first step is to attend ringcraft classes, where you will learn to handle your dog correctly in the show ring. Your vet will be able to tell you where your nearest ringcraft classes are held. Learning to show your dog is similar to learning to drive in that you must first understand the basic manoeuvres and then acquire the skills to implement them. It is only experience that will enable you to become proficient at handling, and you will learn most by watching other exhibitors at shows.

## Why Show your Dog?

There are many different reasons for showing a Bichon for the first time. Sometimes it is merely the desire to learn more about a breed that is still quite unusual, and to meet other people that are as passionate about the breed as you are. Dog shows provide a wonderful opportunity for this. Sometimes it is simply curiosity: you have selected a Bichon from all the other breeds available, and you have carefully chosen a puppy; you are proud of your companion, and at some point you might feel the urge to show him off and find out how he compares with others of his breed. Many breeders show because they feel strongly that only Bichons who have proved their worth in the show ring should be included in breeding programmes. This is often the main reason that an aspiring exhibitor purchases a puppy from someone who has shown their stock: it makes sense to assume that breeders who regularly present their dogs to be judged against the Breed Standard will produce better puppies than the breeders who are not prepared to have their dogs scrutinized in this way. To show your dogs under most breed judges is essentially to ask 'Am I getting it right?' If you continually have poor results in the ring, or your dogs do not have the temperament or the overall quality at least to achieve a Stud Book number, then the answer has to be 'No'.

The other main reason for showing your dogs is probably the one that in the end is the most compelling, and that is the thrill of winning. You may long since have established what you are achieving with your breeding programme, but you cannot resist the desire to do better, to win more, and to win bigger. Once you have made one dog into a champion, you will find yourself looking for another puppy of similar quality to consolidate your initial success. It quickly becomes a very absorbing hobby, and one that easily starts to take precedence over everything else. Before you know it you are daily making decisions around your showing commitments. If you work, it is necessary to have a job that permits you to choose your days off because many championship shows schedule the toy group for a weekday. You will start to take your two weeks' holiday during the height of summer so that you can attend as many as three championship shows. Gone is the fortnight abroad that you used to look forward to. (It is in any case a thing of the past because you now have too many dogs to consider having a holiday without them.)

Attending so many shows in a relatively short space of time can be exhausting, not least because of the strain of travelling that it always involves. Many exhibitors get over this to some extent by purchasing a caravan. Most shows arrange for caravans to use a nearby site. This is an ideal solution to the recurring problem of finding overnight accommodation on the occasions when you have had to travel so far to a show that a return journey on the same day becomes quite impossible. Staying overnight also presents an excellent learning opportunity, for where else can you find so much time to talk to other exhibitors? Certainly not outside the show ring, when everyone is more concerned with the business of showing the dogs. Indeed, some of my best memories of dog shows include the time spent on the campsite with like-minded people.

This brings me to another very important reason that I continue to show my dogs, in spite of the expense and work involved. When you have been showing dogs for any length of time, you realize that the people with whom you are sharing this hobby have become friends. In all, we tend to spend more time at shows together, and then talking on the telephone during the week, than we spend with family members. Life-long friendships are made, and although the competitive nature of our sport means that they can be quite bumpy from time to time there is no one like another 'Bichonist' when you need to mull over problems or seek advice. The social side of dog showing can be quite important, and we have had some great characters in our breed. In the early days especially, there were those who would travel a good distance to a show, only to have such a wonderful time in the bar that they forgot to show their dogs.

# Types of Show

## *Exemption Shows*

These are usually held as a charitable event, and offer a number of different classes. In addition to four classes for pedigree dogs, there is usually a number of fun classes in which any dog, including crossbreeds, can be entered. Since exemption shows are exempt from Kennel Club rules, entrants do not have to be registered with the Kennel Club. You just go along on the day and enter one or more of the pedigree classes. The classes are usually very large, and each will include a number of breeds. Exemption shows provide an excellent training ground for your dog and a good place to meet other exhibitors, although they can be a bit tiring for your puppy, especially if it is a warm day. The judges are usually very sympathetic if they are aware that you are a novice exhibitor practising for the more competitive Kennel Club shows.

## *Open Shows*

An open show is run by a local canine society and includes classes for many different breeds. Each breed is usually given four classes: puppy, junior, post-graduate and open. The winners of each class compete against each other and a Best of Breed and a Best Puppy declared. Each Best of Breed then competes for the best in their group (the toy group in the case of the Bichon Best of Breed), and then the seven group winners will compete for Best in Show. The whole process is repeated for the puppies.

*The Bichon Frise Club of Great Britain Open Show, November 1993. Best in Show, Ch. Vythea Jacks the Lad at Melsel (left); Reserve, Ch. Bobander Magic in the Air (middle); Best Opposite Sex, Ch. Louisiana Highland Fling.*

These are the shows where you will gain most of your experience in the early days. There may be breed classes for Bichons, in which case you will meet other Bichon exhibitors and their dogs. If there are no classes for Bichons, there will be variety classes for toy dogs, and you can enter your Bichon in these and enjoy the day out. Unfortunately, Bichons have lost many of the classes that were allocated to them because they were poorly attended. If exhibitors start to support the open shows again, perhaps the societies will think about restoring classes for Bichons.

## Championship Shows

These are very large shows, often held over three days or more. Essentially they are the shows at which Challenge Certificates (CCs) are on offer. The Kennel Club decides how many CCs to allocate to any one breed. Without CCs, a dog cannot gain the title of Champion, so the incentive to attend these major events is high. The championship show that most people will be familiar with is Crufts. There are many shows like Crufts held up and down the UK throughout the year, mainly in the summer months, and the majority of serious exhibitors will attend a large number of them. At these shows most breeds are featured, and even if Challenge Certificates are not on offer for our breed there will be many Bichons there and competition will be high.

You can attend any of these shows providing your dog is registered with the Kennel Club and you have transferred the ownership of your puppy into your name. The exception is Crufts which, owing to the number of entries that would otherwise be received, imposes a further restriction: to be eligible for entry at Crufts, a dog must have won non-specific awards at other championship shows.

## *Club Shows*

These are my favourite type of show. They can have either open show status or championship show status, but in either case they are held by the breed clubs so are exclusively for our breed, which makes them quite special.

Club shows are especially useful for the novice exhibitor because they are generally more relaxed and friendly, and you will have a better chance to watch other exhibitors and ask questions. Everyone has more time to talk than they do at other shows because the classes are spread throughout the day, dogs in the morning and bitches in the afternoon. Sometimes there is a different judge for each sex. Our breed has four clubs at present, so we can have as many as ten club shows in a year.

## Entering a Show

The first thing to do is to subscribe to one of the weekly newspapers for dog exhibitors which will advertise shows that are coming up in your area. To begin with, enter only one local open show rather than a championship show. Entry fees for open shows are much less than those for championship shows and, in any case, it is a waste to enter several shows only to find that on your first outing your dog (or for that matter you) hates it.

When any Kennel Club-registered canine society holds a show, a schedule is printed, and the show is advertised to attract as many exhibitors and their dogs as possible. You can telephone or write to the secretary for a copy of the schedule, which will contain all the information about the show. The schedule will include an entry form for you to fill in with the relevant details about you and your dog. You must indicate clearly which class or classes you wish to enter. If your dog is still a puppy then it is best just to enter the puppy class, which is for dogs aged six to twelve months. The junior class is for dogs between six and eighteen months, and the novice through to the open class is for dogs of any age. If you are starting to show with a dog that is no longer a puppy it is wise to stay in the lower classes such as graduate or post-graduate until you feel more confident. Your success on the day will depend on many factors, most of which will be beyond your control. You have no way of knowing how many other dogs will be in your class, nor any idea of the quality of those dogs compared to yours.

It is essential that you fill in your entry form clearly and correctly. The completed form should then be returned to the secretary along with the entry fee and any membership fees or additional costs for car-parking tickets or a catalogue if you want one. There will be a closing date for entries, so be sure to send it off in plenty of time.

Showing dogs is a gamble, which is what makes it exciting; but it makes sense to give yourself the best possible chance by entering a class that is appropriate for your dog.

## Preparing for Show

When you have been to one or two shows and decided that you want to continue showing your dog, you will probably need to make a few adjustments to the way you care for your Bichon if you wish to be successful in the show ring. It may be necessary to take a little more care over his coat, especially his furnishings, so they do not become stained. Some exhibitors wrap the moustache and beard to keep them white, and this is because staining is better prevented because it is extremely difficult to

*Ch. Harene Beatrice Anne at Pamplona.*

109

remove. More regular and careful bathing may be necessary, and greater care should be taken to prevent your dog's soiling his coat in the garden. I found it easier to replace my lawn with patio slabs – they are far easier to keep clean and cannot be excavated by Bichons.

Regular exercise is essential for a show dog: pavement walking in particular will keep your dog in hard condition and his weight in check. It is impossible to keep a Bichon in full show coat while at the same time following the usual advice about keeping your dog with a collar and identifying disc. I have never kept a show dog in a collar. However, this means that it is essential to take other precautions to ensure the security of your dog. My rear garden has been made completely escape-proof and inaccessible from outside. There is no way anyone can carelessly leave a gate open.

Having made these changes to your routine care of your dog, you need to consider investing in some basic equipment. The first necessity, I think, is a carrier of some description in which you can keep your dog safe, clean and dry when travelling to shows. I prefer the folding metal cages for this purpose. Be sure that the cage is a strong one and big enough for your dog to turn around and lie down in, for he will probably spend a fair amount of time resting in it between classes. Keep in mind that you may eventually show more than one dog, so there must be room in your car for another cage as well as all the paraphernalia that accompanies you to a show. Like me you may reach the conclusion, quite quickly, that you need a bigger car.

In addition to the cage, there are a few items that you should take with you to a show. It makes sense to keep a bag specifically for the purpose, and to keep it ready packed so that you can avoid last-minute searches for essentials. Your bag should include a spare show lead, your grooming kit (or, better still, a second grooming kit that is kept specifically for shows), a spare towel or blanket for lining the bottom of the cage, a secure container for carrying fresh water, a water bowl, and a few spare plastic bags for cleaning up after the dog. As you become a seasoned exhibitor, you will add items to your show bag as you learn from experience what you are likely to need.

Plan to arrive at the show in plenty of time. Your dog will need to stretch his legs, and you will need to allow time for last-minute coat presentation. When you get to the show, find out where your first class is – there is often more than one ring – and make sure you know when you should be there. Find the show secretary, or other show official, and make sure that you have everything you need, such as your ring number.

# In the Ring

The judge has to assess the quality of the dogs before him and place them in order of merit. The best one is first, the next best is second and so on, until there are five dogs in the final line-up. The procedure is followed in each class until all the dogs have been judged. To assess the quality of each dog requires a considerable amount of knowledge of the conformation of the Bichon. The judge must know the Breed Standard and understand it in every detail.

It is worth bearing in mind that the judge will probably start making his assessment as the dogs enter the ring. Some dogs will catch his eye because they are full of their own importance; similarly, some may escape his notice because the tail is hanging down or because they are having to be dragged into the ring. So think positively as you enter the ring. Think about enjoying the experience, and you will find that your attitude will be reflected in our dog's demeanour.

Line up in the way indicated by the ring steward. Each dog will then be assessed or 'gone over' on the table. Most judges begin their examination at the head. He should feel the overall width of the head, which should be quite broad and slightly rounded but not domed. There should be a well-defined stop and the eyes should be dark, round and forward-facing. The eyes should be quite large but never protruding, and there

*It is necessary to pay attention at all times when exhibiting your dog in the ring! Here, the author handles Ch. What Ho Bertie.*

111

should be no white showing when the dog is looking forward. He will check that the outer corners of the eyes and the tip of the nose form an equilateral triangle, and that the muzzle to skull ratio is 3 to 5 (he will flatten the head coat to confirm this). Ear placement should also be established at this point, and he will bring the ear leather along the side of the head to see if it reaches half-way along the muzzle. If the ear is set too high this will be difficult. Pigment should be solid and complete around the eye-rims and nose. The haloes should be dark, but are best described as shaded rather than solid. He will look inside the dog's mouth to assess the teeth, and at the same time will check the pigment on the lips. It helps considerably if your dog is well used to having his mouth opened and inspected. (Some judges will ask the exhibitor to open the mouth for them.) The judge will be looking for complete dentition and will probably take some time to check for this. It is not uncommon for exhibitors to have crooked incisors removed and then trust that four or five tidy teeth will be less noticeable than six untidy ones. Nine times out of ten this deception is successful. He will check that the premolars are present, and that there is a scissor bite and a strong jaw line. So often we see snipey, narrow jaw lines, associated with jumbled, crowded mouths.

Having assessed the head, the judge will usually run his hands down the neck, which should be fairly long, and feel the shoulder placement. He should feel for a well-pronounced chest and a good depth of brisket. If your dog is overweight, the judge will have difficulty in feeling these structures. The front legs should be straight when he views them from the front. He should also check that the elbows are tucked in close to the sides of the chest. Viewing the dog from the side he must assess the overall shape. In view of our breed's stature, this must be done while the dog is on the table. The judge will then feel beneath the coat and the illusions created by styling to check that the dog is really longer than tall: to do this he will assess the distance from the withers to the ground (or table). The body should have substance and be well rounded. The muscles should be well developed and firm. The tail should be felt along its length: any kind of kink in the tail should not go unnoticed. At this point the judge should check that dogs have two testicles present and fully descended, although dogs are now allowed to be shown if they have been castrated.

Next comes an inspection of the hindquarters, and the judge will flatten the hair over the hocks to determine how well the rear is angulated – he should not rely on what his eyes tell him for here, too, clever scissoring can make a dog seem better than he really is. Pad pigment has to be checked, and most judges do check all the pads for complete pigment, for it doesn't follow that if the first pad that you pick up is completely black the other three will be black as well. The overall coat quality must be soft and silky to the touch: coarseness will probably feel quite different to most other coats in the class.

When the judge has gone over the dog in this detail, he will usually take a last look at the dog's head. By now he will have decided either that he likes him or that he is disappointing. Having examined conformation in this way, the experienced judge will have a reasonable idea of how the dog will move. He will ask the exhibitor to move the dog first in a triangle, and then up and down. This is not just for the purpose of assessing movement. It is also an opportunity, in our breed especially, to assess whether the Breed Standard's all-important line, 'Gay, lively, happy little dog', is an apt description of this dog. A judge can hardly be expected to assess this when the dog is being firmly held and made to keep perfectly still while the judge moves slowly along the line of dogs or examines him on the table, although he will no doubt have gained an impression of the dog's personality as he came into the ring. While the dog is being moved away, the judge should notice whether the dog's rear action is correct – that is, legs moving straight along the line of travel with pads showing. The judge's vision of the hind movement should not be obscured by the tail flowing behind. The tail should be over the back, although not so far over that it causes an indentation in the coat, and certainly not so far that it makes contact with the spine. When the dog is performing the top part of the triangle the judge can assess reach and drive – that is, how far the dog is able to extend in front and behind, and the manner in which he does it. He should make it look effortless, as if he could keep going all day. He shouldn't be bouncing up and down with his legs going nineteen to the dozen and yet going nowhere. He should hold his head and neck up proudly, not thrust forward like an Old English Sheepdog nor thrown back in a completely unnatural position. He should not be strung up on his lead so that his front legs are hardly in contact with the ground, and when he is coming back towards the judge his front should be straight and true. He should be confident enough to return to a stranger and not back away when the judge leans down towards him. The judge will then ask the whole class to move around the ring together, sometimes to compare just two dogs that he is preferring over the others.

By now he should have decided on his winner, for in most classes the better dogs stand out. He will, however, line the dogs up again for a last look before indicating his final choice. How the judge assesses the size will be down to personal preference: some specialist judges

*Bichon Frise Club of Great Britain Open Show, November 1993. Reserve Best in Show, Fougere Baggy Britches (left); Best in Show, Bobander What Ho Bertie (middle); Best Opposite Sex, Rusmar Magic Flame.*

(people that have bred or owned the breed they are judging), will in the case of Bichons favour the smaller dogs; it is not surprising that the all-rounder judge (someone who judges many different breeds) will often be attracted to the bigger Bichon that, in full coat, can look stunning and catch the eye more easily than a little one.

Judges will vary in their manner and ability to judge, and how good a day you have at a show should depend not only on whether your dog has been placed highly but on whether you have performed well. The most important judge of your dog is you, for it must be said that whether you win or not will depend on much more than having a quality dog. How you present your dog is important to our breed; whether or not we agree that this is right does not change the fact of it. How well you train your dog to behave can be an advantage: some judges prefer a dog to move around the ring on a loose lead; others like you to move them slowly. It helps if your dog will respond well to these eventualities. Even your choice of class can make a difference to how well you do: if a class is very large and there are many good dogs in it, it might be wise to enter your dog in a slightly higher class that has fewer dogs. As long as your dog meets the qualifications for the class you can enter him. Remember also that, like us, dogs can have 'off' days. Judges must assess the dogs in the class as they present themselves on that day; they cannot take off days into account.

It is not always wise or necessary to win your way through the classes. Your aim should be within reach. Set yourself little goals, perhaps a placing at first, then a higher placing as you and your puppy gain in confidence. Before you know it you will be looking to qualify for

Crufts – and you will, if you keep a level head and don't expect too much too quickly. Just remember to have fun, you and your dog.

## Sportsmanship

In an article written in 1988 in the Bichon Frise Club of Great Britain's year book, Den Thomas writes:

How many times at shows do we hear a judge's intelligence, knowledge or integrity questioned or ridiculed, often by people who have actually paid money for this very judge's opinion? Would it not be easier to avoid showing under someone you don't respect? This is providing you can find anyone else with whom you totally agree. Judging is, after all, expressing an *opinion* based on knowledge, experience and an eye for quality. No two people will ever share the same background, so will never see a dog in the same way. Everyone has a different set of values relating to individual faults and virtues. The perfect Bichon has not yet been bred, and if you know your dog's good and bad points it seems logical that the judge will also see them. It is his job to weigh up the points of each dog, then balance them in his mind, and with personal insights and experience arrive at a decision, which is ultimately based on opinion. If you can see no good in others' dogs then perhaps it is not the judge who is at fault.

Another instance of lack of grace is implied in the use of the expression 'face' judging. A 'face', presumably, means a well-known, successful exhibitor who has spent time and effort learning the art and has used experience and intuition to breed successive generations of winning dogs, each one painstakingly trained and groomed to show to advantage in tip-top condition. Strangely enough, these are the last people you will hear using this expression. It almost always comes from another type of show goer: the one that has bought a pet and then decides to show. The dog is often poor quality and in inexperienced hands, completely untrained and badly presented. This mediocre Bichon will then be mated to another of equal merit and the best of the resulting litter be hailed as the next show dog – still poor quality and, with the same standard of handling and grooming, it will again be beaten by others. Thankfully, in our breed, enough sensible new owners learn about correct type and conformation and spend time perfecting the training and grooming of their pet. In these cases the effort pays off, and the number of champions belonging to first-time owners gives a testimony to the fact that quality – of dog and handler – will out. The next time you look along a line at a show, find the well-presented exhibit, trained to show off its virtues and full of quality; then find the dog and handler who look as if they are waiting for the bus, and ask yourself which will be the winner and which will be complaining later of 'face' judging.

A subject that also causes problems for certain people is the 'friends of the judge' syndrome. It is an uncomfortable situation, but is often unavoidable. Very often the first contact between two exhibitors is to admire one another's dogs. This will sometimes develop into a friendship, and a sharing of ideals and ambitions. Friends will exchange views and influence ideas on type and movement, and so on. We often do see groups of friends with dogs of similar breeding and type, so why is it so surprising that when shown under each other, these dogs – so similar in so many ways to the judge's own – are favoured?

The other aspect of this situation is that quality dogs owned by others will be mutually admired and placings understood, we hope. Lack of integrity, in all forms is here; and sadly, it always has been, although instances of it are fairly isolated. Let's not take the pleasure completely out of dog shows by always jumping automatically to the worst conclusions. We should look at a situation from all angles, and then, if still dissatisfied, accept with good grace and remember that dog showing is, after all, a sport. Sportsmanship is the art of accepting victory and defeat with equal grace.

# Making a Champion

Making a dog into a champion is every show exhibitor's dream. It is what everyone strives for. Some people are fortunate enough – or not, depending upon how you look at it – to make their very first dog into a champion. Of course, if your first dog is of champion quality then he will surely gain his title, but so often I see the disappointment when the exhibitor has neither the experience to breed a good second dog nor the good fortune to acquire one. If you have the correct attitude when showing your dog, and enjoy the sport as a pleasant pastime for you and your dog, you will probably enjoy yourself more. On the whole it is better to achieve little milestones on the road to success than to win everything with your first dog.

In order to become a champion in the UK, a dog has to win three Challenge Certificates, each from a different judge. Every breed is allocated a number of sets of CCs (each set comprising one for the best dog and another for the best bitch). The CCs can be awarded throughout the year at championship shows. For Bichons there are currently twenty-six sets of CCs on offer each year at shows throughout Britain, but since the shows are spread across the country this can mean considerable effort must be expended in order to stand a chance of winning the necessary number. You can understand why some people need a caravan if they are to attend all these shows.

The competition varies considerably, too. At Belfast in Northern Ireland there can be as few as thirty Bichons competing for the one set of CCs, while at Crufts or Windsor there can be as many as 150. The judge on the day is not obliged to award the CCs if he does not consider the best dog or bitch to be worthy of the title Champion. However, such is the quality of the dogs in Britain that withholding of CCs is extremely rare.

It is generally understood throughout the world that Great Britain is the most difficult country in which to gain the title of Champion. There are more dogs of high quality, and fewer opportunities for exhibitors than there are in other countries. While I am sure that the best dogs from any country worldwide are equal in quality to Britain's, it never ceases to amaze me how some very mediocre UK dogs are sold abroad and go on to gain their titles with relative ease. On the other hand, the British system allows a Bichon that already has his title to carry on gathering CCs, a practice that prevents some very good dogs from ever gaining theirs. It also means that a dog has to be even better than existing champions before the CC can be awarded to him, which might appear to be an impossible task for any dog. However, older champions pass their best or have an 'off' day, different judges favour different types, and younger dogs come into their prime; thus the system does work. Only when an outstanding dog is relentlessly shown at every available show does the system fall down a little. Dogs can be shown from six months to ten years old. The older ones are usually in the veteran class (for dogs over seven years) but we have very few Bichons in these classes because it is so difficult to keep their teeth and coats presentable enough to show. I would love to see more older Bichons entered at club shows, whether they have a full set of teeth or

*Bichon Frise Club of Great Britain Championship Show 1985. Best Puppy in Show, Jangerra Uptown Girl (left); Best in Show, Sulyka Snoopy (middle); Reserve, Ch. Hunkidori Personality Miss.*

117

not. It is of great importance for exhibitors old and new to see some of the older dogs that so often feature in their pedigrees. The puppy classes at most shows are very well attended. Hopes are high for these little ones, and for the exhibitor there is not quite the pressure that exists in the higher classes. Rarely does a judge find so little of top quality in the older classes that he feels justified in giving a Challenge Certificate to a young puppy. The judge does, however, choose Best Puppy from the winners of the puppy classes.

When the dog CC winner has been decided from the dog classes, the bitches are judged in the same way. The runner-up in each case is awarded a Reserve CC. A Reserve does not count towards gaining a title unless the CC winner is for some reason subsequently disqualified. The two CC winners compete for Best of Breed. At all-breed shows, all the breeds are placed in their groups. Bichons are in the toy group. Because of the great numbers of dogs involved there are usually only one or two groups shown on any one day. This is another excellent reason for owning a caravan: you can watch the other groups on the other days and be there for the Best in Show award at the end.

The Bichon Best of Breed then competes with the other Best of Breed winners in the toy group, which is judged by a different judge. The winner of the group will compete at the end of the show against the other group winners for the Best in Show award. Bichons tend to do very well in the toy group because they are generally so sound and stand out so well. However, only one Bichon has ever gone right through to Best in Show, and this was Ch. Tiopepi Mad Louie at Pamplona.

NZ Ch. Exquis Sugar N
Spice.

118

*Ir. Ch. Penrose Bucks Fizz
at Glandore.*

In Ireland, dogs are made into champions through the Irish Kennel Club's 'Green Star' system. A dog requires forty Green Star points to gain the title of Irish Champion, and of these it is necessary to have gained four 'major' Green Stars; these major awards vary from five to ten points in value. Each year, the value of the Green Stars is assessed. For example, at the present time, it is necessary for five Bichons of the same sex to be present in order for one to gain a five-point Green Star (other breeds vary). However, if the Best of Breed is a dog and there are only three dogs present, while there are five bitches, then the dog and the bitch are awarded five points each as the Best of Breed cannot receive fewer points than his opposite sex winner. If the Best of Breed Bichon then wins the toy group he will receive the Green Star equivalent in value to the highest Green Star value of any other breed in that group. A dog may use only one group win towards his title of Irish Champion. The system is complex, and means that a Bichon who wins five Green Star points at a show could end the day with ten points. The Irish title of Annual Champion is awarded each year to the Bichon that has won the greatest number of Green Stars in the breed. Because of the complexity of the system, it is possible for a dog or bitch to be declared Annual Champion and yet not have achieved his Irish title. If however a dog or bitch wins this title twice consecutively, he is awarded the title of Irish Champion. At certain shows, FCI (Fédération Cynologique Internationale) awards are on offer, as well as Green Stars, and these count towards the title of International Champion.

The system in the USA is not dissimilar from the Irish one in that points are accumulated and used to count towards the title of Champion. In order to become an American champion, a dog must accumulate fifteen points, which must include at least two wins of three points, each won under a different judge. The amount of points on offer at a show varies between one and five. Only champion Bichons can compete for the title Best of Breed, leaving the non-champion dogs to compete for points towards their titles. The system means that more dogs can become champions than can their UK counterparts, so great success is measured more by Group and Best in Show wins.

In New Zealand, Challenge Certificates are awarded for Best of Sex. To gain the title of Champion a dog has to win eight CCs under different judges. An extra title of Grand Champion is awarded to dogs that have won fifty CCs and three Best in Show awards at all-breed shows.

# Junior Handling

Junior handling classes are an important part of the show scene. They provide an excellent opportunity for the young exhibitor to practise ringcraft skills in a competitive, and therefore authentic atmosphere. The importance of this cannot be overestimated, for the standards of presentation that will prevail in the future will be determined by today's young show enthusiasts.

Most open shows hold junior handling classes for children of all ages. Classes are held for two age groups: six to eleven years old and twelve to sixteen years old. When both classes have been judged, a best handler is declared. Classes are also held at championship shows, which can take the appearance of a very large variety class.

In giving you an idea of what junior handling is all about, I cannot do better than to quote the words of one of our most successful junior handlers, Tamara Dawson:

> Competition in the great junior handling classes is sometimes very high, and it is necessary to learn some very difficult manoeuvres in order to demonstrate that the handler can remain in complete control of his dog. However a good handler will need to remember that although it takes much hard work and lots of practice, showing any dog should always remain enjoyable, especially for the dog.
>
> Becoming involved in junior handling is not difficult. It is possible to learn the basic skills just by handling a dog at ringcraft classes and small shows. Other juniors will often help you, and it is possible to learn a lot about handling just by watching the older handlers go through their paces. It is a very exciting sport to be involved in, and if your parents are already exhibiting their dog it is an excellent way to share their hobby.

The size of your dog can be important. It is hardly sensible, or safe, for a six-year-old to handle a Great Dane. Bichons are ideal in that they are small, compact, easily controlled, and eager to please, so even the smallest children can manage them. And, of course, Bichons have an added advantage in their white coats, which make them more likely to stand out in a large class.

The dogs are not there to be judged; it is only the skill of the handler that is assessed. So it is not essential to have a top-quality dog, although it helps if the dog moves well, is in good condition and is well presented.

Some very well-known exhibitors in the breed gained much of their experience whilst competing as a junior handler, and this gives a clear indication of how particularly suitable our breed is for this branch of the sport. Anthea Pleasants (then Colvin) started very young with Lhasa Apsos, and then with Bichons when they first arrived in the UK. She won the national title of Junior Handler of the Year, which is a competition for all children who have won specific junior handling classes. They are entered into a semi-final competition, held every year at Richmond Championship Show in September. The finalists from those classes compete for Junior Handler of the Year at a very prestigious final, sponsored by Pedigree Chum. The title winner represents the UK in the international competition at Crufts which attracts competitors from other countries worldwide.

Marita Rodgers (then Gibbs) was another very well-known junior handler who was also successful in the breed ring. Tracy Alexander handled her mother's Bichon to many wins during the 1980s, and in 1989 became the second Bichon handler to take the Junior Handler of the Year title. In 1995 and 1996, I won Junior Handler of the Year consecutively, setting a new all-breed record, as well as enjoying success in the breed ring.

I started showing Bichons when I was nine years old, although I had owned my first one since I was four. My mother, Val Cumstey, showed other breeds before I was born and bought our first Bichon puppy from Vera Goold. We bred a litter and kept the best dog, but he wasn't good enough to show. We then used Sue Dunger's dog, Ch. Sulyka Puzzle on our bitch, and bred our first really nice Bichon. This bitch, Tamalva Belle Ami, however, would only behave for my mother, so we bred another litter so that I might have a puppy of my own. I had some success with the next bitch and she helped me considerably to develop my handling skills. She did very well in the breed competition as a puppy, but never really developed. I then started to use Sue Dunger's dogs in the major junior handling competitions, and in 1991 I won the semi-finals of the Junior Handler of the Year, judged by Chris Amoo.

Over the next few years my mother bred more litters of Bichons, and for one reason or another would always part with the pick of the litter until, in 1993, we mated Belle Ami to Asilene Paperback Writer. My mother agreed to let me keep the best bitch from this litter, and I called her Tamalva Keep The Faith. In September 1994 I had handled Faith in the Junior Handler of the Year semi-finals at

121

*Tamara and Faith in the Group at Crufts.*

Richmond and won the class. I then went on to handle her at the finals, which we won under Frank Kane. I think we had done better this time because I had been showing my own dog regularly and had developed a much better rapport with her. Winning the Junior Handler of the Year meant that I was to represent the UK in the international competition at Crufts. It was all very exciting because I wanted to show Faith in the breed classes as well, which meant that it was going to be a very hectic day. The international competition took place first, and for this I was to handle a different breed, not my Bichon. The dog was a flashy American Cocker spaniel called Olivia. I won it! Everyone was thrilled, but amid all the excitement I had to rush off to another part of the building where I was just in time to show Faith in the Bichon ring. We won this too. Faith was awarded her first CC and Best of Breed by Marita Rodgers. In the toy group she came fourth, and she was still only nineteen months old. She became a champion at Windsor later that year, where she went on to win the toy group under judge Kari Jarvinen. By the end of 1995, she had accumulated six CCs and was Top Bitch in the breed.

In 1996, Faith went on to win five more CCs and also the toy group and Reserve Best in Show at Paignton Championship Show. She was Top Bichon for this year. At the Junior Handler of the Year semi-finals, I handled Faith again and won it. Against all odds, I went on to win the final under Terry Thorn, and in winning the title for the second consecutive year I created a record that has so far not been broken.

We have retired Faith now and mated her to Ch. Sulyka Happy Hurbert. We have kept the best bitch from this litter, and I shall continue to enjoy my showing with her. Not, however, in junior handling – at eighteen, I am far too old.

# Make Haste Slowly

Buying in another dog to show and then perhaps breeding your first one is the course that many new exhibitors naturally take. However, try to progress slowly at first: don't be in too much of a hurry to buy in dogs from other lines, and when you do, choose carefully, for the choices that you make early on will influence your later success.

It is wise to remember that every dog that you purchase in an effort to start your own successful kennel will need as much care and attention as a single family pet. It is unfair to the dogs that you buy, and to yourself and your family, if you overstretch yourself emotionally and financially. Think hard about how you will cope with any number of dogs if you are ill; to their cost many fail to take account of such factors. If your family shares your enthusiasm for the sport and is willing to share the responsibility, dog showing can prove to be second to none as a family hobby. Without the family's support – or at least co-operation – dog showing can be too much of a strain, both for you and for the family members who are expected to share their home, spouse or parent with a number of dogs. I have known many very enthusiastic and dedicated lovers of the breed that have known considerable success with a single Bichon, or even a second one, stop completely because the inevitable next step would be to own a third dog, and this, for a variety of reasons, was impossible.

Having said that I hope that I can encourage anyone who owns a Bichon to come along to a show at some time just to have a small taste of the showing world. If you belong to one of the clubs, you will receive a newsletter from time to time giving you details of future events. The clubs put on other events, such as Christmas parties and seminars, as well as shows. Sometimes these events are staged for the pet owner specifically, and important groups such as breed rescue may benefit, so it is important that everyone has the opportunity to be involved.

Even if you feel that dog showing is not the sport for you, you may still enjoy a day out seeing so many Bichons all beautifully prepared and looking wonderful. It is a very special sight for anyone who loves this very exceptional breed.

# 7

# Judging

To become a judge in the UK requires no academic qualifications, nor any formal training in understanding the construction and characteristics of a dog and how to assess them. One's knowledge and understanding of the Breed Standard is not tested in any way other than that implied by one's performance as a judge in the show ring. However, certain criteria must be fulfilled if a judge's name is to be included on one of the judging lists. Judges are graded according to the criteria they meet, and their names are then placed on the appropriate list.

The top-grade (A) list contains the names of judges who are approved by the Kennel Club to award Challenge Certificates. In order to be approved, it is necessary for you to have judged a large number of dogs in your breed and, usually, to have judged at a club show (which is in itself a recommendation for it indicates that a club committee has sought your opinion). Before inviting you to judge at a club show, some breed clubs will require evidence that you have achieved some success as an exhibitor. The principle behind this requirement is that the first test of your ability to judge must surely be your skill in assessing your own puppies when deciding which ones to keep for show. If you consistently fail in this – in other words, regularly show dogs that never reach top honours – how can you expect other exhibitors to value your opinion? I believe that it is not unreasonable to expect that someone who can award CCs has at some time during his career received them (or a similar award if he is from outside the UK).

The second (A2) list is for those that satisfy the criteria for a place on the A list but have not yet received an invitation to judge at championship level. Approval by the Kennel Club is not usually sought until such an invitation has been made.

The third (B) list contains the names of another group of people who have been judging for around seven years and are gaining experience. In order to be included in this list, the judge will be expected to attend lectures annually, although responsibility for seeking any specific training rests with the individual.

The fourth (C) list contains the names of those who are just starting to judge. In most cases, they will have been actively involved in the breed for a few years before receiving an invitation to judge. Many such people seek a judging opportunity because they are quite sure that they can do a better job than someone else (who is usually the person who last judged their dogs and didn't place them). It is not until a canine society gives them a chance that they realize that it is not as easy as they thought.

The Kennel Club is looking at new ideas for improving the quality of judging in the UK. In the meantime, more and more breeds are beginning to realize that aspiring judges should be provided with some formal training and, increasingly, attendance at club-organized training events is required before they can be given a place on a judging list.

## Stewarding

Stewarding offers an excellent grounding for those who wish to become judges. Such is the general recognition of its value that experience in stewarding will soon become a condition of an aspiring judge's inclusion on the judging lists.

The steward's job is to assist the judge. He will check that all exhibitors and their dogs are present, and he will prepare paperwork

*Bobander Chasing Rainbows.*

125

and hand out prize cards. Generally, he will ensure the smooth running of the proceedings and make sure that there is no interference from outside the ring. Stewarding is in itself a responsible job, but for the aspiring judge it is also a valuable way to become familiar with the judge's responsibilities and to learn the various ways that different judges will approach the task.

It is always interesting to observe the judge's placings (especially if you are stewarding your own breed) and, later, to read the judge's critique so that you can compare your observations with his.

# A Good Judge

Not everyone has the ability to judge. Some people can assess quality with ease, whether it is with a glance at a group of puppies running around the garden or with the handling of a youngster when bathing and drying him. Such a person may not have the command of the terminology to describe or explain his assessment, but the 'eye for a dog' is undoubtedly there. Conversely. there are those who can attend lectures, read books, and display an unquenchable thirst for knowledge, but still judge a class of two dogs and place them in the wrong order.

When you show your dogs regularly and exhibit your dogs under many different judges it is possible to decide for yourself which are the good judges and which you consider to be the bad or indifferent ones. Even though some may have left you unimpressed, you will often give them a second chance if they happen to be judging at one of your favourite events. The best judges are not necessarily the ones that have awarded your dog top honours but those that you feel have been fair. As an exhibitor you will want to feel that your dog has been examined fairly and thoroughly, and that the judge was not rough when he handled your dog. You will expect his manner to be friendly and any instructions to be clear and precise. You will not always agree with his choices, but you will go under him again if you feel he has been fair.

No one can ever expect to agree with all the decisions that any judge makes. No matter how carefully you watch the proceedings from the ringside you will be unable to assess the dogs in the ring in the same way as the judge can. Even if you have had the opportunity to judge most of the dogs yourself shortly before, you will still be unable to make an accurate comparison between one dog and another, on that day. There are so many factors that vary from day to day and from show to show. Fluctuations in body weight, presentation, attitude and coat texture, even the way a particular floor surface affects the dog's movement, are all factors that will affect a dog's performance and may ultimately result in his being placed differently on separate occasions. However, it must also be acknowledged that some dogs find themselves consistently placed in the top spot not because they are the best Bichons but because they have 'gathered momentum': if a dog does quite well at a few shows, wins a group or even two, some of the weaker judges may find it hard to place other dogs over him, even when he stops looking so good or moving as well.

Being a good judge is not just standing centre ring and placing the dogs in some order. This can be done by almost anyone who can subsequently explain that, for whatever reason, he simply prefers one dog to another. Judging well is assessing a dog's attributes. In what areas does he excel, and where does he fail? There are no disqualifying points, so any fault that is found has to be considered according to its severity. This is the main area where, in my opinion, some judges make a mistake. They 'fault-judge'. They find a fault on a dog and mentally dismiss him. On examining other dogs in the class they find a nice little dog with nothing in particular wrong with him. He is placed first. The dog with the fault, whether it is a missing tooth or an off nose, may have other qualities, better movement, good overall pigment, or a stunning head, but for that judge the fault was too big an obstacle: it blinded him to the dog's attributes and a plainer dog won.

There is always room for improvement when it comes to the finer points of judging dogs. But everyone who takes on the role of judge will automatically become sympathetic towards other judges as they realize how difficult some decisions are to make. Formal training in ring procedure would ease some of the pressure placed on many judges as there are many rules that have to be adhered to and uncertainty of them can create unnecessary tension. However, those people who are constantly decrying all judges' ability to do a good job are in my opinion those people who have poor dogs. Their dogs rarely win, but instead of taking a step back to look constructively at their dogs and perhaps recognize why they fail, they blame the judging. They consider that the really good judges are the ones that put their dogs up, when in fact the opposite is true.

I am of the opinion that there are not many really bad judges. I know many people will disagree with me, but I do believe this to be true. There are many judges who place certain points on a dog higher in the order of importance than I do. There are others who favour a certain type of Bichon because they really believe it to be the one that fits the

Standard most closely. It is also true that there are those judges who fault-judge and therefore always end up with mediocre dogs; and there are those who judge class after class looking for a single point – such as large dark eye, or extra length of leg or whatever – dismissing all dogs in whom that point is not the strongest characteristic. Nevertheless, I am convinced that however a judge approaches the job of placing our dogs in order of merit, the vast majority go into the ring and consciously do the best they can and try very hard to get it right.

I can remember an experienced judge in Bichons saying to me many years ago that she judged a little better at every appointment. She illustrated this by comparing judging to learning to drive a car: though you may pass your driving test, it is the subsequent years of practice and experience that enables you to become truly proficient. This makes a lot of sense to me. Each time we judge, especially at championship show level, we learn more; it is only after we have made a decision and are truly comfortable with it that we know it to be the right one. But if we make a mistake, that too adds to our experience.

## The New Judge

Most exhibitors who have been involved with the Bichon for some time, and who are familiar with all aspects of the breed, will at some stage or another, wish to try their hands at judging. Many aspiring judges hold the firm belief that they can master the task with comparative ease because they have the knowledge to perform it, and to do well. However, having an in-depth knowledge of a breed is not on its own enough to equip you for the task. You must also have the character to cope with those aspects of judging that do not involve the direct assessment of dogs. The judge must have the ability to make a decision, under pressure, and without any consideration for the politics that exist in the ring.

Any judge will find some decisions particularly difficult. You might imagine that the most difficult decisions are those that have to be made when there are many good dogs to choose from. But while it is true that a judge will feel sorry that they cannot all take first prize, classes of good-quality dogs create fewer problems than those in which all the exhibits are poor. In a class of low standard, there is still the requirement to place the dogs in order of merit, which is easier said than done. If it is a championship show it must be remembered that a high placing may qualify a dog for Crufts: and if all the exhibits are poor the judge will find such a prospect difficult to accept. The only way that a judge can prevent it is to withhold the top placing, and thus to permit his disapproval to be noted by everyone present. To be able to do this you must have both the confidence in your ability to determine quality and the courage to stand by your decision, not only in the ring and on that day but for as long as people remember it – and those exhibitors that are directly involved will.

Your class winners will line up in the challenge. Whether they were the only dog in their class, and therefore in the final by default, or the winner of the biggest class of the day, someone will compare the dogs in the line-up to see if they all look to be of a similar stamp. In making such a comparison, the onlooker will measure your ability to judge to type. In any case, you can be quite sure that the majority of those around the ring will be assessing the dogs for themselves and, chances are, their conclusions will differ from yours. Whichever dog you finally choose, whether it is the 'best' one or not, you will have to cope with some disapproval. The very nature of the sport dictates that there will be those who disagree with you. It is a well-known fact that if several people witness the same sequence of events, each of them will recall them differently; the same happens when judging.

Even those people who were not actually there will have formed their own ideas about which dog should win, and which should stand second or third. And so when the results are relayed to them they will have definite views on whether or not your decisions were the right ones. Rarely is any consideration given to all the different factors that may have affected the order of things; only the judge's ability to do a good job is questioned. Some individuals are really unable to cope with this kind of criticism, and as such they do themselves an unkindness by accepting a judging appointment – whether it is for a little open show or for Crufts – and subjecting themselves to it.

It is for you to decide whether you have sufficient strength of character to deal with the more blatant efforts of some to apply pressure. If you do not, the fact will eventually come to light: exhibitors will work out which judges are susceptible to such pressure and will usually stop exhibiting under them.

## The First Appointment

If you are lucky enough to do enough winning in your formative years to receive an invitation to judge, think hard before you accept it. It will not reflect badly on you if you decide that you would rather wait until you have gained more experience; nor will anyone blame you if you decide that you do not want to subject yourself to the pressure.

At the moment, a society can invite you to judge purely on the grounds that it considers you fit for the task, but it will soon be necessary for you to have your name on a breed club's judging list before the society can consider you as a candidate. Some clubs demand that you attend lectures on judging the breed, and this must not be seen as an obstacle. If organized well, these events are an excellent opportunity to learn more about the breed and to gain hands-on experience of judging before you take up your first appointment. You will be amazed how much you will already know, gained primarily through choosing puppies for show and exhibiting them. No experience is wasted. I have learned more about the construction of a dog whilst being given tips about trimming than I have from any other source. Nevertheless, you will find it very valuable to learn more about the technicalities, such as, where the withers start and what 'lay of the shoulder' actually means. Most people will find there is at least one technical detail they have misunderstood. Whatever your personal strengths or weaknesses, never be afraid to ask questions.

Local ringcraft classes are an excellent relaxed environment for you to practise your judging skills. As we have seen, being a good judge means more than merely placing the dogs in a sensible order. It means going over a dog well, which requires you to be thorough, but gentle, and to have the skill to put the exhibitor at ease without being over-friendly. It requires you to be aware, especially with puppies, that you are a stranger to the dog and to be sure that you do nothing to upset him. All this requires practice. If you are confident in your ability to go over the dogs well while making the exhibitors feel at ease and then to choose the best dog, then you can do no more.

However confident you are of your knowledge and understanding of the breed, you may find arriving in the ring for your first appointment quite a daunting experience. For there is no one to assist you or advise you: you are left to your own devices. This is when some training proves to have been worth while: it will have given you confidence in your ability to conduct yourself in the correct manner, and thus you will feel able to concentrate on judging the dogs before you without having to worry about whether you are following the correct procedure. This said, there is no substitute for the real thing, and it is not until you are faced with your first class that you will be able to judge your own ability to do the job.

One of the difficulties you may come up against is trying to decide between two dogs that are of very similar quality. Try to picture them in place in your mind; now, reverse the order. Which decision are you

*Reserve group winner at Scotland in 1985. The breed judge was Jackie Ransom.*

most comfortable with? If you are still not sure, take a little more time; do not feel under pressure to make a snap decision.

You may also feel a little intimidated that the person handling the dog is someone who does a lot of winning. Again, imagination is a useful tool: picture the dog in the hands of a novice; is he still as attractive? You will learn that it is necessary to evaluate every dog on his merit on that day. You cannot take into account what the dog may have looked like yesterday or last week. We see very respectable judges slip up by putting up a dog they assume to be a big winner because a certain person was handling him, only to find out later that they have been misled, sometimes unintentionally, because the dog's usual handler was showing elsewhere.

Always bear in mind that because the whole world of dog showing is based solely on the opinion of the judge, there are times when discussions become heated and tempers frayed. If you consider it a privilege to be invited to judge, rather than take the view that your judging is necessary for the good of the breed, you will find that in time people will appreciate your opinion. Of course, such respect has to be earned, and many years of experience, knowledge and sound decision-making go into making the few judges whose opinion is really valued.

# Critique Writing

In Britain, at open-show level, judges must write a critique on the class winner. At championship-show level, the critique goes further in that the first and second dogs are described and the placing sometimes explained. Critique writing is an art. There are very few judges who can write in sufficient detail to satisfy the reader as to why the dog placed first was preferred to the second one, and yet not reveal to all and sundry every fault any one dog possessed.

A well-written critique can help the exhibitor to progress. If enough judges comment on his dog's lack of muscle, for example, he may realize, to the dog's advantage, that more exercise is needed. There is much to be learned about type, and why one dog appealed to this particular judge more than another. Any exchange of information has got to be a good thing. Judges who shy away from writing a constructive critique are usually either lazy or unable to explain themselves (probably because they lack confidence in what they have done). Of course, there is the odd occasion when it is not possible to write, but these are few.

When writing a critique, it is infinitely easier and less time-consuming to make very general, non-committal comments. However, I consider these to be of little use to anyone other than the exhibitor who has won on the day. Derogatory generalizations, such as, 'heads were awful except in my primary winners', or 'movement overall in the bitches was appalling', convey nothing but an overwhelming impression of doom. If an area of weakness has to be highlighted, it should not be exaggerated merely for effect. It is considerably more constructive to make the criticism in a sober manner while at the same time balancing the point with a more positive observation. There is always something encouraging that can be said.

For the seasoned exhibitor, critiques can serve as a useful guide to a judge's personal preferences, which can then be taken into account in the future.

# 8

# Breeding

Breeding a litter should never be entered into lightly. You must decide what your motives are for breeding and whether they are the right ones. If your only reason for breeding is to make money then you are bound to be disappointed. For the breeder with a financial incentive, Nature has this surprising knack of producing a litter of problems that will require the costly services of the vet, along with a huge surplus of puppies from other breeders, making the litter more difficult to sell.

Your main reason for breeding should be a desire to produce quality puppies from which you will endeavour to start your own line and from which the breed as a whole will benefit. Of course, not every litter is bred purely for the show ring, but the desire to breed good, healthy dogs must remain any breeder's driving force. It is unfortunate that there are still a few owners of bitches who are led to believe that it is advisable for a bitch to have a litter before she is spayed. This is not good advice. There is no evidence to support this theory; indeed there is much to suggest that spaying early reduces the incidence of mammary tumours.

Another common reason for breeding is a desire to produce another puppy like the much-adored family pet. It can be very difficult to argue the case against going ahead with a mating when the owners are very keen and the bitch is of sufficient quality. It must be remembered that not everyone can go to shows or even see it as a sensible way of spending weekends, and this should not automatically exclude them from the experience of breeding a litter. In fact some such litters have considerably more thought put into their planning than have some that experienced breeders produce for the show ring. Whatever your reasons for breeding, it should be understood that if the experience is to be a pleasure, and not one that you come to regret, great planning and thought must go into it. The results of this mating – whether it is your first litter or your twenty-first – will stay with you forever: regardless of where these puppies end up, you must bear the responsibility for their existence. Your aims must be very clear; and you must be prepared for disappointment as well because nothing in the breeding of dogs is certain, and much is out of our control.

# Breeding Systems

## *Line-breeding*

Line-breeding is the mating of a dog and a bitch who have at least one common ancestor. It is the most consistently successful method used by dog breeders. The theory is that if the ancestor was a particularly good dog, his qualities will appear in both breeding partners and will be perpetuated in future litters. The more champions and known good dogs there are descended from him, the greater the evidence that his qualities appeared in his offspring. However, the further back in the pedigree that the ancestor appears, the greater the chances that inferior dogs will have been introduced to the line, so nothing is ever guaranteed.

## *Inbreeding*

This is the mating of closely related dogs, for example father to daughter or, closer still, brother to sister. It is occasionally done with very good dogs in order to fix qualities in a line. However, it will also increase the likelihood of faults occurring, so it should never be attempted unless you are very experienced and dealing with your own extremely familiar lines.

## *Outcrossing*

This is the mating of dogs who are from different lines and share no common ancestors. Outcrossing is commonly recommended every three or four generations to inject new vigour into a line. In choosing an outcross, a breeder will look at lines that possess qualities that are weak or diminished in her own line. However, it is not quite as simple as it sounds because besides the desirable qualities – such as a darker eye or a better coat – you may introduce to your line faults that previously had not been there.

Some breeders feel that they can inbreed and line-breed indefinitely without ever having to outcross. This is usually because they see other lines only in terms of their faults, and they are therefore critical of all of them. Eventually, their own dogs become more and more exagger-

*Ch. & Ir. Ch. Sulyka Snoopy.*

ated and their own line's faults more difficult to avoid. However, even people who think they are outcrossing in Bichons will realize that it is very difficult to do so in the true sense, as I can illustrate for you with a tale that has become a small part of dog-breeding history:

In March 1985, I mated my bitch Shamaney Manhattan of Bobander (Jody) to Ch. Sulyka Snoopy on days ten and twelve of her season. Two days later, while I was out, my own dog Bobander the Muffinman (Blue) also mated her. There was now no way of being sure who the sire was: since the two matings had taken place only two days apart, the date of the whelping did not confirm either one. I eventually made up my mind not to register the puppies and instead to sell them as pets only. However, the litter contained two bitches and a dog, and one of the bitches (Toots) looked very nice. Di Johnson (of Dicarl Great Danes and Boxers) suggested that I might run this bitch on and register the litter with two sires – it had been done before. I followed her advice and in due course Toots became a champion, but I knew that the fact that she was registered with two sires would always be a problem, especially when it came to registering any of her own litters. Furthermore, I would not be able to sell any of her puppies abroad because at that time many countries would not allow registration of a dog with such an unusual pedigree.

With the help of *Dog World*, I was given the opportunity to use ICI's new technology to have the dogs DNA tested and the true identity of Toots's sire revealed. Blood had to be taken from Toots, Jody, and the two

*Shamnaey Manhattan of Bobander.*

sires, Blue and Snoopy. The DNA extracted from the white blood cells in each sample was processed into bands, or 'fingerprints', and the bands compared in order to identify one whose differences from the others would eliminate it as that of Toots's sire. It proved to be a difficult task because Snoopy is Blue's sire, and so their DNA had many similarities. It was further complicated by the fact that in producing Blue I had used Snoopy on my Jarlien Petite Cherie (Tallulah), whom I had thought to be completely unrelated to Snoopy (and therefore an outcross). However, Tallulah and Snoopy had a common ancestor five generations back in Am. Ch. Chaminade Mr Beau Monde. As a result, there was only one line in Toots's band that was present in Snoopy's but not in Blue's. This identified Snoopy as the sire. On this basis, a case was presented to the Kennel Club whose general committee decided that Blue could be erased from the pedigree – the first decision of its kind in Kennel Club history.

Dr David Morton, the vet at Leicester University who had performed the testing, asked me if it was common practice to 'inbreed' so closely. Having explained that the UK Bichon started out a decade previously with a very small gene pool, I went on to point out that, since then, many other dogs had been introduced from overseas and that as a result most pedigrees were very different (as illustrated by Tallulah's pedigree, which was different from Snoopy's over no less than five generations). He was insistent that regardless of the apparent differences in the pedigrees, the DNA proved that, genetically, Bichons were being inbred.

While this story illustrates how difficult it is really to outcross, it also contains another very valuable lesson: that of ensuring you keep your mated bitch well away from other dogs!

# Like Begets Like

Some breeders make a great study of genetics in their endeavour to come up with the right choice of stud-dog for their bitch. However, in selecting breeding partners on a scientific basis – rather than by the age-old means of following your instinct – you must have some idea of the genetic make-up of each dog in the potential partners' pedigrees. Like me, most breeders are armed with only a basic knowledge of the subject and yet manage to breed successfully through knowing their own dogs and by following the principle of putting a good-looking dog to a good-looking bitch. Having said this, I think it is important to acknowledge the value of a basic understanding of why what a appears to be a good, healthy breeding pair will occasionally produce offspring that do not apparently do justice to their parents.

All living beings inherit from their parents characteristics that in turn have been inherited from previous generations. All these characteristics, good and bad, are carried in the genes, and the genes are contained

*Ch. Kynismar Heaven Forbid.*

137

in pairs of chromosomes. One of the chromosomes in each pair is inherited from a dog's sire, the other from his dam. A problem arises when the information contained in the genes of the sire's chromosome conflicts with that contained in the dam's. To deal with this, Nature has devised that some genes are dominant and others are recessive. This means that if a dog inherits conflicting genes, the dominant gene will 'win' and the dog will display that dominant characteristic. A simple example can be found in the inheritance of coat colour. If a dog inherits the gene for a black coat from one parent, and the gene for a white coat from the other parent, he will have a black coat because black coats are dominant. However, such a dog will still retain the recessive gene (in this case white coats) in his make-up; and if he is then mated to a bitch who also carries that recessive gene, that recessive characteristic may suddenly appear in one or more of their offspring. The difficulty for the breeder lies in the fact that until two recessive genes come together in this way, recessive characteristics are invisible. And since a recessive gene can be carried through any number of generations before it visibly manifests itself, a breeder can be completely ignorant of its existence until it suddenly appears in a litter.

In addition to a rudimentary understanding of the relationship between dominant and recessive modes of inheritance, the successful breeder requires quite an active imagination. When I assess a potential breeding pair, I try to picture the resulting puppies in my mind. This is made easier if the pair has a fair amount of characteris-

*Int Ch. Tarzan De La Persaliere, and his son Ch. Rank's Tar-son Du Lejerdell.*

138

tics in common. I generally assess the qualities in my bitch, and then look for a dog with similar ones. If she has faults, which of course she does, I make sure that the dog of my choice does not have the same ones. If possible, I try to determine whether the recent ancestors on either side appear to be clear of these faults, although I should add that it is impossible to address every fault that can occur as the result of a mating: the size of the Bichon's gene pool dictates that the various breeding lines are ultimately similar, and this means that similar faults can be found in most of them; but it is possible to reduce the frequency with which they might occur by adopting a system of selective line-breeding.

## Hereditary Defects

It is unfortunate that hereditary defects are primarily carried on recessive genes. This means not only that their incidence is difficult to predict but that their complete eradication is scientifically impossible. Nevertheless, they become a major problem only when they are ignored by those who persist in inbreeding to affected animals. We are fortunate in that the Bichon is relatively healthy. This may not remain the case indefinitely, and when new problems do emerge we must have the will to address them. I am particularly aware that for the breeder who finds a problem there is very little help available, and information is scarce. I can remember when I bred a puppy with hydrocephalus (*see* Chapter 10); only one other breeder would even acknowledge that the condition existed at all, so I was left feeling as though it was a problem that I alone had invented.

This is understandable in a way, for some people depend so much upon the stud fees and puppy sales to finance their sport that they will find it difficult to acknowledge that their lines might not be completely perfect. It may seem easier to keep quiet about any problems and allow it to appear that they happen only to other breeders, but really very few people are fooled.

When researching any problem, whether it is one that has been well documented or, as yet, still quite unresearched, there will always be diversity of opinion regarding whether something is hereditary or congenital and why. It can be very difficult to decide whether to discard a dog or a bitch from one's breeding programme because they have produced a puppy with, for example, patella luxation. Many think it foolhardy to remove a dog completely from a breeding programme only to replace him with one that may bring with him a different set of problems from another line; instead, the solution might appear to be to avoid a repeat mating but continue to use one of the carrier dogs elsewhere. The problem with this is that even if you can be sure that the next partner is clear of the recessive gene, some of the subsequent puppies will not be; and if they in turn are unwittingly mated to another carrier dog, history will repeat itself.

Whenever I have come across a defect in our breed – whether or not it has appeared in a puppy that I have bred – it has often been quite difficult to find non-conflicting information about it. Vets are usually able to diagnose a problem, and may sometimes be able to prescribe treatment, but they are rarely able to offer advice on how this will affect your breeding programme. I have found that the majority of vets will recommend that you do not breed from any dog unless it is completely trouble-free. This sounds like excellent advice in theory, but it is near impossible to follow in practice. Libraries can sometimes help; so too can your breed club and the Kennel Club, especially if it is not a new problem but merely one that has not emerged for a while. A newly discovered defect should be given the full attention of the breed clubs and the correct and relevant information gathered and made available to any member who needs it.

There is much yet to learn about the nature of hereditary defects, and some breeders will want concrete proof that a condition is the result of a recessive gene before they remove a dog from a breeding programme. Hereditary defects undoubtedly carry with them a stigma, and too often the reaction to their occurrence is the generation of a witch-hunt within a breed. This is counter-productive, for defects know no boundaries: they can occur in any dog from any line. Tracing back suspect dogs through the pedigree may make the owner of a carrier dog feel a little better and less responsible, but the sooner the facts are faced the better. Mutations may periodically appear completely by chance, so there isn't always an earlier generation to 'blame'. In any case, blaming a single parent for a defect is a nonsense, for it must be understood that it is necessary for both parents to be carriers of a recessive gene before it can manifest itself in some of the offspring.

Since defects can be difficult to predict, it is sometimes easier to avoid a dog whose structural type is likely to predispose him to a condition. In many of the bigger breeds, hip-scoring has helped considerably in the fight against hip dysplasia and, in the future, a similar programme may help us and other toy dog breeders to overcome our problems with the slipping patella.

In conclusion, it is not the existence or non-existence of hereditary defects present in a line that separates the good dogs from the better dogs and the responsible breeders from the irresponsible ones. Rather, it is how the breeder copes with the problem once it has appeared, and how she deals with the disappointed owner now that his puppy is lame, its show career over and all future hopes dashed. All the time we are breeding dogs, whether for ourselves or for future breeding by others, it is essential that we accept responsibility for the health of puppies that are born.

# Planning your Litter

Good planning is a major part of the skill involved in breeding. It is as important to the health and overall quality of the resulting puppy as any other stage in the process. Many breeders make their main mistakes at this point. They drift on for many years breeding mediocre bitches to strange dogs and as a result make very little progress with their breeding programmes. Occasionally, they stumble across a good dog and use him on a bitch that is better than their usual, and from this union they produce a single champion; but since this single success was achieved by accident, and since they do not analyse the reasons for it, they are unlikely to repeat it. It is essential to have goals, and then to work out how to achieve them. If it requires a change in direction, or help, then take it. In order to breed a litter that will be a credit to you, you must look closely at what you are achieving and be honest with yourself: if you are five years into a breeding programme and disappointed with your progress, you must analyse why and be prepared to make changes accordingly.

*A litter of six puppies.*

You might be fifteen years on and running into problems with particular hereditary faults. Never be afraid to change course or even start again with a new line. Previous experience will not be wasted for you can apply all that you have learned already to a new breeding programme.

The ultimate aim of the dog breeder is to produce the perfect dog. This might be impossible in itself, but the continual striving towards it is what enables the breeder to produce better and better dogs and, ultimately, that big winner. Whatever your specific goal – whether it is to produce your first champion or your twentieth – careful planning is the essential factor in increasing your chances of achieving it.

## The Breeding Pair

It used to be said that you should buy a bitch puppy for the show ring on the grounds that if she doesn't make the grade you can at least breed from her. Why should this be true of a bitch and not of a dog? If you are hoping for puppies of quality then surely the bitch has to be as good as the dog. We would not consider taking our champion bitch to a pet dog that we have come across in the park, so why do people consider this to be acceptable in reverse? Common wisdom also has it that you should buy the best bitch that you can afford from a well-established breeder; but this is not foolproof, for some such breeders lose their way and yet continue to trade on old success long after the reason for it has gone. Be careful about where you obtain your first Bichon, for the path

*Rusmar Sea Angel of Zudiki, a significant dam for the Rusmar kennel.*

142

you subsequently follow under the guidance of that person will greatly influence your progress in the breed.

Bear in mind that although you may have bought a bitch puppy with a view to breeding, there is no guarantee that she will fulfil her promise. When the time comes for mating, you must make an honest assessment of her qualities and her failings. The breeder may help you here. You must be sure that she is healthy and still apparently free from any defect or disease that she could pass on to her puppies; and she should also be as free as possible from faults in breed type, such as poor pigment and light eyes, which are very easily passed on to the progeny. It is wise to visit your vet, tell him of your plan and have her checked over. She will need her heart checked, and her stifles checked for patella luxation. It is not enough to allow the bitch's breeder to check the stifles as I am convinced that many of them are unable to assess these with any accuracy.

You will soon realize that there is much to consider when deciding on the suitability of your bitch, but the most important two factors are good conformation and temperament. There must be no exceptions to this: a bitch that is not correctly made and balanced cannot hope to produce quality puppies, no matter how influential the dog is. And an even temperament is essential. Never imagine that a nervous or aggressive attitude will improve with a litter of puppies; if anything it will be worse as nothing is more stressful for a bitch than having a litter. This is the only area in which the bitch actually contributes more than the dog, because although behaviour may be inherited it is also partly learned from the dam.

Having established that your bitch is a good, sound specimen of her breed and that she is in good health and firm condition, you must find a stud-dog for her. Before settling on a particular dog, have a look at his progeny in the show ring and study the lines that he has been put to already. If his puppies are being shown, their exhibitors must be reasonably satisfied with them, but avoid using the latest big-winning puppy just because he is currently popular with other breeders. He will be an unknown quantity for some time to come, and he may yet develop a previously unknown fault, such as failing pigment or even a bad temperament. Always look to a more experienced dog, or even the puppy's sire if he too has the qualities you seek; this is especially good advice if you have a maiden bitch.

As with all breeding, faults as well as qualities can be inherited, and since recessive genes can skip generations it is wise to gather as much information about the other dogs in the chosen dog's pedigree. As a rule,

*Ch. Sulyka Puzzle (right), and his son Garfield.*

it is far better to line-breed back to a dog that you have seen yourself. Other people's memories of a dog can be unreliable, especially when they are embued with nostalgia. Try not to be affected by others' opinions: you should not persuade yourself to use a particular dog or to breed to a particular line when you really prefer the qualities found in another. Your final decision to use any dog should be made because you like the dog for himself, not just because his pedigree looks impressive.

Don't be too put off by a long journey if it means being able to use the dog that you feel is the best one for your bitch; but if there are two or three dogs you wouldn't mind using, choose the nearest one. This is especially sensible if this is the first time your bitch will be mated, for it may be necessary to make a few visits in order to be sure that she has conceived. In any case, many people find that the stress of making long journeys reduces the chances of conception. If it is necessary to travel some distance, I find it better to take overnight accommodation so that the bitch has a chance to relax before she is taken to the stud-dog.

# Mating

Allow yourself plenty of time to prepare for the mating. You must work out when your bitch will be in season and when it would be convenient for her to have the litter. If mating her at the next season would mean having a litter of puppies in the dining room over Christmas, it would be wiser to wait until the next season. Plan ahead so that you can be sure you will be free to give your bitch all the attention she needs when the time comes, and for quite a time afterwards.

144

Before your bitch actually comes into season, check that her vaccinations are up to date and seek your vet's advice about a suitable worming programme. You should approach the stud-dog owner and agree terms, which will include the fee and any other arrangements, such as provision for a second service if your bitch does not conceive the first time.

Timing is critical. A bitch's season lasts for around three weeks and usually occurs twice a year. During the first nine or ten days of the season (called pro-oestrus), the bitch will discharge blood. In the second stage (oestrus) the flow of blood will cease and she will begin to discharge a clear, straw-coloured fluid; oestrus lasts for another nine or ten days, after which the bitch will be no longer be willing to mate. Most bitches are ready for mating on the tenth day, as oestrus begins. It is often difficult to be sure when a bitch is ready, but a good sign is when she becomes very flirty with any dog and swishes her tail hard over to one side if the area around her tail is touched. A more accurate method of testing for ovulation involves taking a swab, a procedure that can be performed by your vet, but I would enter into this only if it was otherwise impossible to predict. One case might be the bitch who has 'clear seasons' (which are not uncommon): such a bitch does not bleed visibly but instead produces a colourless discharge throughout the season. This makes it more difficult to know when the time is right and, as a consequence, success is less likely.

As soon as the bitch comes into season, inform the stud-dog owner so that he knows approximately when the mating will take place. Avoid bathing your bitch in the day or so prior to the mating, for while a keen stud-dog will not be discouraged by the shampoo's unnatural masking of the bitch's scent, some other dogs will be less enthusiastic.

Not all stud-dogs behave in the same way. All of mine have been individual in their approach, as have been the stud-dog owners in the way they treat the situation. Some owners will allow the dog the freedom to court and play, and generally to take things as nature intended. This is favourite with most breeders, and probably also with bitches who are more likely to co-operate if they are relaxed and happy. The problem with this approach is that it may set in the dog a tendency to resent any assistance from humans, even when this is just to steady the bitch, and of course it may result in the dogs' failure to mate at all. Occasionally the stud-dog will be introduced to the bitch on a bench or table and held by the owner. Although this is a very controlled situation, and with a very experienced stud-dog a mating nearly always takes place, the bitch whether co-operative or not has little chance to display her readiness to be mated. When the dog actually penetrates the bitch during

145

such a mating, it is wise to quickly and very calmly take support of her, for it is at this point that the obvious discomfort may incite her to object and perhaps even to try to get away.

Once the dog has penetrated, the pair will probably 'tie': the base of the dog's penis will swell and the bitch's vaginal muscles will grasp it, preventing the pair from separating. During the tie, the dog will usually turn himself around so that the partners are standing tail to tail. Any attempt to separate before the natural cessation of the tie will be painful and possibly damaging, so it is important to continue to support the pair throughout and to provide restraint if either decides to pull away prematurely. The tie can endure for what might seem like for ever, but typically it will last anything from a few minutes to twenty or so. The duration of the tie is often used as an indication of how successful a mating is likely to be, but there is no scientific basis for this belief and indeed I have known litters to be produced from matings with no tie at all.

When the pair separates, take the dog somewhere quiet to recover. The dog's sperm will last up to two days, so it is not essential to repeat the mating, especially if all appears to have gone well, but if you repeat it two days later you may increase the size of the litter, and certainly the chances of conception if the bitch has been slow to ovulate. The most common reason for failure to conceive is getting the timing wrong. New breeders especially – afraid that they might miss the deadline – are likely to take their bitches for mating too early. Try to resist this: bitches usually stay receptive for at least five days after the end of pro-oestrus, and as a rule I find that the later they go to the dog the more eager they are to mate.

*Ch. Avava Madam I'm Adam.*

# 9

# Pregnancy and Whelping

## Signs of Pregnancy

Once your Bichon has been mated, you will look for signs that she is in whelp. The litter will not cause the abdomen to distend until about five weeks into the pregnancy, but before this time you may notice slight changes in your bitch: the vulva will be swollen, the teats will start to enlarge, and she may start to behave slightly differently. However, without tests, it is difficult to confirm pregnancy for certain as bitches are prone to phantom pregnancy, the symptoms of which are identical to those of a genuine pregnancy and can ultimately include milk production and guarding behaviour (although the guarded babies will take the form of a favourite fluffy toy). It may seem comical to the human onlooker, but it will be very real to her. Try to distract her from her purpose through encouragement rather than force and increase her activity – in other words, do what you can to take her mind off it. If symptoms do not subside consult your vet, who will probably prescribe hormone therapy.

## Care of the Pregnant Bitch

After the mating the most natural thing to do is to treat your bitch normally, but being very careful to keep other dogs well away from her until her season is over. The only concession I make to a bitch in whelp is to take her for more secluded walks when she goes out: I feel it is not advisable for them to come into contact with strange dogs, and I do not advise anyone to take an in-whelp bitch to a dog show. If you wish to continue showing a bitch you must postpone mating. It is pure greed to show a pregnant bitch and put the puppies at any risk, however slight, just for the sake of another award, no matter how important it may seem at the time.

I feed my bitches normally until around the seventh week when I divide the meals into two smaller ones and give a little extra. Howev-

147

er, even if she appears to have an enormous appetite, you must be careful not to overfeed because a bitch that is fat will have a more difficult delivery. Many people are concerned with the levels of calcium in the bitch's diet. Calcium is important for more than just healthy bone and teeth formation: a deficiency can cause eclampsia, a very dangerous condition that can be fatal (*see* Postnatal Problems, page 155). However, the old common practice of giving extra calcium during pregnancy is now considered harmful as it can have a detrimental effect on the bitch's natural calcium levels.

Towards the end of the pregnancy it is a good idea to trim your bitch's coat short: a long coat will make her hot during whelping and will in any case become very messy. As the day of the whelping approaches, introduce your bitch to the whelping box, which should be situated in a warm, quiet place in the house. It should be easy to clean and large enough to allow the bitch to lie comfortably with her litter without being so large that it is draughty.

## The Birth

The dog's gestation period is sixty-three days, although the puppies may be born any time between days fifty-seven and sixty-five. My bitches tend to whelp at sixty-one days, and usually at night. There is a lot of waiting around involved and the most important thing to remember is to stay absolutely calm. Your bitch will very quickly pick up any anxiety that you feel, so it is important to be well prepared for every event.

Line the whelping box with layers of old towels or sheeting. I avoid using newspaper as it makes such a dreadful mess of anything wet it comes into contact with. You will also need:

- A pair of sharp, disinfected, round-nosed scissors.
- Cotton wool.
- Several old towels to dry off the puppies as they are born.
- A small box or carrier containing a thickly wrapped hot-water bottle or a heated pad.
- A clock and notebook to record times of birth. (You must keep aware of the time that elapses between each birth so that if any problems arise you can give details to the vet. It is also worth keeping records for future comparisons.)

Try to arrange for someone else to be at hand to answer the phone, make the tea or, at worst, drive you to the vet if necessary. Do not have other pets wandering around: no matter how well you think they all get on you cannot know what effect their presence may be having on the bitch. This applies to small children too. The whole environment must be quiet and totally unthreatening to the bitch; the only person to keep her company (discreetly) should be the one she knows well and trusts. It is far better for her to be attended by you, with no experience, than by a more experienced person whom she doesn't know.

Your first idea that something has actually started to happen may be the lowering of your bitch's temperature. From around fifty-six days, use a sterile, lubricated thermometer to take her temperature first thing each morning. The dog's normal temperature is about 101.5 °F (38.6 °C); when it drops to below 99 °F (37.2 °C), the puppies will usually be born during the next twenty-four hours. She will start panting and become restless, and she may show signs of discomfort. This stage can last anything from one hour to all day. She may take little naps, and she should be allowed the peace and quiet to do so while she can. During this stage, some bitches refuse food but will always drink. Milk is often a good compromise, but water must always be available to her. She will be aware that something is going on and although you will be amazed at how automatically your little pet takes on the role of mother, she may still be a fraction frightened and will want you with her. It is not the time to go off to work and leave her.

The next visible sign may be some blood loss, which may be quite watery and copious. This happens as the contractions start to move the puppies down the birth canal. Soon afterwards, signs of pushing become evident. (Those owners who have wondered whether they would know when the bitch is starting to push can be assured that they will be in no doubt.) Make a note of the frequency of the pushes, which will become less frequent as more puppies are born. Very prolonged pauses and half-hearted pushes may indicate a problem, so observe your bitch's behaviour closely. Note-taking is important if it becomes necessary to describe events over the phone to your vet. When the puppy starts to emerge, it should still be encased in its membranous sac. As soon as the puppy is born, the bitch will normally lick the sac away; but some maiden bitches may seem confused about what to do, in which case you can gently tear the membrane from around the puppy's face and wipe the liquid away from the nose before the first gasps are taken and fluid is inhaled. It is important to make sure that the airway is clear. I find that some bitches are more interested in the afterbirth, which follows the puppy. She will probably want to eat the afterbirth and sever the umbilical cord with her teeth. However, if the bitch is reluctant to sever it, or the pup seems in need of revival before the afterbirth has been expelled from the bitch, you may need to cut the cord yourself. Unless it is an emergency, time should be allowed for as much blood as possible to transfer itself from the afterbirth to the pup. There is no panic to separate the pup from the afterbirth. I have fiddled around with bits of cotton thread in an effort to tie off the cord before cutting it with sterile scissors; but it is an enormously time-consuming job, especially if you are alone and the bitch then spends her time frantically removing your handiwork anyway. It is usually enough to apply pressure to the cut, which should be made about half an inch (1.2cm) away from the puppy's navel. It will bleed even less if you can emulate the bitch's teeth by tearing the cord with your thumb nail; this is in any case the preferred method if the afterbirth is still attached to the bitch and you need to revive the puppy.

Subsequent puppies will be born either almost immediately or hours apart; some will come head first, others tail first (usually the two presentations alternate). If the bitch was reluctant to pay atten-

*Mother and her litter of pups.*

tion to the first puppy, give her the opportunity to step in with the second one: she will usually cope better. Although the time between each birth will vary, an hour is a good guide. Provided your bitch is not straining furiously for more than an hour, she can be allowed to decide her own pace. But if she becomes distressed or is straining fruitlessly for more than an hour, you should contact your vet for advice. Most litters will be born without event if the whole process is allowed to happen with the minimum of fuss and the least amount of disturbance for the bitch.

Newly born puppies will quickly latch on to the nearest teat, but it may be necessary to move them to a corner of the whelping box when the next pup is being delivered to avoid their being trodden on. Do not remove them from sight however as this will invariably upset her. Offer her a warm milky drink during the whelping. If she consumes all the afterbirths do not worry unduly: it may make her stools loose for a day or two, but I am quite sure that the benefits of letting her have them outweigh this inconvenience. Although there is little evidence to support the old theory that consuming the placenta encourages the milk to flow more freely, it may nevertheless contain useful hormones or proteins. I happily allow my bitches to consume the afterbirths that they get to first, but in a big litter I try to remove a couple of them to reduce the likelihood of vomiting and subsequent diarrhoea. In any case, make sure you keep a note of how many afterbirths are expelled (there should of course be one for each puppy). This is very important because a retained placenta can cause serious problems: if you suspect that your bitch has not passed all the afterbirths, consult your vet.

Quickly examine each puppy as it is born. Besides noting the obvious, such as the sex and whether they have all their toes, look around the jawline and inside the mouth for any obvious deformity such as a cleft palate. Some puppies may appear quite blue when they are born, usually because they have been a little slow in taking in enough oxygen. However, most puppies recover quite naturally and are soon a nice healthy pink colour. Through the bitch's licking and stimulation, what looks to be a very scrawny, cold little scrap becomes a warm, dry, rounded and much healthier-looking bundle, sucking away at his first feed.

When you are sure that there are no more puppies to be born – your bitch is no longer restless or pushing and hasn't done so for at least two hours – you can give her some clean bedding and settle her down with her puppies. Allow her some peace and quiet for this, and resist the temptation to allow the family and hoards of neighbours in to tell her what a clever girl she has been. She must be disturbed as little as possible for a few days. Some bitches will have to be prised away from their pups before they will go and relieve themselves, but while she is away you can take the opportunity to examine and weigh the puppies without upsetting her.

It is hard to get the balance right between keeping an eye on the new family and interfering. It can take up to forty-eight hours for the litter to settle down and they can seem particularly noisy at first, especially when your are trying to get your first night's sleep in three days. It is easy to imagine that the cries you are hearing are being made because one is being lain on or because they are hungry and the bitch doesn't have enough milk. Such fears are usually groundless, but tiredness will make you more anxious. This is a good time to enrol the help of your partner so that you can get some rest. You will be no use to your bitch if you are tired and edgy.

## *Whelping Complications*

It is unpleasant to contemplate anything going wrong, but occasionally a problem will arise and it will need to be dealt with. The most common one you may have to deal with is reviving a puppy that has failed to start breathing. First check that there is nothing blocking the airway, then rub the puppy with a towel. This is usually enough to stimulate breathing, but if there is no result hold the head back and the mouth open and blow gently over the face. Great care must be taken to ensure that you do not exhale into the lungs but just direct the flow into the airway, as too much force can damage tiny lungs. Do not be tempted to shake the puppy violently. If you think there may be fluid in the airway, hold the puppy firmly in both hands; then, with the puppy facing away from you, and your hands supporting the head and neck, swing the puppy smoothly downwards. As long as you hold the puppy securely, and make sure that your hands are fully supportive, this swinging action repeated a couple of times should remove the fluid without damaging the puppy.

Sometimes it becomes obvious that the bitch is having trouble passing a puppy. If the contractions are weak and unproductive, or they cease altogether, she may have secondary uterine inertia and you will need to call your vet for help. Inertia can be caused by exhaustion or by an obstruction, and it is most likely to occur in either very small or very large litters. An injection will usually resolve the problem, although if the inertia is caused by an immovable obstruction a caesarean may be necessary. An obstruction is also the most likely explanation if contractions are still strong, and your bitch is working hard at pushing, but to no avail. An oversized puppy, or two puppies side by side, may block the canal, or the puppy may be abnormally presenting and unable to negotiate the canal. There is little you can do yourself, and it is unwise to delay calling your vet, who will identify the cause of the problem and take appropriate action. If a caesarean is necessary then you can rest assured that it will not prevent her from whelping normally in the future.

# Early Days

The first few days are always the most traumatic for you and your bitch. She may settle very quickly and assume her role as a mother without any problems at all, or she may take much longer. I have found that the ability to cope with a litter is a distinct trait that is passed from mother to daughter, and a bitch that copes easily is a treasure. At birth, a puppy has a very low body temperature, sometimes as low as 94 °F (34.5 °C). And since puppies do not shiver, they have no way of generating their own heat and must be kept warm. The bitch's body heat is usually sufficient, but if she leaves the box for any reason the puppies may become chilled if there is no other source of warmth. (Remember that even in the height of summer the temperature may drop sufficiently at night for the puppies to suffer if the bitch is away for long.) A heated pad is a useful heat source – in the bitch's absence the puppies will gravitate towards it – but only if the whelping box is big enough for the bitch to be able to keep away from it, otherwise she will overheat.

Usually by day three everyone has settled down into a routine and this is a good time to give your bitch a much-needed bath. If you have trimmed her coat down, bathing shouldn't take long. If you intend to have the puppies' dew-claws removed, which will necessitate a visit to the vet, then a bath is an excellent way to occupy the bitch while the puppies are away.

Unless you are feeding the bitch or changing the bedding, try not to interfere with the puppies at all. It is quite easy to weigh the pups quickly while mum is outside (if you can prise her away!), and she need never know that you have done it. Even if it is necessary for her to have her whelping box in the corner of your sitting room it is still possible to observe her right to privacy. Do not allow visitors, for even if she knows them well she will not be the docile pet that they know

153

*Eight weeks old.*

and the chances are that she will guard her puppies furiously, perhaps treading on them in the process. There is plenty of time for visitors later. If your bitch keeps on picking the pups up and trying to hide them, it usually means she is trying to find a safer place for them. You can help by not reacting adversely when you see her do this – it is a perfectly natural way for her to behave. Try covering the whelping box up so that the pups are concealed, and if the box is not already in a pen then section the area off altogether so that her space is more defined and therefore more secluded.

While she is nursing her puppies, your bitch will require more food and a diet that is higher in protein than usual. I also offer her goat's milk, which is a valuable source of calcium that doesn't upset her. However, I always have to hand a good-quality milk substitute formulated for puppies in case the bitch begins to find the puppies' demands too great and I need to supplement her milk supply.

## Postnatal Problems

The most immediate problem that may arise is that the bitch seems not to have a clue what to do, or seems not to want to lie still for the puppies to remain on the teat for long enough. Be patient with her and try not to fuss as you will only increase any anxiety she may feel. When faced with a bitch like this, your first action must be to ask your vet to check her over for any physical causes of the behaviour, such as a retained afterbirth or an infection. (You should in any case ask the vet to give the whole family an early check-up, even if there are no problems at all.) Your main concern will be that the puppies are not getting enough food, although in most cases they will be, despite the bitch's apparent lack of interest. Try to resist the temptation to take over the feeding unless you are absolutely sure that she has insufficient milk and the puppies are failing. A normal, well-fed puppy will be quiet, sleepy, warm and round, and will feel firm and solid to touch. If you gently pinch the fold of skin on the back of the neck it will quickly return to shape when you let go. An abnormal puppy will feel cold and clammy; it will persistently cry and have a bluish tinge to the skin.

If the vet has confirmed that the bitch is well and has no reason to reject her puppies, it can help to put these puppies on the teat while you comfort the bitch, encouraging her to keep still while they feed. Do this as often as you can, for it can make all the difference to pups that have had a difficult start. After each feed, you should watch to see that the bitch licks the puppies: the action of her tongue on the abdomen and around the tail will stimulate the puppies to pass urine and faeces, which is important because they are incapable of spontaneously emptying the bowels and bladder. If she does not perform this task, you will have to simulate the dam's tongue with a piece of warm, damp cotton wool. Having said all this it should be pointed out that this supplementary rearing will be of use only if the puppies are otherwise healthy and are merely being hampered by a young and inexperienced mother who is taking time to adjust. It will not work if any of the pups are destined to fail for some other reason.

Even if the new family has settled down and is progressing well, the conscientious breeder will continue to be vigilant. There are a few other problems that may arise in the first few days or weeks, but two in particular are especially worth mentioning here.

The first is eclampsia, which is a very serious and unfortunately not uncommon condition that occurs in the bitch as a result of calcium deficiency. It is most likely to appear in bitches with large litters when the pups are between two and four weeks old and milk production is at its highest. Onset is quite sudden, and will cause the bitch to be restless and then to move in an unco-ordinated fashion. She may salivate copiously, and ultimately she will be unable to stand. Eclampsia is an emergency requiring immediate veterinary attention. If it is caught soon enough, the cure – calcium administered intravenously – is almost instant. Most experienced breeders will have some first-hand knowledge of the condition. The dam of my very first litter collapsed with eclampsia twelve days after birth, and if she had not received a calcium injection quickly she would have died. Her recovery was remarkable, but she was unable to care for her five puppies properly so I had to hand-rear them – a task made more challenging by my frantic bitch, who couldn't understand why I had taken her precious puppies away from her. Eventually we compromised: I gave her back the one puppy that refused to be bottle fed, so everyone was happy.

The second problem is mastitis, which is an inflammation of the teats. The teats will be painful and excessively swollen, and they will feel hot and hard to the touch. In mild cases the symptoms may be relieved by expressing excess milk, and the teats may then settle down as the milk supply adjusts to demand. In any case, you should consult your vet, especially since mastitis may result in an infection which can then be passed on to the puppies.

*Rusmar Magic Moments (left); and Ch. Rusmar Xmas Magic.*

156

# Growth and Progress

At around twelve days old your puppies' eyes will have opened. By this time they should have more than doubled their birth weight. By four weeks, they should be walking, running and playing vigorously, and they should be leaving their sleeping area to relieve themselves; their hearing will be more acute and some may even bark when you approach them. At this age, you will usually be able to dispense with the heated pad and to begin weaning, which should be a gradual process of increasingly supplementing the dam's milk with a puppy food formulated for the purpose.

At five to six weeks the puppies will play games with each other, such as chasing and hiding. They will have better control when running and have some co-ordination skills. The baby teeth will be coming through. The dam will be becoming more reluctant to feed them, and their main source of nutrition will be that provided by you. By seven weeks, mother's visits will have become far less frequent and she will be away from them completely at night. By now, each puppy will have developed his own distinctive personality and a pecking order will have been established.

# New Homes

At nine weeks your puppies will be ready to go to their new homes, preferably not all on the same day. They should be bathed the day before and ready to depart as early as possible on the appointed day so that they can settle into their new homes before night-time. Bitches are rarely concerned at their babies' departure and seem to take it in their stride. You will probably be more upset, but if you are very careful about whom you sell your puppies to then there should be no need for any real anxiety.

If you are selling more than one puppy, it makes sense to keep notes of which puppy is going to whom and when. For each puppy I keep a coloured folder in which I build up a dossier of information for the new owners. On the front goes the details of the new owners and the name of the puppy; inside I keep all the paperwork that will accompany the pup when he goes. This includes:

- A correctly completed pedigree.
- A sales receipt, with the purchase price and any other agreements clearly stated on it.

- The Kennel Club registration document, signed by me to enable the new owners to register the puppy in their name.
- A diet sheet. I make sure that instructions are clear and quantities precise as most telephone calls in the first few weeks are about food.
- Worming certificate.
- Insurance certificate: I insure my puppies against loss or illness for the first six weeks in their new home.
- A general puppy-care booklet, containing useful tips and guidelines to be studied at leisure.
- A contract, to be signed by the new owner and me. This includes a promise from the new owners that they are buying the puppy as a pet for themselves and that they will treat him well. They also agree to return the puppy to me alone if their circumstances change and they are unable to keep him.

When I have had as many as five puppies to go, I have been very glad of this folder system as it helps to ensure that nothing is forgotten.

The responsibilities of a dog breeder do not end when the last puppy is sold. If you have behaved responsibly and supplied the new owners with a contract of sale (as above), you will be held liable for his quality, and you should make yourself available for the puppy's return if anything goes wrong, which includes the development of a fault with which the new owner is unable to cope. This may seem like an unreasonable demand – and in some circumstances it is – but you must nevertheless be prepared to meet it. If you feel that you are unable to do this then it is unwise to breed at all. The breed-rescue organizations are kept busy with problem pets that should really be the responsibility of the breeder – and indeed would be if the breeder was informed of the need. But too often the breeder is unaware that one of her dogs has needed help until he has been through the rescue system and found a new home.

# 10

# Ailments and Diseases

All dogs require veterinary treatment from time to time. Even a healthy dog that is well cared for by the most conscientious and sensible owner may have an accident or catch an infectious disease. We cannot always prevent this from happening, but the way we treat our dog and the speed with which we respond can make a lot of difference to his recovery. As a matter of course, all responsible dog owners will vaccinate against the major infectious diseases. Some, especially those whose dogs are in close contact with other dogs, may want to vaccinate against other viral infections, such as kennel cough.

In Bichons, there are a few problems that occur more frequently than others, and these are described in this chapter along with the more generally common conditions. Some may require the attention of your vet; some can be dealt with at home. In any case, if you suspect there may be something wrong with your dog, you should always consult a vet. Never ignore symptoms, however vague they seem to you. And never put off a visit on the grounds that you may not be able to afford it: apart from causing unnecessary suffering to your pet, you may find that delay has resulted in a worsening of the condition and, ultimately, greater expense than you would otherwise have incurred. Veterinary treatment can be expensive, so it is well worth considering pet insurance. There are various types of policy available, so you are bound to find one to suit your needs. If, for whatever reason, you do not wish to buy insurance, you must be quite sure that you can afford unforeseen veterinary fees before you buy your dog.

## General Symptoms and Conditions

### *Bladder Stones*

Bladder stones occur as a result of an accumulation of excess minerals and waste deposits in the urine. Traces of blood in the urine is a symptom. But if one of these stones blocks the urinary tract, your dog will also have great difficulty in passing urine at all and his abdomen will appear very distended because the bladder is unable to empty. Usually, however, the stones stay very small and only particles can be found in the urine. Diagnosis involves testing the urine to determine the presence of stones; the stones will then be analysed to discover what minerals they contain. Treatment will usually involve the prescription of a special diet, designed to break down the stones so that they can be passed, but if the stones are big it may be necessary to remove them surgically before the diet is followed.

## Coprophagy

This is the term used to describe the eating of faeces – either the dog's own or that of another animal. This extremely objectionable habit is one that any breed of dog may develop and, unfortunately for the owner, it is also one that can be difficult to cure, especially if you have several dogs. The simplest and most effective way of dealing with it is to ensure that you do not leave your dog's faeces in the garden: pick it up immediately. A change of food can help, as dogs that indulge in the habit are usually attracted only to a firm stool, but the theory that a dog may do it in order to resolve some nutritional deficiency is an improbable one, especially now that proprietary dog foods are so carefully balanced. I have heard of many strange remedies for it, including adding fruit to the diet, or shaking pepper on to the stool as a deterrent, both of which have apparently worked for some. But whatever solution you try, it must be remembered that it is a natural thing for dogs to do, especially nursing mothers who are impelled to clean up after their pups long after it is necessary (sometimes in this household it is a mad dash to see who can clean it up first – the bitch or me). However you cope with the situation, be assured that your pet is not a freak and it would be unfair to punish him for it. We tend to humanize our dogs, which is natural when we care for them so much; but it means that at times like this it can be something of a shock to remember that they are, after all, animals.

## Diarrhoea

Diarrhoea may result from simply changing a dog's diet or from an upset caused by the dog's eating something to which his system is unaccustomed. However, it is also a symptom of a number of other diseases and conditions – some of which are very serious – so if diar-

160

rhoea persists for more than a couple of days you should consult your vet. One of the serious side-effects of acute diarrhoea is dehydration, so it is essential that you do not restrict your dog's access to fresh water.

## Hot Spots

These small areas of redness on the skin may appear anywhere where the coat is dense. Because it causes irritation, the dog will lick the area (or scratch it if he can't reach it with his tongue), intensifying the irritation and eventually causing a bald patch characterized by red, raised skin that is hot and firm to the touch. If left untreated it will usually subside after a short time, but the damage to the coat is quite extensive. My vet considers a hot spot to be the result of an infection, which may go on to ulcerate; others consider it to have a dietary cause. This may account for the diversity of treatments that have been offered by different vets and might explain why treatment is not always very effective. The incidence of this condition does seem to lessen considerably in dogs whose diet is both low in protein and gluten-free. However, I also know that a predisposition to this condition does seem to occur in lines. In this household it occurs only in one grandam, her daughter and her grandson. In my opinion, the causes of 'hot spots' are various, and may differ from one dog to another.

Immediate treatment is better kept very simple, and it is wise to keep the area free from any cream, powder or potions that may irritate it further. It is possible to keep the area clean by bathing it in warm saline solution (one teaspoon of salt to one pint/half a litre of water), at least until it has been seen by your vet and an more accurate diagnosis made. If it is necessary to bath your dog when he has a hot spot, use a very mild shampoo especially if the skin is broken. While the treatments for hot spots are varied, recovery is quicker and damage to the coat minimized if the area is kept completely dry. This will encourage the formation of a scab, and once this has occurred the dog will usually leave it alone.

## Hypothermia

This condition is not one normally associated with toy dogs with thick coats, but the problem can be a real one in certain circumstances and I have known it claim the life of two Bichons. If your Bichon becomes wet or his coat heavily covered with snow then he will be at risk in very cold weather. If it is not removed and the coat dried, the dog's body temperature can drop quite quickly and dramatically. The dog will shiver quite violently and yet become lethargic and unresponsive. Unconsciousness follows; and if the dog is not found quickly and treated, he will die. It can be great fun to see your Bichons playing in the snow, but you must be prepared to dry your Bichon quickly with the dryer as soon as you can coax him back indoors.

## Kennel Cough

This presents itself exactly as the name implies. The dog will cough, sometimes with a retching sound, and may also bring up a small amount of white foamy liquid. The temperature is often raised. However, the severity of the symptoms varies: what may be a mild infection in one household may be very serious in another where the dogs may be more susceptible to it. (It most often affects elderly dogs and of course the very young.) The condition is caused by an airborne virus, and it is therefore extremely infectious. For this reason it is essential to keep affected dogs indoors: you should never be tempted to take them to a dog show or anywhere where they will come into contact with other dogs. Antibiotics may be necessary and paediatric cough mixture can also help, but when you take your dog to the vet be sure to leave him in the car until he can be seen.

## Travel Sickness

This can be a frustrating problem, especially if you are travelling to a show with a young puppy and you are particularly keen to make the experience a positive one. The type of car you own, and whether you keep the travelling cage covered or uncovered may make some difference, but if you have a dog that is regularly sick in the car it can make both your lives a misery. The fact that many dogs are affected on the way there, and yet are problem free on the journey home, is probably significant. In any case it is notoriously difficult to deal with because any number of factors – such as excitement, fear, or simply dizziness – may contribute to it. There are a number of medicines that may help to relieve the symptoms, but some may cause drowsiness (which is an important side-effect if your destination is the show ring). If your dog is prone to travel sickness, give him plenty of loosely folded bedding and make sure that the floor of his cage is non-slip. If you can, take the longer route if it is straighter, and make regular stops to check him. If your dog continues to find travelling a misery, it would probably be kinder to leave him at home. Most dogs, however, do grow out of the problem by the time they are about eighteen months old.

# Parasites

## *Worms*

All dogs should be wormed at the age of four weeks, and regularly thereafter for the rest of their lives. It is not enough to assume that your dog is not at risk because you keep everything scrupulously clean and have never seen a worm.

The two types of worm that most commonly affect dogs are the *Toxocara* roundworm and the *Dipylidium* tapeworm. There are various species of each, but the one that is most familiar to the public is *Toxocara canis*. Alarmists constantly report on – and frequently exaggerate – the dangers posed to children by this particular roundworm; and the anti-dog fraternity are quick to jump on the bandwagon, even though cats and foxes pose a greater risk because these animals are less likely to be wormed regularly. That said, it is important for dog owners to adopt a responsible attitude and ensure that they implement a sensible worming programme.

There are some excellent wormers on the market that are very safe and effective against tapeworm and roundworm. Your vet will advise you on the most appropriate ones for your dog.

## *Fleas and Ticks*

All dogs are susceptible to flea infestation, especially in the summer months. However, in common with some other dogs, many Bichons are also prone to flea allergy – a reaction to flea bites which causes the skin to become inflamed and sore and the coat to become very sparse and coarse. A severely infested Bichon will also go a typical rusty colour, caused by the flea's blood-stained waste products being trapped in the coat and by the dog's saliva staining the coat as he licks to relieve the irritation. Since we bath our Bichons so regularly, keeping them free from fleas should not be difficult: if you regularly use a good-quality insecticidal shampoo, it will prevent the odd flea that your dog may pick up from becoming established in your home. There are also preparations that can be taken in tablet form once a month, and these are especially useful if your dog is constantly exposed to a source of infestation, such as a neighbour's cat or visiting foxes. The topical gels that are applied to your dog's neck are generally considered to be very good, but they have been known to irritate a Bichon's skin.

When treating your dog for fleas, it is extremely important to treat at the same time any other dogs and cats you may have, and also your dog's environment. The female flea lays its eggs in the dog's bedding and in any other soft furnishings, including carpet, so you must treat all these areas with a preparation designed for use in the home if you are to ensure that flea control is effective.

Ticks can also be a problem, especially if you exercise your Bichon in wooded areas or places where sheep have grazed. If you find a tick on your dog, *do not* be tempted to try to remove it unless you are experienced. Ask your vet for advice and the right preparation to kill it. If you have to attempt removal, apply alcohol to the tick before using tweezers to twist it out in an anti-clockwise direction. This is important because otherwise you may leave the head of the tick embedded in the skin, and this will cause the area to become infected. Ask your vet to demonstrate the procedure for future reference.

# Hereditary Conditions and Defects

## *Hip Dysplasia*

Dysplasia means abnormal growth. In the hip it results in a failure of the femoral head to sit firmly in the socket in the pelvic joint, causing the joint to become unstable. The joint deteriorates, and the ligament that holds the head of the femur and the acetabulum (the socket in the pelvic bone) together becomes stretched. The cartilage between the two bones becomes eroded and in an effort to re-stabilize the joint, osteoarthritic new bone develops around the neck and head of the femur and the acetabulum.

Like patella luxation (*see* below), it is a hereditary condition whose mode of inheritance is polygenetic (i.e. carried on several genes); it may also be influenced by diet, exercise and trauma. The degree of incapacity resulting from hip dysplasia can vary considerably. Although we know it exists in the British Bichon because cases have been recorded, I have no personal experience of it. The incidence seems to be higher in America, where breeders routinely X-ray their dogs before breeding from them. It is surprising that although all UK and US Bichons originated from the same sources, so few British breeders have experience of it.

## *Open Fontanelle and Hydrocephalus*

All puppies are born with a membranous gap at the top of the skull – a fontanelle – which allows the skull to be compressed so that it can pass down the birth canal. After birth, the bony plates should fuse together to close the gap. However, in some puppies there is an abnormal delay in closure, or the skull fails to close altogether, and such puppies are then said to have an open fontanelle.

Since an open fontanelle is normal at birth, the condition is not identifiable as a defect until the pup is over two weeks of age. And since the majority of breeders would not even think to look for it, delayed fusion of the plates is rarely identified because in most cases closure will usually be complete by the time the pup is seven or eight weeks old. However, in a few puppies it is associated with a condition called hydrocephalus (water on the brain). From birth, a hydrocephalic puppy will have a very characteristic appearance: the head will seem disproportionately large, and the eyes large and very widely spaced; the whole of the face will appear to be in the lower half of the head. There will probably be some evidence of an infection, most likely a discharge from the nose. The puppy may survive if the bacteria causing the infection is quickly identified and the correct medication given, but there is no guarantee and the puppy may die or have to be put to sleep if symptoms of brain damage are observed.

Although hydrocephalus is recorded as a congenital deformity (caused perhaps by an infection or the presence of toxins prior to birth), rather than a purely hereditary one, we have to consider the possibility that there may be a genetic factor until there is evidence to the contrary. Because of the severe nature of hydrocephalus it is extremely unlikely that affected dogs have ever been bred from, although pups with delayed closure of the fontanelle may have been bred since they develop and mature normally.

An open fontanelle is fairly common in breeds whose skulls are domed, as in the Chihuahua. The Bichon skull should be only slightly domed and quite broad, and compared to the Chihuahua's it should feel relatively flat. It could be that with some narrowing of the skull, which we know is not uncommon in the breed, sufficient doming might occur to prevent the successful closing of the fontanelle. However, without considerable research this theory would be difficult to prove. In the case of hydrocephalus, I personally feel that the presence of infection is the main factor in its occurrence: when an antibiotic is administered to a puppy with an open fontanelle, the skull fuses without event.

165

## Patella Luxation

A luxating patella is commonly referred to as a slipping stifle (the stifle being the equivalent of the human knee.) Because it is fairly common in the smaller breeds, the condition is often trivialized – which is extremely regrettable, for while it is not life-threatening it can be debilitating and painful.

The patella sits in front of the knee joint and is held in position by ligaments. When the dog bends his leg, strong tendons facilitate the patella's movement up and down the trochlear groove (which can be best described as looking like a stick of celery). In a normal dog, this celery-like groove is sufficiently deep to retain the patella within it and to prevent it from sliding in a lateral direction. In the dog with patella luxation, the groove is very shallow, which means that the patella can slip outside the groove. When this happens, the dog is unable to move the affected leg and will usually stand with it suspended awkwardly. The more the patella slips, the more the edges of the groove become worn and the worse the condition becomes. The tendons also become stretched.

Some leading orthopaedic vets consider a luxating patella to be symptomatic of a problem in the hips. While I am sure that this might often be the case, we have far too many dogs with problem stifles but normal

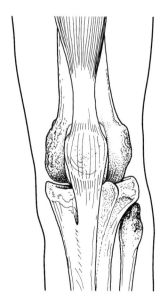 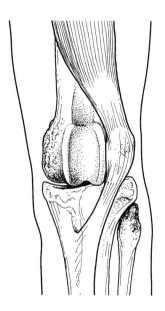

*The correct position of the patella.*  *The patella displaced.*

hips to consider the association to be a strong one. While the genetic link is undisputed, we also know that in the absence of correct diet and exercise, bone and tissue formation can be compromised, so husbandry is a contributory factor. The condition can be instigated in one leg by trauma, such as a dog's damaging one of the supportive ligaments in an accident, but even on these occasions it is not unusual for the other leg to fail in time, indicating an underlying weakness that an accident highlighted. Because several genes are involved, the incidence of the condition is sporadic and hard to predict. There is no real physical attribute that can identify a dog as being more or less likely to be affected: well-angulated dogs seem just as likely to develop a slipping patella as his poorly angulated cousins. The only certainty is that if the presence of such a weakness is ignored, and a breeder continues to include affected dogs in her breeding programme, the incidence in that kennel will increase.

To begin with, an affected dog may not show any symptoms at all (unless they have presented as the result of a fall). Many dogs perform and function quite well and the owner is quite oblivious to the condition; but when the condition worsens, the dog may find it increasingly difficult to walk without pain, especially if the joint becomes arthritic. Even then, it is tempting to dismiss the symptoms as being quite mild, for it is easy to forget that dogs are very stoical and probably suffer more than we might imagine. Although the joint can be corrected surgically, the operation is only occasionally successful. Any affected dog should not be bred from, nor should he be shown. If you are in any doubt about the soundness of your dog's patellae, you should ask your vet to check them for you; and if you intend to breed and show, the dog should be checked regularly. Any judge with experience of the condition will feel a badly slipping stifle when she examines a dog's pads for depth of pigment: there is no mistaking the feel of an affected joint.

## Perthe's Disease

The full name for this condition is Legg Calve Perthe's disease. It is caused by a reduced supply of blood to the femoral head, and this results in the destruction of the tissues in this area. It affects mainly small breeds, and will usually occur when the dog is between four and ten months old. It usually presents itself in one hip, unlike hip dysplasia which normally affects both. The condition develops quite slowly, and manifests itself as increasing lameness. The affected dog may make a little skipping movement every few steps. Wasting occurs in the muscles of the leg and osteoarthritis forms around the femoral head in an attempt to stabilize the joint. In the advanced stages, the dog will be unable to weight-bear.

A firm diagnosis can be made only by X-ray, although there is evidence that not all diagnoses have been correct and some X-rays have been inconclusive. When the diagnosis is undisputed, the ball of the joint looks more like a sponge instead of a solid-looking bone. Some dogs have recovered spontaneously but surgery is usually indicated. The femoral head is removed to encourage the bone to produce a fibrous joint that will function quite well and enable the Bichon to walk without pain.

Studies made on other breeds have revealed that unlike hip dysplasia and patella luxation, in which there are many genetic factors that may or may not be involved, Perthe's disease is inherited by way of a single recessive gene. However, as with many other inherited diseases, outside factors – such as, trauma, diet, type of exercise, and any number of other influences that may be brought to bear during this vital stage of the puppy's growth – may determine whether it manifests itself. More research has yet to be done on Bichons specifically, but certainly we should never breed from affected dogs.

## Spasm of the Soft Palate

Although this condition undoubtedly exists, I am unable to substantiate its name. It is not a serious condition but it can be quite alarming to any owner experiencing it for the first time. It happens in many small toy dogs, most often when walking on the lead. The dog will stop, appear to have difficulty in catching his breath, and make a loud snorting noise through his nose and throat. It is believed to be caused by a spasm in the soft palate at the back of the mouth, similar in a way to our hiccoughs. Whether or not a dog is affected may depend on the structure of the palate, or at least its thickness. In any case, experience shows that it is a very definite trait that has a hereditary pattern.

It can be quite a nuisance to the serious exhibitor as it has an uncanny habit of occurring just as the dog sets foot in the show ring. It can be extremely disruptive if, when the judge says, 'Take them round please,' you and your dog are immobilized because he is gasping and quacking like a duck. The immediate answer is gently to pinch the tip of the nose over the nostrils. This will stop the noise instantly; and it will also make the dog swallow, which seems to help the spasm subside. There are no permanent solutions, however. A wider collar (or show lead) helps considerably, as does avoiding excitement, but this is hardly a solution. Selective breeding is the only long-term answer.

# 11

# The Bichon Around the World

As a rule, dogs imported to the UK must face six months in a quarantine kennel, which means that it is easier for UK breeders to send dogs abroad than it is to bring them in. In other parts of Europe, breeders and their dogs are more easily able to travel between neighbouring countries; as a result they are able to take part in a wider breeding programme and they find it relatively easy to have a champion crowned in more than one country. However, the UK laws relating to quarantine are currently under review and it may be that UK breeders will eventually be able to import and export dogs with the freedom that exists for their European counterparts. Many British Bichons have gone abroad and have proved to be very successful both in the showring, and when bred into the lines that already exist in the destination country. And the breed is now quite well known in many countries, not only in the western world but also in the East. The breed is strongest in the USA, Australia, New Zealand and Sweden.

Every four years a World Congress is held in a host country, giving many enthusiasts a chance to meet and exchange ideas. The third one was held in San Diego in America in May 1998, and the fourth, in 2002, will probably be hosted in one of the Scandinavian countries. The accessibility of new technology means that the world is becoming an increasingly smaller place. Communication through the Internet is brisk, and one of its great advantages is that it enables the new pet owner as well as the experienced breeder to be involved and to contribute. Ultimately it will widen everyone's horizons and introduce new people to this delightful breed.

In this last chapter I hope to offer a brief insight into the breed's profile around the world. Wherever possible, representatives from the various countries, and individual UK kennels, have described the breed's development in their own words.

# Australia

### (By John and Wendy Hutchinson)

The Bichon Frise has enjoyed considerable success in Australia over the last ten years. Although there is not a large number of breed fanciers in each state, the standard of presentation and ringcraft has been very high and many top awards, such as Best in Show at all-breed shows, have been achieved by those who show our breed regularly.

Of the many influential Bichon males, we consider that our own Eng. & Austral. Ch. Leijazulip Jazz of Zudiki has been the most significant. Before becoming an important addition to our Monjoie kennels he gained his UK title, won two Best in Show awards, and was also the first Bichon to win a toy group at a championship show in Great Britain. In Australia he was Best in Show at The Bichon Frise Club of Victoria two years running, and then at the Bichon Frise Club in New South Wales. But it was as a sire that Jazz really left his mark. He is the breed record-holder in Australia, with thirty-four champion offspring to his credit. Jazz passed away in January 1998 at almost seventeen years of age, leaving his progeny to find success all over the world.

Julia Jeffery's Ch. Zipadedoda Hidden Meaning is another important sire who has won many Best in Show awards at both all-breed and breed-club shows, as has the highly successful Eng., Austral., & NZ Grand Ch. Rusmar Magic Rainbow, imported from England by David Green's DJHS kennels. Other sires of note include the Dobrana kennels' Ch. & NZ Ch. Dobrana Debonaire, who was campaigned in Australia and later sold to Ngaire Ross in New Zealand; Denise Moriarty's Ch. Petadina Tres Jacque (later sold to Julia Jeffery); Jill Eerden's Ch. Daejilon Song N Danceman; and our own Ch. Monjoie Ima Devil.

*Nagazumi Mr Frosty of Zudiki imported by Azara kennels from the UK.*

Rennie & Warman's Austral. & NZ Grand Ch. Shandau Fame Seeker (handled by Caroline Lill), originally from New Zealand, was very successful in the ring, and still competing at eight years of age. Another import from New Zealand, Gerry Greig's Ch. Shandau Lyfiz Acaberay, was the Best in Show winner at the Bichon Frise World Congress Show in 1993. A UK import that has been particularly valuable for our Monjoie kennels is Eng. & Austral. Ch. Honeylyn Timmy Tiptoes to Sulyka, who has won a number of Best in Show awards. Many other males have been successful in the ring, and these include Jill Eerden's Ch. Revencre of Valindra (NZ), Monica Smith's Ch. Monjoie Oliver Twist, Valerie Harrison's Ch. Dobrana Timelord, Katherine Berwick's Ch. Parfait Magical Man ( NZ), Gail Robinson's Ch. Monjoie Traditional Jazz, and her Ch. Monjoie Artful Dodger (whom we campaigned ourselves).

The bitches that have made an impact on the breed include our Ch. Azara Mabelle Ami, who holds the bitch breed record for the most Best in Show awards (eight in all). We bought her from breeders Rudy Van Vorst and Frank Valley, who were among the few people who pioneered the breed in Australia and brought in great early dogs such as Austral., Fr. & Int. Ch. Jazz de la Buthiere of Leijazulip, and Fr., Ger., Swiss, Austral., & Int. Ch. Looping de la Buthiere. As a dam she produced thirteen champions (all by Jazz) from only sixteen puppies, including champions in Australia, New Zealand, Canada, Finland, Sweden and Norway. Their progeny have included champions in all those countries as well as Denmark, UK, USA, and Brazil. It would be fair to say that Ami has been behind many successful kennels throughout the world.

Although the bitches have done very well in the show ring, they have not reached the heights attained by the dogs, mainly because puppy-rearing prevents their being campaigned so extensively. Those that have achieved notable success include: Ch. Monjoie Angelica, Top Toy of the Year winner and breed Best in Show winner, Ch. Monjoie Devils Desire, a multi-group winner and runner-up Best in Show winner, and Ch. Monjoie Sweet Georgia, an all-breeds Best in Show winner; Julia Jeffery's Ch. Chismene Isabella, winner of seven Challenges as well as being an all-breeds Best in Show winner, and her Ch. Zipadedoda Royal Result, a Royal Show puppy group winner; Gerry Greig's Ch. Corene Back to The Future ( NZ), who won the CC at the Bichon World Congress Show in 1993; Jill Eerden's Ch. & NZ Ch. Dobrana Divine Miss, a multi-group winner.

All in all the breed in Australia is very strong; despite the fact that we do not have large numbers shown, we see our breed consistently in the top awards. Australia has been fortunate in importing a number of high-quality dogs and bitches over the years. Many of these have come from the UK, and some from the United States and the Continent. New Zealand has also contributed to our stock, although many of these have their origins in Australia or the UK. The Australian Bichon Frise has certainly earned his reputation for quality; and, through the dedicated work of our breeders, our Bichons can compete anywhere in the world.

# Canada

## (By Dale Hunter)

The breeding programme in Canada has been greatly influenced by the introduction of the British gene pool during the past ten years. The first World Congress held in London in 1988 enabled many breeders and fanciers from around the world to perceive the ideal Bichon Frise. Looking back, the importance of such an event cannot be underestimated. Since 1988, it has been difficult to find a top-winning Bichon that doesn't have some English bloodlines in his pedigree; before that time the reverse could be stated.

Ann Yocom, a very dedicated Canadian breeder, has imported some very influential bloodlines into Canada. The first big winner was Am. & Can. Ch. Wendar Fly the Flag, a son of Ch. & Ir. Ch. Tiopepi Mad Louie of Pamplona. Pilot, as he is affectionately called, became the top-winning Canadian Bichon of all time, winning an incredible fourteen Best in Show awards. Even more importantly, Pilot has become a very influential sire as breeders across the country have recognized his wonderful showmanship. His many champion offspring include Ch. Vassaly Vilor The Baron and Ch. Winsome Southern Belle (both Bichon Frise Club of America National Speciality Show winners), as well as many grandchildren that have also won Best in Show awards.

Another important import was Can. Ch. Sulyka Pandora, who was imported in whelp to Ch. & Ir. Ch. Sulyka Puzzle. This mating produced four outstanding males that were placed in show homes across Canada. Their influence has been monumental as three of them have become multiple group winners. One of them in particular, Ch. Yoannewyn Col. Billericay (co-owned and handled by Sandy Greenway) became 1993 top-winning Bichon in Canada and Number 6 Non-Sporting dog, with three all-breed Best in Show awards. His daughter, Ch. Sanbree's Rainbow Cadillac (Reba), out of Chaminade, Chamour and Craigdale lines, went on to beat over a hundred other Bichons to the Best of Winners title

172

*Am. & Can. Ch. Wendar Fly the Flag.*

at the 1997 Bichon Frise Club of America National Specialty Show, judged by the well known all-rounder Ann Rogers-Clarke. Another particularly successful Bichon was Best in Show winner Ch. Ballidier at Trafalgar Square, owned, bred and handled by Julia Dickinson. From another mating from a brother of Col. Billericay called Yoannewyn Capt. Barnstaple and Am. & Can. Ch. Kibbats Craigdale Joy, close line-breeding on the Chamour and Chaminade lines produced Am., Can., & Int. Ch. Craigdale Yoannewyn El Toro. Toro went on to become a top winner in the United States, taking the American Specialty in 1996 and becoming the Number 2 Bichon Frise in the States.

It will be interesting to see how these lines develop further as the combinations seem to be meshing and outstanding puppies are being produced. I feel the Canadian Bichons could compete successfully with any Bichon Frise in the world.

# Ireland

### (By Pat Keery)

The south of Ireland, or Eire, has its own kennel club based in Dublin, while Northern Ireland comes under the jurisdiction of the Kennel Club in London. Northern Ireland canine clubs and associations hold many shows during the year, but there is only one championship show in Belfast where Bichons can compete for Challenge Certificates. It can

*Ch. & Ir. Ch. Spelga Sweet Heaven at Lamoda.*

be difficult to gain the three CCs required for a UK championship title. However, exhibitors from Northern Ireland can become associate members of the Irish Kennel Club (IKC) and compete at IKC championship shows.

There are no large breeding kennels in Ireland, but several people have had considerable success. Michael Coad was one of the first to show and breed his Pamplona Bichons, and Rita McCarry Beattie, also one of the first, has campaigned several Bichons to their Irish titles. Eileen O'Connor (Penrose) was very successful, and Marie Renehan (Lamoda) also bred and owned several Irish champions. At present Marie owns the only Irish champion bitch, bred and residing in Ireland, to have travelled to Britain and gained her UK title as well: Ch. & Ir. Ch. Spelga Sweet Heaven at Lamoda is by Ch. Kynismar Heaven Forbid, out of my Bobander Theme for a Dream at Spelga. Heaven was the top Bichon in Great Britain in 1994. She won Best in Show at the Bichon Frise Club of Ireland's Championship Show and won the CACIB at the first international show held in Ireland.

In the north of Ireland the successful breeders include Ann Bailie of the Aloria Kennels and Lindy Watton with her Tullyheron Bichons. My Spelga Kennels that I own with my husband Glen have been involved with Bichons since 1981. We have owned and bred several Irish champions and are particularly proud that we have also bred, as well as Heaven, Ch. & Ir. Ch. Spelga Solitaire (by Kynismar Show Me Heaven and out of Alareen Precious Gem of Spelga); he too was born and bred in Ireland and the only Irish champion dog to have gained his UK title. He won the Irish Toy Dog of the Year in 1994 and also the CACIB at the first international championship show held in Ireland. Northern Ireland does not have a Bichon Frise club, but the Bichon Frise Club of Ireland does have members from both the north and the south, as well as some from England. The club's breed championship show is always the highlight of the Bichon year.

# New Zealand

Although New Zealand is further from Australia than the UK is from France and Scandinavia, the two countries complement each other's breeding programmes and are familiar with each other's show scene, working together to produce lovely dogs. Although there are considerably fewer dogs and enthusiasts in New Zealand than there are in many other countries, the overall quality of New Zealand's Bichons is often commented upon by British judges who are invited to judge there.

One of the earliest pioneers of the breed in New Zealand was the husband and wife partnership of Jean and David Fyfe from Auckland, whose Mutiara affix is very well known. From the UK, they imported Leander BeauMonde Snow Puff in the mid-1970s and, later, Kynismar Hidden Destiny who soon gained his New Zealand title and became particularly influential as a sire as well as a big winner in the show ring. Another early pioneer who is still breeding and exhibiting her Bichons is Elsie Rennie, who owned the very first Bichon in the North Island of New Zealand in 1978: NZ Ch. Leander Snow Jingle, by Am. Ch. Vogelflights Choirboy of Leander (an American UK import), out of Leander Snow Witch. Another from Wendy Streatfield's Leander kennel in England was Snow Petal of Leander, by Am. Ch. C&D's Star Maker of Leander (another American import), out of C&D's Little Snow White of Leander.

Shandau Snow Flurry – by BeauMonde Snow Puff, out of BeauMonde White Wine (imported from the US in 1979) – was mated to Cluneen Jolly Jason to Hunkidori, and both then left for New Zealand's Shandau kennel. Puppies from these matings left their mark on winning dogs for a long time. One of White Wine's puppies, NZ Ch. Shandau Iceberg, was the first Bichon Frise to win a toy group in New Zealand (under world breed specialist Richard Beauchamp). Iceberg passed away in 1997 aged sixteen and a half. His litter-sister, Shandau Snow Muff, is the dam of Austral. Ch. Shandau Lifizacaberay, a top-winning dog in Australia for a long time who was awarded Best in Show at the second World Congress

*Austral. & NZ. Grand Ch. Shandau*
*Fame Seeker.*

*Ch. Parfait Just a Breeze.*

Championship Show. A bitch from the other mating of Snow Flurry is the great-grandmother of Austral. & NZ Grand Ch. Shandau Fame Seeker, a multi Best in Show winner in both Australia and New Zealand. The Shandau kennel also imported Puffin Billy of Sulyka (Fame Seeker's sire) from the UK's Sue and Roger Dunger; Billy was to become the very first Bichon to be awarded the title of Grand Champion. The Shandau kennel continues to breed their own dogs but also appears to value the introduction of new dogs into existing lines by purchasing more dogs from England. Among them was NZ Ch. Tamalva Union Jack, out of Eng. Ch Tamalva Keep the Faith owned by Tamara Dawson.

Raewyn Rainsford and Steve McDowell's Parfait Kennel was established in 1986 with a puppy from Jean Fyfe's Mutiara kennel – Petit Bijou Charm. On her first visit to England, she bought a dog called Rusmar Magic Knight, who became a New Zealand grand champion and set a record in Bichons by winning twelve Best Puppy in Show awards and thirteen Best Junior in Show awards. He was set to achieve even more acclaim until his father, Ch. Rusmar Xmas Magic, showed up following Raewyn's second visit to England. Xmas Magic's influence has been particularly significant in New Zealand. With these two dogs Raewyn dominated the show scene for quite a time, and the quality of her kennel's progeny has helped to establish her kennel in Australia as well as New Zealand. Her latest NZ champion, Parfait Just a Breeze, is being campaigned alongside a little bitch called Dupanache Just a Flirt who at twelve months is only one point away from her title.

Ally Crabe and Morris White own the Trouvaille kennel, which was founded in 1988 with Jean Fyfe's NZ Ch. Casino of Mutiara; they now have five champions. Barbara Crum started in the breed in 1989 with

Ch. Blancheur Exquis, a daughter of Austral. & NZ Grand Ch. Monjoie Damour (imp. Australia). Her kennel has since produced six champions, with progeny in both Australia and New Zealand.

# Norway

## (By Ester Stray)

In 1977 two Bichons arrived in Norway from England. They were Leijazulip Danielle and Leijazulip Phillipe, imported by Mr and Mrs Robinson, and Norway's first Bichons. When the Robinsons moved to the United States with their Bichons, they left Danielle and Phillipe's progeny. Their Perito White Mustique was mated to Tresilva Don Azure, an English dog who was exported to Sweden. This mating prduced a dog (Int. Nord. Ch. Sankt Obri Snohvit, owned by Elvi Glette) and a bitch (N.S. Ch. Sankt Obri Chivas, owned by Berit Nilsen); from these two dogs, many of Norway's present Bichons are descended.

Norwegian and Swedish (N.S.) Ch. Sankt Obri Snohvit became the first Norwegian-bred champion bitch. The first Bichon in Norway to become an international Nordic champion was Huntglen Nollie, born 3 October 1980, and imported from England by Gerd and Haakon Strand. Huntglen Nollie and Sankt Obri Chivas were mated, and their son Lollipop My Boy became the first Norwegian-born dog to gain the title of International Nordic Champion. Lollipop My Boy produced Int. Nord. Ch. Violar Excellent-Raphsodi (owned by Wivi-Anne Olsen), who became the first Norwegian Bichon Frise to win Best in Show at an international show arranged by the Norwegian Kennel Club.

Among the more recently imported Bichons that have made their mark in Norway is N.S. Ch. Sergeant Pepper from Ligray (imported by Wivi-Anne Olsen) and Int. N.S. Ch. Kynismar Bugsey Malone (imported by me). Most of the recent Best of Breed winners have been produced by one of these dogs or their offspring. At the latest Norwegian Winners Show (the equivalent of the UK's Crufts), in Hamar in 1997, the Best of Breed and the Best Opposite Sex were grandchildren of Pepper and Bugsey. Bugsey consistently produces quality offspring who have his wonderful temperament. A Pepper son, Int. Nord. Ch. Petit Ami's Starmaker, owned by Wivi-Anne Olsen, is currently the Bichon Frise with the most Best in Show awards in the breed's Norwegian history. He is a wonderful dog with incredible showmanship.

The only Bichon imported from England to achieve the coveted

*Nor. Ch. Kynismar Bugsey Malone.*

Norwegian Toydog Club's title of top-winning dog is Int. N.S. Ch. Kynismar Winterlude Angel, owned by me and bred by Myra Atkins. She is also the Bichon who reached the highest score of all the top-winning Bichons since the competition was started in 1981. Angel, the half-sister of Bugsey Malone, is an extremely sound bitch with great movement.

This breed has become very popular in Norway. From five registered Bichons in 1978, and only six in 1979, the breed's numbers escalated and reached their peak in 1991 when the Norwegian Kennel Club registered 928 puppies. Since then the number of registered puppies seems to have stabilized at between 500 and 600 a year.

## Sweden

### (By Catarina Harde)

The first Bichons were imported to Sweden from England and the USA in 1976. Today the Bichon is one of the most popular breeds in the group of countries whose canine affairs are governed by the FCI (Féderation Cynologique Internationale). Every year, around 500 Bichon puppies are registered with the Swedish Kennel Club. The Swedish Bichon Frise Club was founded in November 1982 by some Bichon fanciers, and it is now the world's largest Bichon club, with a membership of around 1,500. The club is very active and offers seminars about general care, grooming and scissoring. Every year there is at least one special show for the breed.

In 1981 Int. Nord. Ch. Leijazulip Guillume, bred by Vera Goold and Derick Chiverton, was imported from England by Jane Martinsson-Vesa. He was by Austral. Ch. Jazz De La Buthiere of Leijazulip, out of Leilah de la Buthiere of Leijazulip. Willie, as he came to be called, was a wonderful dog who enjoyed great success as a show dog and, more importantly, as a stud. One of his offspring – Nor., Swed., Int. Ch. Xanbos Sir William Thomsey (out of Xanbos Love Illusion), bred by Barbro Jonsson and owned by A. Fransson – came to have a great impact on the breed. He was very successful in the show ring at the beginning of the 1990s. In December 1991, he won Best of Breed at Stockholm and thereby became Swedish Winner 1991. Thomsey is a particularly good Bichon with his wonderful expression and perfect proportions in head and body. These advantages have been inherited by his offspring and particularly by his son, Swed. & Dan. Ch. Xanbos Sir William Shakespeare (out of Xanbos More Amore Illusion), who is a wonderful breed representative. Shakespeare's daughter, Swed. & Dan. Ch. Chonfri's Lady Macbeth (out of Swed. Ch. Chonfri's Eminent Lady, bred by M. and C-G. Bergstrom and owned by my kennels), shows that line-breeding to excellent dogs can produce champions through four generations.

During the 1990s, Rigmor Ottosson's Bichonette kennel has had great success with her breeding groups. In Sweden, a breeding group consists of four dogs from the same breeder shown in a given competition. The Bichonette kennel has won a lot of these classes, and in 1996 Rigmor Ottosson became fifth on the Best Breeder list for all breeds. Mrs Ottosson has also been successful with KBHV-96 Nord. Ch. Bichonette's Pantomime Nice'n Easy (by Twinley Pantomime King,

*Swed. & Dan. Ch. Xanbos Sir William Shakespeare.*

out of Swed. & Nor. Ch. Sandfeld's Endless Surprise). Easy has won innumerable Best of Breed awards and has been placed in the group finals many times. In 1996 the Swedish Kennel Club arranged five international shows in nine days, and Easy won Best of Breed at all of them! A great-grandson of Willie's – EUW-97 KBHV-97 Nor. Ch. Perlett's Yeoman Junior (by Nord., Int., Swed. & Dan. Ch. Petit Ami's Yeoman, out of Nord. Ch. Petit Ami's Ayla), bred and owned by A. and G. Lingblad – has had success in the late 1990s. Before two years of age he had already become Swedish, Danish and Norwegian Champion as well as European Winner 1997 and Copenhagen Winner 1996. A Bichon that has done extremely well in Europe is WA-96 DT. BSG-96 VDH-SG-96 Int., Ger., Dan. & Swed. Ch. Chonfri's Ghostbuster (by the British-bred Swed. Ch. Dunlavin Divine Madness, out of Swed. Ch. Suchon's Jingle Bell), bred by M. and C-G. Bergstrom and owned by our kennels. Besides winning all these show titles, Ghostbuster is a great flyball dog: and his team mates – all Bichons – participate in a lot of events, proving that a Bichon is not only a show dog.

# UK

In this section, many breeders candidly share their experiences of breeding and exhibiting the Bichon. You will see that the path to success is not always a smooth and easy one, and that it is not always possible to determine at the outset whether that path will prove to be the right one. And success can bring with it its own problems – not everyone rejoices in another's triumph. Acknowledgement of a fault in your line can have repercussions when it is seized upon by the foolish; only breeders whose confidence in the overall quality of their dogs can comfortably rise above this and enable future 'top breeders' to benefit from their experience. I am very grateful to all those who have provided such a unique insight into the world of Bichons.

## *Alareen*

Maureen and Alan Miles's kennel is relatively new compared to the majority of those that follow, but their success has been quite rapid. They decided quite early on that it would be necessary to breed their own dogs if they were to make any real progress. After purchasing Judamie Precious Bettina, whom they campaigned alongside her kennel-mate Ligray Bobby Dazzler, they experienced enough success to whet their appetite.

*Ch. & Ir. Ch. Alareen Precious Sundancer.*

Bettina was mated to Ch. Sulyka Puzzle and produced a litter of four – three dogs and a bitch. They decided to keep two of the dogs, Alareen Precious Sundancer and Alareen Precious Starlight. Maureen is Irish and regularly goes home to visit family, so both dogs were campaigned regularly in Ireland as well as in the UK. Sundancer gained his UK title and, at the height of his career, won Best of Breed at Crufts under breed judge Wendy Streatfield. Another Puzzle daughter, Ch. Hunkidori Miss Serendipidy, purchased from breeder Judy Fender was their next champion. The Miles were becoming well known for their energy in campaigning any dog whether it was this side of the Irish channel or the other. Maureen in particular was becoming very adept at getting the best out of a dog, and it was this skill that has helped others to achieve more. For example, when Pat Keery in Belfast bred Ch. Spelga Solitaire (by Kynismar Show Me Heaven out of her Alareen-bred bitch, Precious Gem), Maureen campaigned him to gain his UK title.

Spelga Dance Y'Self Dizzy (by Sundancer, out of Bobander Love In Air) came to me to start her show career. However, she was impossible to show and I let Alan and Maureen take her, convinced that they could do no better with her than I could. I was wrong: they campaigned her beautifully. She didn't gain her title but she did very well. Another Sundancer son, Akwasulis Chuckles Charlie (bred by Sylvia Thomas), was purchased by Mr and Mrs Neil Baxter. They too had difficulties campaigning their dog and turned to the Mileses for help. In no time at all, another champion was made. While these successes in no way diminish what Alan and Maureen are achieving in their own breeding programme, they serve as a valuable lesson in how essential it is to start off with quality Bichons and how early decisions can affect everything that comes after.

*Cluneen Admiral Aldo at Appleacre.*

## Appleacre

Paddy Holbrook-O'Hara's first breed was Dalmatians, in which Paddy ran an extremely successful kennel. But she was one of the very first breeders to be captivated by this little white Bichon dog when it came into the UK, and her Cluneen Admiral Aldo was one of the first to be born in this country. She exhibited a bitch called Cluneen Good Grace at Appleacre at the very first club show in 1978, and won a third in Maiden. Paddy won her very first CC (in Bichons) with a bitch called, Appleacres Happy Aura (by Zethus De Chaponay at Tresilva, out of Crystal Aureole from Appleacre) at the Ladies Kennel Association Show under judge Joyce Fagin. Paddy used my Bobander Chasing Rainbows to produce a bitch called Appleacres Over The Rainbow, who won two Reserve CCs in 1993. A very successful dog for her was Ch. Appleacres Any Dream Will Do: he took off in a big way by winning his first CC under specialist judge Michael Coad at Darlington Championship Show when he was still in junior.

Paddy was the secretary of the Northern and Midland Bichon Frise Club for a period of seventeen years from 1981 until very recently – a clear indication of the level of respect that is felt for her among her fellow exhibitors in the breed.

## Asilene

When I was first showing my Bobander The Muffinman, Eileen Beeston was handling her daughter's dog, Edelweiss Ebony Eyes. He had the most fabulous pigment and the darkest of eyes. He was Eileen's first ever champion, and was made up at Scotland under Jackie Ransom. On the same day my Toot the Flute got her first CC. It was quite a memorable day for both of us. Eileen's next champion was Fionavar Billy Whizzes about Asilene, a little dog bred by her friend Maureen Reynolds. Eileen's latest bitch, Asilene The Whizz Kid (Billy's daughter) is well on her way to her title. I gave her the first CC while still in junior; her second came from Hilary Stapely at the Ladies Kennel Association show at the end of 1997.

## Atroya

Helen and Alan Banfield are probably best known for starting the Southern Bichon Frise Breeders' Association with Sue and Roger Dunger. Helen was secretary during the early years when the club was being established. Eventually in July 1996, she took over the reins as secretary of the main club, the Bichon Frise Club of Great Britain.

Helen's Pengorse Poldark of Tresilva (sire of the breed record-holder Ch. Si'bon Fatal Attraction of Pamplona), was mated to a little bitch called Dolly Day Dream to produce Ch. Orpheus Orion at Atroya – Helen's first champion, made up in 1989.

Her second champion, Ch. Atroya Punchinello of Languilla, was owned and campaigned by Lesley MacLeod. The third champion to

*Ch. Orpheus Orion of Atroya.*

carry her affix was Atroya Christmas Gift at Colynthia, owned by the Caspells in Cornwall; this dog has done particularly well, winning his latest CC at Crufts in 1998 and winning two groups.

## *Bobander*

I was probably one of the most unlikely people ever to own a Bichon Frise for I had only ever owned Border Collies in the past. One of my nursing colleagues told me that she showed Old English Sheepdogs and a new breed called the Bichon Frise, which from her description sounded lovely. I let Rita Edler know that when she next had a litter I would be interested in buying a bitch. In what seemed no time at all, she rang me to say that her bitch had had a solitary puppy and that she was mine if I wanted her.

Rita encouraged me to enter Tallulah at Portsmouth and Southsea Open Show. She was still only a puppy and I entered her in Any Variety Toy. It was my first experience of showing, but we managed to get fifth place out of six dogs; more importantly, Tallulah had performed well and I actually enjoyed myself. However, we soon realized that Tallulah, as precious as she was, was not going to become a champion, so we decided to buy another bitch – a decision that we justified on the grounds that Tallulah needed the company. We were lucky enough to buy Shamaney Manhattan, a bitch bred by Margaret Flintoft. Her sire was a lovely dog, Ch. Leijazulip Kipling of Shamaney, and her dam was the very pretty Sweet Clare of Shamaney. We had little success with her: I had a lot to learn about presentation and although she had the most exquisite head and the darkest of eyes and pigment she was not very true behind. Competition in the ring was increasing as the Bichon become more popular and it was clear that Manhattan was not to be our first champion.

I always admired Ch. Sulyka Snoopy, so when it was time to choose a dog for Tallulah the decision was easy. She had five puppies but quickly ran into problems, developing eclampsia. We had to hand-rear the puppies, carefully dyeing their tails different colours so that we didn't try to feed the same one twice. One of the litter, The Muffinman (Blue), had his sire's showmanship and soundness and did very well for us in the show ring. He was nearly three years old before his pigment started to fade, as his dam's did, but not before he had won two Reserve CCs and earned us the affix Bobander. (At that time it was necessary to breed a dog and win a post-graduate class before you could choose an affix.)

Progress was slow and steady. I was doing a little better with each dog and learning all the time about the different UK lines and the types of dog they produced. I used Snoopy again, this time on Manhattan, a mating that produced my first champion, Bobander Toot The Flute. She will always be special because she was our first.

In the meantime, I had been admiring everything Kynismar, and Myra Atkins was showing a particularly lovely dog called Ch. Kynismar Blackeyed Boogaloo. Her dogs had the lovely coats and showmanship that I really admired, so luckily she let me have Kynismar Sweet Talkin' Guy (a Boogaloo son) and Kynismar Annie Get Y'r Gun (a Hidden Destiny daughter). With this new blood I was able to take a slightly different direction. Guy was a very eye-catching dog, very stylish, fabulous coat, lovely pigment and dark eye. He won only the one CC and two Reserves, but because of his breeding he was used at stud. From one of the resulting litters I bought in a lovely bitch called Calypso Crazy at Bobander. Cally ended her show career with one CC and five Reserve CCs, but she was to make her name as a brood-bitch: she produced no fewer than three British champions and was awarded the title Top Brood Bitch in 1995 and 1996.

*Glory Be at Bobander.*

*Ch. Bobander Toot the Flute.*

Another little dog, a Boogaloo son called Ch. Rusmar Xmas Magic, was making a name for himself. He was bred similarly to Guy, and I was keen to use him. I had judged him on a couple of occasions and loved his size, shortness of back, and his showmanship. When it was time to mate Toots, who at four years old was a little long in back and had never had a good coat, he seemed like the perfect dog for her. She came into season along with an Annie daughter, Honey. Honey and Toots were mated to Magic only one day apart, but I was glad that I had made the decision when I did for, shortly afterwards, Magic went to New Zealand where he continued to find success.

I kept a bitch from Toots and a dog from Honey. Surprisingly it was from Honey's litter that our next champion was to emerge. Ch. Bobander Magic in the Air was a star from the word go. He had a Reserve CC in Puppy and quickly became a champion. He was everything I had wanted: good head, lovely coat, dark eyes and pigment, and he was as sound as a bell. Of course he wasn't perfect. He had crooked teeth, but they were tucked away from sight and there was nothing wrong with his bite. Calypso Crazy had a perfect mouth but her eye colour had faded. She too was very sound and it seemed only natural that she and Magic should be mated. Line-bred back to Boogaloo, it was a good mating on paper as well as in the imagination. The first mating produced Ch. Bobander What Ho Bertie, winner of nine CCs and the first Bichon ever to qualify for the Pup of the Year final. A repeat mating produced Ch. Bobander Spring in the Air, smaller and more compact than Bertie, and very feminine like her dam. The third and last mating produced a litter of two which included Ch. Bobander Secret in the Air, who was the first winner of the Pet Plan Junior Stakes.

The next generation presented a problem. The breed as a whole has reduced in numbers and fewer people seem to be keeping the stud-dogs from other lines. Many of the dogs share common faults, and it is increasingly difficult to obey the rules of not doubling up on faults. I have very little of my own to put Bertie to, but he was recently mated to a quality bitch and I was very quick to try to repeat history by buying a bitch from this mating. It can be a big test of one's ability to assess quality and spot a potential champion when you are called upon to choose a puppy from unfamiliar breeding. Glory Be at Bobander is already on her way to achieving her title and, fortunately for my future breeding programme, has brought with her the characteristics that can be useful to strengthen the quality of my line, especially her perfect mouth.

There is still much for me to do: Best of Breed at Crufts, a group win or even a Best in Show at a general championship show. To do this it is necessary to breed even better dogs. I will never be able to achieve this if the people in the breed stop working together as a team. We are a team and, as such, should work together: I could never have made up even one champion without the help of the many other breeders who have unselfishly given me advice and encouragement along the way.

## Bylena

Lena Martindale has owned Bichons since they first became popular in the UK. Her first dog, Kingarth Dominique, took one of the early CCs when shown under the late Joe Braddon at Bath in 1982. This dog sired another dog for Lena, Bylena Winner Takes All, who also took a single CC. I have to admit that this dog was always one of my favourites. It must be remembered that at that time there were far fewer CCs on offer, and so many quality dogs went uncrowned. However, Lena has overcome this earlier disappointment and campaigned Ch. Sargetta Davilliam of Bylena to his title in 1992. Lena also bred a lovely bitch called Ch. Bylena Me and My Girl who was owned by Margaret Moss and exhibited in 1995.

## Clanmarret

There is nothing more frustrating for any exhibitor than campaigning a lovely bitch to two CCs but not managing to gain that third and all-important one to complete her title. Marilyn and Terry Holgate have experienced this twice: once with Clanmarret Blue Moon, and again with Clanmarret Liberty Moon. They did however make up Ch. Clanmarret Gemini Moon with room to spare – she had six CCs and nine Reserves by the time she retired at the end of 1993. They have taken no chances with the latest star: when Marilyn became ill while they were campaigning their Clanmarret Out in Style (the breed's Top Puppy for 1996), they let Michael Coad buy him so that he could continue with his career. Now he's well on his way to his title. Four other Clanmarret bitches have each won a single CC and far from being a measure of failure to make up champions, this serves to illustrate how consistent Marilyn and Terry have been in producing top-quality Bichons.

## Fionavar

Maureen Reynolds has always worked very closely with the Sulyka lines, and with Eileen Beeston, to produce Eileen's Billy Whizzes and

187

*Ch. Clanmarret Gemini Moon.*          *Ch. Fionavar Miss Kitty.*

two big winners for herself: Fionavar Elliot Ness (one CC) and Ch. Fionavar Miss Kitty, both by Eileen's Asilene Paperback Writer (an Ebony Eyes grandson). Elliot has a single CC but Miss Kitty is a champion. The highlight of this girl's career was being crowned Best of Breed at Crufts in 1997 – a very popular win. Although Maureen insists that owning several Bichons is just a hobby, she puts enormous effort into it. Her husband John is the treasurer for the Southern Breeders' Club.

## Fougere

Hilary Stapely became involved with the breed in the very early days – long before I did – and over the years she has shown a string of super dogs. In everything they do, all of Hilary's dogs seem to personify that first line of the Standard, 'A gay lively little dog'. A mental picture of Hilary always has her in her capacity as a handler with a very energetic, flashy dog at the end of the lead. If she ever owned a dog or bitch that did not move out then I don't remember it. She has a wealth of experience behind her, much of it gained in American Cockers, so when she takes the centre of the ring in her role as championship show judge it is not difficult to understand why she considers good movement – in a conformationally sound dog in hard condition – so essential, whether it is in a toy or gundog.

Hilary's two latest champions, Fougere Winging Willie and Fougere Baggy Britches, were bred the same way: by Ch. Sulyka Puzzle out of Fanroy Femme Fatale at Fougere. Hilary's husband Norman is a keen amateur photographer, and expert at photographing Bichons because he knows when the pose is right and understands the pitfalls. Many of his photographs are featured in this book.

## Frendors

In 1983, Doreen and Fred Harvey bought Montravia Snow Bell, who was to become a very significant foundation bitch for their new Frendors kennel. Doreen started her breeding programme by going to Ch. Sulyka Snoopy, and continuing to line-breed to the Jazz line for two generations. The second of the two matings produced three sisters, one of which became the dam of Doreen's first champion, Frendors Gorgeous Gabby; the second, Frendors Chantilly Lace, won a CC under Marion Binder at the East of England Show in 1990; and the third, Frendors Little Bit of Lace, is behind my Glory Be at Bobander. Her second champion soon followed. Ch. Frendors Spitting Image (a Gabby son, sired by Ch. Rusmar Divine Rainbow) won his first CC and Best of Breed at Richmond while still a puppy.

Fred died shortly before Doreen made up Ch. Frendors Gorgeous Gabby. Her dogs are now an even more important part of her life, and as well as grooming other people's Bichons she serves on the Bichon Frise Club of Great Britain.

*Ch. Frendors Spitting Image.*

## Hicker

Sid and Mary Hicks would be the first to describe their success in Bichons as far from meteoric. Their love of the breed has always been put before the ambition to win, but it has fuelled a persistence that, after breeding and exhibiting for twenty years, has eventually paid off. They used Brenda Ellis's Honeylyn Sammy Soapsud (not a champion, but proving to be a useful sire), on their bitch Hicker Snowsana, a direct descendant of the breed's first champion, Glenfolly Silver Lady of Sarabande. The resulting litter proved very significant for them: Ch. Luke Who's Here gained four CCs and his litter-sister Hicker Snow Maiden gained one; a son of Luke's, Hicker Here Comes the Son, owned by their new partner Mrs Denise Costen, is a multiple Reserve CC winner. Their latest boy, Hicker Ain't I Smart, was a qualifier for the prestigious Pup of the Year competition and is doing very well.

## Honeylyn

Brenda and Gordon Ellis present themselves as true Yorkshire folk with a love of their terrier breeds. Since they are well known in Bull Terrier circles, their enthusiasm for the quite glamorous Bichon seems somewhat incongruous; and yet the two types of dog thrive in the capable hands of this couple who have a lifetime's experience of dogs behind them. Brenda shows a keen interest in anything to do with our breed, and as breed correspondent for *Our Dogs* newspaper keeps people informed of Bichon news. As an exhibitor and breeder, Brenda is very modest about her own achievements. She is always keen to 'talk dogs'. Other kennels have benefited from her breeding lines through dogs such as Ch. Honeylyn Timmy Tiptoes to Sulyka, Ch. Honeylyn Step in Style to Sulyka, and Honeylyn Sammy Soapsud (who sired Sid and Mary Hicks's first champion, Hicker Luke Whose Here. Brenda has young bitches Honeylyn Oo La La and Honeylyn Luvvy Duvvy both with Reserve CCs as well as Best Puppy awards.

## Hylacer

Brenda and Les Dickinson are well known in dogs. They have owned several breeds over the years, but making their Bichon dog Hylacer Northern Topic into a champion is considered to be a highlight in their career so far. His sire is Ch. Tiopepi Mad Louie at Pamplona and his dam, Hylacer Katcherattit, is also a Louie granddaughter. Besides gaining his title with five CCs he won the prestigious Bichon of the Year Super Match two years running, in 1994 and 1995. The Dickinsons are known for their breed club and rescue work, and their home is frequently offered as a haven to Bichons in need of help.

## Kynismar

### (By Myra Atkins)

My interest in dog showing had already been aroused through my ownership of two Yorkshire Terriers. Then, at the Windsor Championship Show, I fell in love with the Bichon; afterwards I looked for anything I could about the breed in the canine press. In 1979, I saw an advertisement for a litter of Bichon puppies bred by Bernice Perry, so I went along to have a look. (One of the bitches in this litter, Persan Make Mine Mink, later became one of the breed's early champions.) At that time I still knew very little about the breed – only what I had seen at shows and in the dog papers; I knew nothing of coat, pigment or balance. But in the litter there was a pretty little bitch (Persan Madam) for sale. I bought her and called her Pearl.

Fool that I was, I considered that a Bichon would be easier to prepare for show than were my Yorkies, and with this fallacy in mind we took Pearl on a three-month course in ringcraft. When Pearl was just six months, we attempted our first show – an open show held by the South-eastern Toydog Club. We entered her in a puppy class of six. The judge was Bryan Mitchell, who was very experienced in all toy breeds, and Pearl did really well: she strutted her stuff and won the class. I was completely bitten by the show bug, and here began nearly twenty years of travelling Great Britain to breed and make up nine UK champions, with the help of a very understanding husband.

The show report on Pearl had said, 'Feminine, well proportioned, quality head, fair mover; a show girl; a touch straight behind.' Now what on earth does 'touch straight behind' mean? To this utter novice, a judge's critique was not easy to decipher, and I resolved to learn all these words and expressions, and to understand what they meant. The breed was still very new to the UK, and information, especially for the novice, was scarce. I found the best way to learn was to sit quietly and watch people show or trim their dogs.

In 1980, I bought a dog called Kingarth Dapper Dan. He had a very thick coat, good pigment, good bone, a nice head, and he was well balanced. I thought he would complement Pearl, who had a beautiful head

191

with lovely black eyes, but a thin coat, not so good pigment, and rear angulation that I felt could be improved. The result of their mating was our first champion, Kynismar Blackeyed Susie, who won her Junior Warrant at the age of ten months and became a champion on her second birthday. In her show career, she won four CCs and a group. I had also kept her litter-sister, Kynismar Campanula, who was slightly longer in body than Susie. Then, from a repeat mating, I kept another bitch called Kynismar Snowcrocus. During 1981, I bought a dog from Margaret Flintoft, called Shamaney Stepping Out; we showed him until he was two years old, and then stopped because he didn't really enjoy the showing experience. He was mated to all three of our bitches – Susie, Campanula and Snowcrocus – with considerable success. Susie produced Ch. Kynismar Blackeyed Boogaloo and, later, Ch. Kynismar Blackeyed Mr Magoo and Am. & Can. Ch. Kynismar Blackeyed Pixie. Campanula produced Ch. Kynismar Heaven Sent, Ch. Kynismar Boogies Boy, and NZ Ch. Kynismar Hidden Destiny. Snowcrocus was mated only once and produced Kynismar Baron Benjamin, who won two CCs and a Reserve. The three sisters and Stepping Out were a big influence on my breeding programme and established my line.

I kept a number of my own stud-dogs, and I have been able to use a homebred champion dog in every generation of stock. I put Boogaloo to his aunt Campanula, who needed more leg and neck and more of a showman's temperament (like Susie's). Boogaloo had these virtues; but Campanula had the larger frame, which I hoped would be combined with Boogaloo's assets in their offspring. Boogaloo had a great attitude in the ring, and he won ten CCs and a group. His success at stud was such that in 1989 he became the only Bichon to be awarded the title of Top Toy Stud-Dog. He sired five UK champions and many CC winners. His son, Ch. Rusmar Xmas Magic was the first champion for the Rusmar kennel; he then went on to be a very dominant sire in the UK and New Zealand. NZ Ch. Kynismar Hidden Destiny won well in England, including Best in Show at a club show that had 222 entries, and then went to New Zealand where he won forty-eight CCs and sired Ch. Zipadedoda Hidden Meaning (the top Australian champion for two years). Ch. Kynismar Boogies Boy was Top Bichon in 1988 and winner at Crufts in 1988 and 1989. His full sister, Ch. Kynismar Heaven Sent also had a super career. She was Top Bichon in 1989 and won Best Bitch at the Contest of Champions (also in 1989). She was later mated to Ch. Kynismar Billy the Kid who had excellent balance and fantastic, driving action; Billy gained his title in just two weeks (the quickest to date). Breeding is always made easier if you know what your stud-dog is likely to pass on to his offspring,

*Ch. Kynismar Feels Like Heaven.*

and I could always rely on Billy to bestow lovely black eyes. Billy's progeny included Ch. Kynismar Heaven Forbid, Austral. Ch. Kynismar Show Me Heaven and Ch. Kynismar Cherished Heaven.

By this time, my breeding was producing sound, well-balanced dogs with good heads and pigment, thick coats, and excellent showmanship, and I felt there wasn't much more that I could improve on. Cherished Heaven was Top Bichon 1992 and 1993, and Heaven Forbid Top Male 1992; both were group and reserve group winners. Kynismar Show Me Heaven, only a few months younger than Heaven Forbid, went to Australia where Julia Jeffery was able to use him as a stud to the offspring of Hidden Meaning. Before he went, he sired our ninth champion, Ch. Kynismar Feels Like Heaven who, in my estimation, is the closest representation of the Bichon Standard that I can breed. Between August 1993 and December 1995, he accumulated ten CCs and many group placings, and became Top Bichon 1995,

It becomes harder to improve on each generation, as other kennels have found out. But I feel that I have achieved all my ambitions while breeding the best Bichons I can. I was Top Breeder in 1984, 1987, 1988, 1989, 1992 and 1993. I have bred nine UK and fifteen overseas champions, and my dogs have won nearly a hundred CCs. I have judged in Norway, Sweden, Finland, and Ireland, and I shall have the honour of judging this special breed at Crufts 1999.

## Leander

Wendy and John Streatfield's impact upon the breed in those all-important early years was very considerable. They imported many significant dogs from America, including Am. & Austral. Ch. C&D Beau Monde Sunflower of Leander in 1974, who whelped a litter by Am. Ch. C&D Beau Monde Blizzard while in quarantine. Their offspring feature in pedigrees in the UK, New Zealand and Australia, but it was with Am. Ch. Vogelflight's Choirboy that Wendy achieved most success in the show ring in those early days. Wendy's presentation (already well developed through her success with Poodles) served the Bichon well. She was a keen exponent of the glamorous American style at a time when many Bichonists would have preferred to follow the Continent and leave the Bichon in his natural state. But it was this glamorous appearance that was in part responsible for bringing the breed into the limelight, so in retrospect we can see that enthusiasts like Wendy were playing an important part in the breed's ultimate success.

John and Wendy emigrated to South Africa in 1981, and later acquired Ir. Ch. Pamplona Gay Crusader and Ch. Rossage Silver Ghost. Their close friend Sally Wheeler (a well-known and successful exhibitor of pugs) took up the breeding and exhibition of the Leander Bichons and campaigned some lovely dogs, including Ch. Leander The Sundancer and Ch. Leander Snow Cat. She was a long-serving committee member of the Bichon Frise Club of Great Britain and, as such, played an important role in the realization of the committee's ambition to bring about the

*The late Sally Wheeler with one of her champions, Leander Snow Cat.*

194

first World Congress, which was held in London in February 1988. Sally's unexpected death in 1991 was a great loss to all of us who knew her. Sally commanded much respect, especially as a judge who was never afraid to speak her mind and express some very definite ideas about the breed. She also had a great sense of fun, and I am sure it was as much for devilment that she produced an 11-inch measure when she judged at Bournemouth Championship Show as it was for the serious purpose of demonstrating her concern at the increasing number of Bichons whose height was above that demanded by the Standard.

In the meantime, John and Wendy returned from South Africa, where they had continued to breed and show their Bichons with the kind of top-level success that they had enjoyed in the UK. John passed away in 1996, but Wendy is still involved with the breed. She can often be seen at a show and is occasionally persuaded to judge. Her experience and depth of knowledge of the breed will always make her opinion a valuable one.

## *Leijazulip*

Vera Goold had already enjoyed considerable success as a prominent breeder of terriers under her Sidewater affix, when she came across the Bichon Frise on a visit to America and believed it to be a new terrier. Although the Bichon's popularity was beginning to escalate in America, interest was only just awakening in the UK, and it was only when she endeavoured to find out more about it that she realized it was a toy. From Derick Chiverton at the Kennel Club she learned that a Bichon litter had been born and registered by Mr and Mrs Sorstien. Later, when a repeat mating produced a litter of five, Vera purchased Carlise Calypso Orion from them. The partnership between Vera and Derick Chiverton was to produce an affix that has become so significant and far reaching in its influence, it would require a volume of its own to record all the dogs and kennels that have benefited from it.

Having purchased Carlise Calypso Orion (Tulip), Vera spotted another Bichon while on holiday. She asked where it was bred, and was directed to Madam Carmen Desfarges in the town of Buthiere in France, where Derick purchased two puppies, Jazz de la Buthiere and Leilah de la Buthiere. These three Bichons' names, Leilah, Jazz and Tulip, form the affix Lei-jaz-ulip. Six weeks out of quarantine Jazz was shown by Vera's usual terrier handler Tony Giles. This was in the days before there were CCs, or even classes, for Bichons, but he still made an impact in the Not Separately Classified classes. When Leilah came out of quarantine both she and Tulip came into season, and both were

*Ch. Leijazulip Jazz of Zudiki.*

mated to Jazz. In those early years from 1974, Vera's breeding mainly involved these dogs and their progeny. Jazz was sold to Rudi Van Voorst and Frank Valley of the Azara kennels in Australia, but before he went he sired a dog called Leijazulip Guillume, who was as significant in Britain and Sweden as Jazz was to be in Australia. Meanwhile, Vera bought another bitch from Madam Desfarges: Ninon de la Buthiere, given to her close friends Margaret Flintoft and David Black who lived near Saffron-Waldon.

The mating of Guillume and Ninon produced two significant dogs to carry the Leijazulip affix, Ch. Leijazulip Kipling of Shamaney and Ch. Leijazulip Jazz of Zudiki. Guillaume went to Sweden, to Jane Martinsson-Vesa where he became a Swedish champion; and Jazz went to John and Wendy Hutchinson in Australia. Jazz was owned and campaigned in Britain by Jo Brown (now Emmerson) and sired foundation Bichons for many of the successful kennels in Britain today. Kipling stayed with Margaret Flintoft and sired significant champions such as Marion Binder's Ch. Si'bon Jasmyn, who was also the dam of the breed record-holder Ch. Si'bon Fatal Attraction at Pamplona; two champions for Den Thomas; Ch. Roushkas Dancemaster; and Steven Thompson's Ch. Roushkas Song N' Dance, who in turn was the dam of his Ch. Stevo's Stand and Deliver. A Kipling son, Shamaney Stepping Out at Kynismar, sired Boogaloo for Myra Atkins, and my Bobander lines are a combination of both Kipling and Jazz offspring. Another champion that carries this affix is Jackie Ransom's Ch. Jacqueline of Leijazulip at Tresilva, who was by Leijazulip Benjy and out of a Tresilva bitch. Benjy was out of Leilah put to the import Astir De Villa Sainval from Belgium.

The list of champions abroad is very extensive, but after the three UK champions emerged quite early in the breed's short history Vera sat back and became much less actively involved. Presentation became very important and a major part of the Bichon scene. Vera always had to rely on handlers to exhibit her dogs and they were not all keen to take on the Bichon coat. Her judging skills are always in demand and she is a popular judge at home and abroad. Colin and Cynthia Caspall have campaigned the latest Leijazulip, and Leijazulip Repeat Performance already has a CC behind him.

Other kennels that have benefited extensively from Vera's ability to breed good dogs are Judy Fender, with her Ch. Hunkidori Personality Miss (a Jazz daughter), Alan and Maureen Miles with their Ch. Hunkidori Miss Serendipidy (a Jazz granddaughter), Liz Fellows, whose Ligray dogs have a significant amount of Leijazulip behind them through Pyrhaven Amour at Ligray (the dam of Ligray Precious Gift), and Michael Coad whose Eng. & Ir. Ch. Tiopepi Mad Louie at Pamplona is out of Leijazulip Sabina Of Colhamdorn. Of the 118 champions that are UK champions, 108 of them have Leijazulip in their pedigree; of those that do not, most are very early champions bred shortly after their parents arrived in England. Quite a remarkable achievement!

## Ligray

Liz Fellows owned Leander Beau Monde Snow Puff (one of the first Bichons born in quarantine), and was at the first inaugural meeting of the Bichon Frise Club of Great Britain. She also instigated the formation of the Northern and Midland Club. When she met her partner Brian Diaper he was probably better known for his Whippets, which he showed under his Gamelea affix. Brian is a great organizer, and with his help Liz set up the Mid-Eastern Counties Bichon Frise Club; they have both held office, Liz as secretary and Brian as chairman, ever since. Besides this, they have found time to breed quite a few good Bichons: the dam, Ligray Uptown Girl, and the sire, Ligray Precious Gift (a Snow Puff son), of Ch. Ligray Smarty Pants at Ricanna; and, with Judy Lloyd (Judamie), Ch. Ligray Mr Beau Geste. Liz also bred Ch. Ligray Desperate to Be Dan for Mr and Mrs Lewis. Mr and Mrs Dennis Diamond campaigned Ch. Ligray Diamond Lil, and a number of other exhibitors and breeders have benefited from Ligray breeding. Pat Farmer campaigned Ligray Sweet Alyssum, who was very unlucky not to get his crown. He won two CCs in 1982, when

*Ch. Ligray Diamond Lil.*

there were only eleven sets on offer, and many Best of Sex when there were no CCs. Ligray Mr Mistoflees (owned by Jill Buxton) was a particular favourite of mine, and I remember him getting the CC under judge Percy Whitaker at Birmingham in 1984. Ann Toogood owned Ligray Mr Raffles, who nearly made it too, and finished his career on two CCs.

As a couple who introduce new people to Bichons and start them off on the road to success, Brian and Liz are unparalleled. Kennels such as Kennichen, Honeylyn, Teracita, Alareen, Avana, Effaldees, Eithlynn, Harene, Riordan, Penwyvern, and Simway have each produced a champion with Ligray dogs and bitches.

## Lynelba

Major Barry Gisborne and his wife Linda started in Bichons at around the same time that I did. Their first breed was Old English Sheepdogs. They became very firm friends with Richard Blackwell and Chris and Reg Belcher of Melsel fame, and after gaining much experience with Montravia Crystal Ice they were in a prime position to spot a potential champion in Chris's litters. Linda campaigned Ch. Melsel Kiss Me Kate in 1988 and Barry Ch. Mesel Mystic Moses at Lynelba in 1990. These two champions were mated to produce their first homebred champion, Lynelba Kiss Me Freely, who won the group at Scotland when she won her first CC under Michael Coad.

Linda and Barry are not regular exhibitors – Barry's career since leaving the army prevents this – but they show their dogs sufficiently to gain a title or two. Their latest champion, Lynelba Per Se, gained his first CC while still a puppy and became one of the breed's youngest champions.

## Mahendi

Margaret Hoad started in the breed with another Afghan enthusiast, Jo Brown. She purchased her first Bichon for a substantial sum of money, which was why she was called Abbey (the money had come out of a building society account!). Such was the demand for quality Bichons when the breed took off in the early 1970s.

Margaret chose to keep only bitches in her small kennel, and although she bred a string of very successful CC-winning dogs – such as Mahendi the Vandelizer, Mahendi Music Man, and Mahendi Red Hot and Blue – it was with her bitch, Ch. Mahendi Miss Bliss, that she hit the high spot. For many years, Margaret juggled a thriving grooming business with showing her dogs and running the Bichon Frise Club of Great Britain as secretary.

## Melsel

Chris and Reg Belcher teamed up with Richard Blackwell to show their first Bichon. They found considerable success very early on in their career in dogs. Most of us that were showing in the early 1980s can remember warmly their first two champions (Snarsnoz Dancing Rhythm at Melsel and Snarsnoz show Quest at Melsel) winning the Best Brace in Show at Birmingham National Championship Show in

*Ch. Mahendi Miss Bliss.*

199

*Ch. Melsel Cracklin' Rosie.*

1983 – a very big day for all Bichon exhibitors. Their next champion, Ch. Melsel Cracklin' Rosie, was a Quest daughter who won her first CC as a puppy under the late Joe Braddon and never looked back. She gathered a total of twenty-one CCs and held the bitch record for some time.

Richard and Chris served for a long time on the Bichon Frise Club of Great Britain committee, but as Richard was experiencing increasing pressure from a demanding career we didn't see quite so much of them in the show ring. Although their latest champion, Vythea Jack's the Lad at Melsel, gained five CCs all with Best of Breed, they are most frequently seen in their capacity as championship show judges. They are often at the ring side, and it is clear that Bichons are still a major part of their lives.

## Montravia

Peter and Pauline Gibbs and their famous daughter Marita (now Rodgers), were involved with Bichons from very early in the breed's UK history. Ch. Montravia Persan Make Mine Mink (a dog bred by Bernice Perry) was made up with ease during 1980 and 1981, when there were only six sets of CCs on offer a year. Ch. Montravia Snow Dream was campaigned at the same time, and she not only gained her title with the same speed but went on to gather a total of nine CCs. She remained the breed record-holder for many years.

The family are interested in various breeds, but their love for Poodles and Afghan Hounds in particular took precedence for a long time. The results of this dedication and hard work were rewarded with a Best in Show at Crufts on no less than two occasions: once in 1983 with the Afghan Ch. Montravia Kaskarak Hitari, and again in 1985 with Ch. Montravia Tommy Gun (a black Standard Poodle). Perhaps next time it will be with a Bichon Frise. Peter and Pauline are very busy running a successful kennel, but they have always kept a keen eye on what is going on in the Bichon world and for many years Peter was our chairman for the Bichon Frise Club of Great Britain.

## *Pamplona*

### (by Michael Coad)

I was successfully showing Standard Poodles and Pyrenean Mountain Dogs in Ireland, when in 1977 I visited Wendy Streatfield's Leander kennels and saw my first Bichon Frise. I fell in love with the breed and came home from there with Snow Shamrock of Leander (Flip), whom I owned with my old friend Olive Hanna. Along with Flip, Lameda Irish Dancer and Lameda Irish Lace began the success story of the Pamplona Bichon Frise. Irish Lace was the first Irish champion and the first to win a group in Ireland. I also bred the Ch. Pamplona Dragonfly (owned by Mary Conroy who now lives in Australia), the first Bichon to go Best in Show in Ireland at an all-breed show. Irish Lace and Dragonfly dominated the Irish scene for many years. Other Irish champions included Ch. Pamplona Gay Crusader, Ch. Pamplona Debutante and Ch. Pamplona Pussy Patrol.

On another trip to England I visited a friend of many years, Clare Coxall, who had just bred a litter. In it there was a very special puppy dog and I persuaded Clare to let me have him. He became Eng. & Ir. Ch. Tiopepi Mad Louie at Pamplona. He was handled to all his wins by my partner Geoff Corish. Louie is still the male record-holder and the only Bichon ever to win the toy group at Crufts and he is the first and only male to have gone Best in Show at an all-breed championship show. In 1987 he was runner-up for Dog of the Year. In my humble opinion he was the greatest and will never be replaced. Yes, he had his faults, but he was a hard dog to beat and had wonderful showmanship and charisma. He also had superb angulation, which he passed on to his progeny.

At this stage Marion Binder was not showing very much and she decided to part with Si'bon Fatal Attraction at Pamplona. She was a youngster when we had her but it was not long before she swept all before her and gained her championship title. A memorable win for the Pamplona kennel was at Crufts, under breed specialist Jackie Ransom, when Fatal took the bitch ticket and Best of Breed. The Dog certificate winner that day was a Louie son, Molly Harris's Ch. Pamplona Chances Are. Fatal was a multiple group winner, with twelve group firsts in a row; she was also a multiple Best in Show winner and the first and only Bichon to be Dog of the Year. She remains the breed record-holder and the top-winning British Bichon of all time.

My biggest disappointment was when I mated Fatal to Louie. I was expecting great things, but with breeding you don't always get what you expect and this was the case here. Yes, we had champions from this union but not what I had wanted. Fatal was a career girl and that was that. Louie, on the other hand, had sired some lovely progeny and subsequent grandchildren. Rick Beauchamp (Beau Monde) from America gave Louie Best of Breed at the Scottish Kennel Club Championship Show; in his critique he said how wonderful he was and later, that his biggest wish was to mate Louie to Am. Ch. Devon Puff N' Stuff, the number one Bichon in the USA.

Louie led a restricted stud life especially while we were showing him. We were always aware of the danger of his being overused at stud – in

*Ch. & Ir. Ch. Tiopepi Mad Louie at Pamplona.*

my opinion it is unhealthy for any breed if too many bitches are mated to the same dog – and we felt it wise to restrict his use. Brenda Dickinson used him and produced Ch. Hylacer Northern Topic for herself. and the dam of Harene Beatrice Ann at Pamplona, a lovely, showy bitch that we were able to buy from Irene Ellis and quickly make into a champion. Betty Satchell used him too on her Ch. Rossage Silver Locket and produced Ch. Rossage Silver Ghost.

On a visit to us, Wendy Streatfield fell in love with Ir. Ch. Pamplona Gay Crusader. She took him back to South Africa with her and very quickly he became that country's Top Toy for that year. Shortly afterwards, Jane Martinsson-Vesa from Sweden, who was one of the early breeders in that country, took Pamplona Femme Fatal and Pamplona The Entertainer, both of whom became Swedish champions.

To Jean Gee in New Zealand we exported Ch. Pamplona the Rainmaker, and to Mr and Mrs Jacobs in Holland we sent Pamplona Happy as Larry, who gained his German title as well. On a visit from Malibu, California, came Jill Cohen, who was looking for something special to found her kennel. At that time we had another dog from Marion, Si'bon Sloane Ranger at Pamplona, but he was young and we wanted to show him here first. He soon became an English champion and then left for his new home where he became an American champion in just thirty-six hours! He was handled by Eddie and Lesley Boyes, top handlers in the States. A year afterwards we visited him in his new home and found that his bed was a chair overlooking the Pacific Ocean! He is certainly living the life of luxury along with his kennel-mate Ch. Pamplona Lucy Locket.

Another overseas visitor was Anne Yocom from Canada, who was looking for something really good to found what was to become her well-known kennel. At that time we had another of Louie's sons waiting to be shown, Wendar Fly the Flag at Pamplona. She took him and it wasn't long before he started winning. He gained his Canadian title very quickly, became a multiple group and Best in Show winner, and was the top non-sporting dog in the same year. He is still the biggest-winning Bichon in Canada.

Breeding lovely Bichons has extra benefits. I judge regularly in Sweden, Norway and Finland, and have also judged the Bichon Frise Club of California. I try to breed to the Standard, rather than follow fads. We show our Bichons fearlessly, under all judges; and they lead a carefree life, which shows in their wonderful temperaments. I have always tried to breed for correct temperament because, in my opinion, a Bichon that does not have the correct temperament is not a typical Bichon.

My Pamplona kennels have won nearly a hundred CCs, and more groups and Best in Show awards than any other Bichon kennel, past or present – and there is more to come!

## Penrose and Glandore

### (by Eileen O'Connor)

I started showing Dachshunds in the early 1950s, and since then I have progressed through the utility and toy groups and to judge all breeds world wide. The Penrose partnership with the Pamplona kennel spans many decades. My interest in Bichon Frise began when Michael Coad's bitch, Pamplona White Shamrock, produced a lovely litter in March 1983. As my daughter Joy was also interested in the breed I decided to buy a bitch puppy for her birthday in May. Michael gave us the pick of litter, and we called her Penny. She became our first Bichon Frise champion and the foundation bitch for what is now called the Dream Team. Our Bichons are presented by my friend Marie Hamil whose affix is Glandore. Penrose/Glandore Bichons are the only Bichon kennels in Ireland to win Top Irish Show Dog, Top Irish Toy Dog and Pup of the Year competition. We also hold the Irish breed record with 180 Green Star Points.

We chose Penny for her beautiful head and expression, and her adorable personality. She gained her Irish title in 1985, accumulating 100 Green Star points – a breed record that she retained until her son Buster took over in 1989. Penny produced four Irish champions and is grandam to four more champions. In light of this I feel justified in stating the importance of a good foundation bitch, and we could not have asked for a better one than Penny. When she died in the summer of 1997 at the age of fourteen years, she still had the beautiful head, expression and outstanding neck and shoulder that so impressed us when we chose her at six weeks old. She gave us many years of fun and pleasure and we shall always have fond memories of her.

Her son, Ch. Penrose Mr. Snugfit (Butch) was born in April 1985. He caught my eye as soon as I saw him and as the weeks went by I liked him more and more. My confidence in him was justified when this happy little dog won the first All-Ireland Toy Dog of the Year Match in 1987. At around this time it became obvious to me that my recurring hip problem would soon prevent me from handling my own dogs, so Marie took over the presentation of the dogs and shared the handling with my daughter Joy. Butch gained his Irish title in 1987 and later sired Marie's champion bitch Hayley.

*Ir. Ch. Penrose China Doll at Glendore, competing at the Pup of the Year final in Ireland.*

I have always considered that the importance of type should not be underestimated when breeding. With this in mind, I decided to mate Penny to Ch. Tiopepi Mad Louie at Pamplona, and I was not disappointed with the results: Ch. Penrose Crazy Lady (Daisy-May) had style, elegance and was very much to type. She was not always an easy lady to handle – her strong personality and her feminine ways made every show a challenge – but she won the hearts of many judges. She gained her Irish title in 1987 and became Annual Champion the same year. Daisy-May produced only two litters, one of which contained Marie's Ch. Penrose China Doll at Glandore (Hayley). Marie had waited two years for Hayley. As a daughter of Daisy-May, she was a lady with a mind of her own, and what a show-off! She loved showing, and with great drive and style she qualified for Pup of the Year in 1989, and came runner-up. She gained her Irish title and went on to win the Toy Group at the Show Dog of the Year in 1991 and the semi-finalists in the Toy Dog Match.

Marie expressed a desire to have a Penny son and once again with type in mind we all agreed to mate Penny to Ir. Ch. Pamplona Gay Crusader. This mating proved to be a perfect combination. There were two boys to choose from and Marie picked Buster, who was to become Ch. Penrose Bucks Fizz at Glandore. This boy had it all: he had inherited his dam's beautiful head and expression, and all the showmanship and ring presence of his sire. His career thrilled us all. In 1987 at the age of eleven months, he qualified for the first Pup of The Year competition to be held in Ireland. Marie and Buster came through from twenty-four dogs to the final five, and then judge Miss Ferelith Hamilton awarded Buster top honours. Buster's career took off. He was runner up in the Top Show Dog competition (1988) and accumulated 180 Green Star Points – is a breed-record which still stands. Other highlights to his career included two film appearances, and winning numerous Best of Breeds, toy groups, Best in Show at the Bichon Frise Club of Ireland Club Show, and the Annual Competition 1988. Buster retired from showing at two-and-a-half years of age and has sired three champions. He is now in his twelfth year and still holds a special place in Marie's heart and mine.

Ch. Penrose Challenger (Bruno), is Buster's litter-brother and Maura Delmar acquired him at eight weeks old. Rita McCarry took over his presentation and handling, and Bruno won many Green Stars, Best of Breeds and two Best in Shows at all-breed championship shows. He won his title within three years and retired to a quiet life in the country.

My next champion Glandores Touch of Frost at Penrose (Chloe) was produced by Marie's champion Hayley in 1993, and what an ambassador for our kennels she turned out to be. She had excellent drive and at times Marie was hard pressed to keep pace with her. Marie and Chloe developed a style that made them at one with each other. They loved showing, and as a team they won two Best in Shows at all-breed championship shows. They qualified for Top Irish Show Dog, a competition whose atmosphere equalled Chloe's dad's night at the Pup of the Year competition. Having won the toy group, the judge Mr A. Warnock (Canada) awarded Chloe top honours. Chloe retired that night, a champion of champions.

I felt that a half-brother to half-sister mating between Daisy-May and Buster would promote my line and hold type, and my decision proved to be right. The union produced Ch. Penrose Laraheen Daisy Chain (Daisy), the next and latest champion in my line. She carried forward all the qualities of her parents and did not disappoint us. She won Annual Champion 1993, Best in Show at the Toy Dog Society Championship Show, and Best in Show at the Bichon Frise Club of Ireland show in 1994. She is now retired and a lady of leisure. We have had fifteen very enjoyable years in this adorable breed and we look forward to many more.

## Penwyvern

In the ten years since Bichons became their passion, the couple who own the Penwyvern affix have chosen their shows carefully and exhibited infrequently. Still they achieved what many of us are yet to do. Their first champion was Penwyvern Silk Collection, a bitch that gained her title in 1994 without ever leaving the far south of the UK. Her

*Ch. Penwyvern Silk Collection.*

half-brother, Ch. Penwyvern White Diamond, who shares the same dam but is sired by Molly Harris's Ch. Pamplona Chances Are, achieved Best of Breed at Crufts in 1996 when Ellis Hulme judged. He also took the group at Bournemouth in 1997 when Joe Kirk judged the breed.

## Riorden

Nick Skeet has been closely associated with Liz Fellows and Brian Diaper for many years. I can remember him showing his dogs, in particular Riorden The Dream Machine, at the early club shows. He more recently produced a champion, Riordan Beach Boy of Cannengis, for Molly Harris in Cornwall. This dog was campaigned by Michael Coad and Geoff Corish, who also helped Nick to campaign Ch. My Leading Lady at Riorden, a bitch he had bought from Ann Stafferton.

## Rossage

Betty Satchell started her career in Bichons with a little bitch called Gabriella of Rosscarne whose sire, Twinley Tiberius, was born in quarantine and whose dam, Amber De Chaponay of Twinley, was imported by Pauline Block. Her other early Bichon was the Leijazulip-bred Barryville Little Mitzi. When this bitch was mated to Leander Beau Monde Snow Puff, another dog that had been born in quarantine, the result was Rossage Royal Snow Queen at Maybeth, Betty's first bitch champion, crowned in 1983. Betty bred and owned many lovely dogs and bitches including Ch. Rossage Silver Locket and Ch. Bumbleridges

Overture of Rossage (bred by Mr and Mrs Nicholls). Her only dog champion was Ch. Rossage Silver Ghost, made up in 1989. He was out of her Ch. Rossage Silver Locket and by Ch. Tiopepi Mad Louie of Pamplona. Another successful dog was Rossage Silver Bullet who, after winning the CC at Darlington under judge Ann Worth in 1990, went to South Africa to Wendy and John Streatfield where he became a very big-winning dog and gained his title.

Betty and her sister Shirley were very keen exhibitors and were driven all round the country by their parents, Mr and Mrs Green, who were also in Bichons right at the beginning (owning Beaupres Claudius, a puppy out of an early litter). When Mr Green passed away we saw Betty less frequently, and then not at all. She continues to breed, and since she was such an enthusiastic and successful exhibitor I would be surprised if she doesn't look at her latest pick of litter and wonder if this couldn't be UK Champion number five.

## Rusmar

### (By Dawn Russell)

I started in showing with Afghans, but acquired my first Bichon, Katy, from Margaret Hoad. Katy was a very affectionate bitch, but she was long and low, with a lighter eye than I like and a sparse coat. However, she had reasonable pigment and medium bone and, when mated to Jo Brown's Ch. Leijazulip Jazz of Zudiki, she produced Rusmar Sea Angel of Zudiki. Jo was to take the second pick of litter but the arrangement was for me to keep the best one. Right from the beginning Angel was my instinctive choice, but from studying books it seemed that I should choose the smaller bitch, Candy. Well, that was a valuable lesson learnt, for two weeks later I bought Angel back from Jo and sold Candy. Ever since then I have always followed my first instincts when choosing a puppy and, touch wood, they have usually proved right.

Angel was a lovely bitch; she was a bit leggy for some but she had tremendous style and personality, as well as a very broad head and lovely expression. Unfortunately her lip pigment was not complete, and neither were her pads, which were a little patchy. Previously, Katy had been mated to Zudiki Double Trouble and had produced a bitch, Cassiopee of Mahendi, for Margaret Hoad, and a dog, Rusmar Shining Star, for me. Cassie was mated back to Margaret's dog Mahendi Mr Music Man to produce Mahendi Ice Cool Music at Rusmar (Dennis), who was mated to Rusmar Christmas Cracker (by Mahendi Mr Music

Man out of Rusmar Sea Angel of Zudiki). Dennis was quite a small, broad-headed dog with a dark eye and good pigment, as well as a profuse coat, but unfortunately he had a wry bite. However, these early matings were significant for me because they produced two bitches, Precious Pearl of Rusmar and Rusmar Iced Diamond, both of whom produced very important dogs for me.

My first big-winning dog, and my first champion – Ch. & NZ Grand Ch. Rusmar Xmas Magic (by Ch. Kynismar Blackeyed Boogaloo, out of my Rusmar Sea Angel of Zudiki) – was pure Magic from the day he was born, and to this day I consider him to be the best Bichon I have ever bred. He was the ideal size in shape and bone, with a broad head and expressive eyes, correct tail-set, and a wonderful personality. His coat could have been denser, but it was really white, and he had very little tear-staining and his pigment was good throughout. His front could have been a little tighter but he had a very good rear. Many people used him on their bitches to try to improve their rear movement. A mating between Precious Pearl of Rusmar and Magic, produced Rusmar Magic Moments, NZ. Grand Ch. Rusmar Magic Knights and Rusmar White Pearl of Strydonia, all in the same litter.

Rusmar Magic Moments had her mother's huge eyes, but she was slightly heavier in bone. She gained two CCs towards her title but then, like so many other good bitches, she lost her nose pigment. Rusmar White Pearl of Strydonia (Lucy), went to Diane Story. Lucy was finer in bone and very much like her mother. She went on to produce a striking bitch, who in turn produced Diane's first champion bitch when put to Ch. Fougere Baggy Britches.

Pearl was a stunningly pretty bitch, with huge eyes and a very short muzzle, correct shape and size. Some said that Pearl was hydrocephalic and that she should not have been bred from. She was not; she had an open fontanelle which did not close until she was four and a half months, which I admit was unusual. If she had been hydrocephalic she would not have survived, let alone shown and later raised a perfectly normal litter of puppies. A year later, when I repeated the mating, she suffered early eclampsia at six weeks in whelp and reabsorbed the puppies. The eclampsia caused her to convulse but I had difficulty convincing my vet that her problems were caused by a lack of calcium. It wasn't until she had a really bad fit during the night, which he was able to witness for himself, that she was treated. An infection occurred and three days later she had to be spayed and was never the same again. At five years old I had to have her put to sleep after a particularly bad night of fits, but Pearl's daughters did us proud.

*Ch. Rusmar Divine Rainbow.*

*Ch. & NZ Grand Ch. Rusmar Xmas Magic.*

I was persuaded to part with Magic. Unfortunately our hobby is an expensive one and I had to raise two children alone. Selling Magic to Raewyn Rainsford in New Zealand meant that I could carry on showing. Raewyn had already purchased a son of Magic's. Rusmar Magic Knights, who did very well for them and became a grand champion.

Before Magic went to New Zealand I put him back to his daughter Rusmar Magic Moments, who produced my second champion Rusmar Magic Minstrel. His pigment was very intense and he was a real extrovert; he was slightly longer in body and had a lighter eye. He was also heavier in bone, which I have found happens when I breed from very closely related dogs. Magic had also been put to Iced Diamond, who produced a little bitch called Rusmar Magic Crystal who to this day still has a profuse coat. Crystal had shorter legs and a longer body, so when I was choosing a stud-dog for her I was looking for longer legs and a shorter back. I had always admired Sulyka stock and wanted to use Ch. Sulyka Puzzle, but this was not to be, so I used his son, Bobander Chasing Rainbows, instead. He was taller, with a lovely head, coat and pigment, and he was not at all heavy in bone. His bottom teeth were jumbled but I felt he had so much else to offer me that I was prepared to take the chance. And I am glad that I did. I had just one puppy from this mating, but what a dog he turned out to be: Beau grew up to become Eng., NZ. & Austral. Grand Ch. Rusmar Magic Rainbow. Beau is stunning, in head, eye and expression, and he has super pigment and a luxurious coat. I should have liked a little more neck and a better lay of shoulder, but he moves like a dream and seems to flow round the ring. He has a couple of teeth slightly out of line, which is why I have always tried to deter anyone from using him if their bitch's mouth was not perfect. Beau produced seven UK champions, including two for myself, Rusmar Divine Rainbow and Rusmar Magic Flame. Ann and Lawrence Lee have produced four champions by him; from one of the litters I had a bitch, Ch. Warmingham Ruby Rainbow at Rusmar. The other champion was Ch. Lynelba Per Se, the best dog sired by Beau.

Ch. Warmingham Ruby Rainbow at Rusmar is a bitch I am particularly fond of. She has a lovely nature with big dark eyes. I mated her to my latest dog Rusmar Magic Quest. Quest is the product of a mating between Rusman Magic Kiss (a Magic Minstrel granddaughter) and Ch. Frendors Spitting Image (a Ch. Rusmar Divine Rainbow son). Ruby has had three puppies from this mating Quest, and one bitch looks particularly promising. This mating combines two lines of my own breeding. It is interesting how strengths and weaknesses can manifest themselves in progeny: four generations back on Quest's pedigree are Magic and his litter-sister Krista; Magic had the good rear, Krista the better front, and generations later both of these can be found in the one dog.

I feel I have been extremely lucky to have produced the dogs that I have over the years as I usually only have one or two litters a year, and they are rarely very big. During this time I have continually struggled to improve on pigment and eye colour. At one time I seemed to produce a larger percentage of bad mouths, so I made a conscious effort to improve this wherever possible. Bichons are a relatively healthy breed but the more we breed, the more problems we shall find coming to the surface. It is very important that people should feel free to discuss their problems and the faults that may arise in their breeding programmes without fearing witch-hunts. No one breeder can ever be blamed for anything specific that appears as a result of their breeding. Since the Bichon is a toy dog, it is only to be expected that there will be problems with mouths and slipping patellas, but this in itself is no excuse to stop trying to improve our stock and breed away from dogs that we know to have problems. Generally, our breed is going in the right direction and is pretty fit and healthy. Let's hope we can keep it this way.

## Shamaney and Davyluvs

Margaret Flintoft and David Black were the people recommended to me when I told my friend Rita Edler that I needed to buy the best Bichon I could. I remember being very impressed because when I bought Shamaney Manhattan from them, Margaret wrote out Manhattan's pedigree without referring to anything – it was all in her head! David is the expert at presentation and was responsible for the fact that Manhattan's sire, Ch. Leijazulip Kipling of Shamaney, always looked so good. He was shown regularly in the Champion and Veteran Stakes and was still doing really well when David and Margaret married and then moved to Alicante in Spain. Margaret often comes to England to judge. Her opinion is especially useful because she can offer a fresh eye when she views the dogs. Shamaney Bichons have provided the foundation stock for many kennels, including my Bobander, Myra Atkins's Kynismar, Margaret Hoad's Mahendi, and Sue and Roger Dunger's Sulyka kennels; and they have influenced a number of other kennels through Kipling, who features in many pedigrees throughout the breed.

## Shoolters

Roy Kelman Jack and his wife Betty share a keen interest in all dogs; but the Bichons are Betty's particular love, and she writes some excellent poetry about the breed for the club's publications. Their Shoolters Bichons won their first CCs in 1987 when Shoolters Marmalade Henry (by Shoolters Shabby Tiger out of Shoolters Griselder) won under the late Mme C. J. Koudijs at the Northern and Midland Bichon Frise Club Show. Marmalade Henry's son, Ch. Shoolters What's is Name, was the result of five generations of Shoolters breeding. He was made up in 1996 at the Three Counties Show under breed specialist judge, Jackie Ransom.

## Si'bon

Marion Binder came into Bichons as a Poodle person with considerable knowledge as a breeder and exhibitor. She only ever kept bitches, and very few of them, so considering these restrictions her success in Bichons has to be greatly admired. Marion is probably best known for her very easy-going attitude to exhibiting: she is always fun to be with and she clearly enjoys the lighter, more social side of showing; she has never taken it too seriously, or if she has she has never shown it. She

*Ch. Si'bon Sloane Ranger at Pamplona.*

had a beautiful bitch called Ch. Si'bon Jasmyn, a Ch. Leijazulip Kipling of Shamaney daughter out of Si'bon Soda Pop who was by Ch. Montravia Persan Make Mine Mink. She won two of her CCs while still a puppy and the third when only fourteen months old.

Marion repeated the mating and the result – a bitch called Si'bon Evita – won a single CC at Richmond under Marita Gibbs in 1985. Three years later Si'bon Busy Lizzy won a Reserve CC at Richmond under the late Madeleine Harper (Huntglen). But when Marion sold her Si'bon Fatal Attraction to Michael Coad she couldn't have realized just how successful she was going to be. Fatal was another Jasmyn daughter (but this time by Pengorse Poldark of Tresilva) and the winner of thirty CCs. Next, Marion put Jasmyn to Michael Coad's Ch. Tiopepi Mad Louie at Pamplona and sold one of the puppies, Si'bon Sloane Ranger at Pamplona, to Michael. He too became a champion.

We still see Marion around at local championship shows such as Windsor and Richmond, usually with her close friend Wendy Streatfield, and we all look forward to the occasions when she awards CCs – you can always guarantee that it is never boring when she does!

## Sulyka

### (by Sue and Roger Dunger)

The Sulyka story started almost twenty years ago when we purchased our first Bichons. They were two cute little eight-week-old pups who had classic heads and wonderful temperaments, but little else, and we soon came to realize that they were not going to become the foundation stock we were seeking.

Following our experiences with Rough Collies, we determined right from the outset that we must select a sound base for our breeding programme. Sound meant healthy, well constructed, without exaggeration, typical of the breed, and conforming as closely as possible to the Kennel Club Breed Standard. To be good enough to breed from meant, to us, to be good enough to show, and we have stuck to that maxim to this day. There are no brood-bitches in the Sulyka kennel: we breed only from show stock.

We were fortunate enough to find Shamaney My Choice of Sulyka (Zoe), but Margaret Flintoft-Black wanted her to come to us on breeding terms that meant she had pick of litter and also that she selected the stud-dog. Zoe produced a litter of six to Leijazulip Jazz of Zudiki (later to become an English and Australian champion). This was the first litter Jazz sired and, of course, he went on to become one of the most influential Bichons in the world. When the time came for Margaret to make her 'pick' she chose a small, pretty, well-balanced bitch who went on to become an American champion. Thankfully she overlooked our choice, a dog who turned out to be Eng. and Ir. Ch. Sulyka Snoopy. His career has been well documented: Best of Breed at Crufts in 1984 and 1985, and the very first Bichon to gain both UK and Irish titles. As a stud-dog he was very influential within the breed.

He was twice mated to Vythea Fragrance, who was herself line-bred to Jazz. They produced Snuggle up to Sulyka (Best in Show at the first World Bichon Frise Congress Show) and NZ Grand Ch. Puffin' Billy of Sulyka, (the first Bichon to gain this prestigious title). This mating produced wonderful broad heads with short muzzles and super pigmentation.

Putting Jazz to Zoe was a master stroke. To quote Catherine Sutton who awarded her the Bitch CC at Crufts, in 1984, Zoe was 'a good honest bitch'. Jazz, however, put his stamp on the pups: they had good heads, style and balance. We have striven to maintain and improve upon these qualities by setting standards, which are probably far higher than we shall achieve in our lifetime but which we absolutely refuse to lower.

We were not without the odd problem however. It is an irrefutable fact that short muzzles will produce some undershot mouths and, as with other toy breeds, relatively fine-boned dogs will produce some cases of patella luxation. We were no different to other breeders in this respect but we decided to do something about it for our line. The decision we took was never to breed with affected stock and, moreover, not to permit our dogs to be used on affected animals. From then on, bitches coming to our dogs had to be certified by a veterinary surgeon as free

*NZ Grand Ch. Puffin'
Billy of Sulyka.*

from patella luxation. We were aware that this was not a popular policy, nor was it the complete solution, but it had to improve the chances of producing unaffected offspring. The results have fully vindicated our stance on this matter. At a later date we took our health checking a stage further when we had all our Bichons hips X-rayed. The results showed them all to have excellent hips and at the time of writing we believe we are one of only three kennels to have taken this action.

Before Puffin' Billy left for New Zealand he was mated to two bitches. Each litter produced a pup destined to be important to our line. Sulyka Sacha did much to fix and continue the qualities we wanted, while Ch. Sulyka Puzzle won ten CCs, was Bichon of the Year, and has several Top Stud-dog and Top Sire competitions under his belt. He made his mark quite quickly and many of today's top show Bichons have Puzzle in their pedigrees. At the time of writing Puzzle has produced six UK champions.

Snuggles was mated to Puzzle and they gave us Sulyka Garfield, a Reserve CC winner at Crufts. Although he was a lovely dog, Garfield hated showing. Even so, our good friends John and Wendy Hutchinson of the famous Monjoie kennels saw potential and took him to Australia where he has produced well for them. When we stayed with them in 1993, we were very taken with a dog in their kennel and we brought him home with us. Monjoie de Lumiere a Sulyka (Louie) is the sire of Ch. Sulyka Happy Hurbert. It should come as no surprise that John and Wendy like our stock and we theirs: we share common principles, breed from similar bloodlines, and strive to produce the same sort of results – so much so that our breeding programmes are fairly well entwined. It's a pity we have so many miles between us and that quarantine restricts the passage of dogs between our two kennels.

*Ch. Sulyka Happy Hurbert.*

We are very much aware of the dangers of breeding only with our own stock, so from time to time we look to introduce 'outcrosses'. It is impossible to totally outcross in our breed because the gene pool is so small, but we try to select good specimens that are not too closely related (although we like to see a common ancestor in the past three or four generations).This philosophy produced Ch. Honeylyn Step in Style to Sulyka and Eng. and Austral. Ch. Honeylyn Timmy Tiptoes to Sulyka. Step in Style was the result of mating Puzzle to Honeylyn Sweetheart, a bitch we had long admired, and Timmy the result of mating Bossy Boots of Honeylyn and Honeylyn Silken Tassle (a Puzzle daughter). We also used a very under-rated dog, Honeylyn Sammy Soapsud, on Sulyka Sasha to produce Sulyka Belinda Bubbles, who in turn produced Happy Hurbert.

We continue to set ourselves very high standards and, consequently, very few Sulyka-bred Bichons appear in the show ring. There are a small band of people throughout the world who have our stock, and these folk have had the patience to wait for something that we have considered worthy to send them. Mostly they have proved to be winners in the show ring and good producers for their owners. Sulyka dogs have been influential foundation stock in many kennels in the UK and abroad, notably the Leewards kennel of Jaana Leinonen in Finland (the destination of Sulyka Boomerang who won many titles throughout Scandinavia and

216

Europe); Avana Mickey Mouse of Sulyka, a Puzzle offspring, was sent to Brazil where he has become a very famous champion as well as being the basis of Roberta and Cristina Da Veiga's Dreams Came True kennel.

## Tamalva

Val Cumstey and her very well-known daughter Tamara Dawson share this affix. It is fast becoming a considerable success story with a champion in each of their breeds, Bichons and Tibetan Terriers. Tamara's handling skills are second to none. Their Ch. Tamalva Keep the Faith for Mistama, a bitch with eleven CCs and two group wins, has gone on to produce another lovely bitch, Tamalva Runnin' On Faith, who I have no doubt will follow on in her dam's footsteps.

## Tresilva and Suanalu

It is impossible to write about these affixes separately because the two kennels work together as a team. Jackie Ransom (Tresilva) had some success in the early days with her home-bred Bichon, Ch. Gosmore Tresilva Zorba (at one time owned by Audrey Dallison) and handled by Geoff Corish when he became the first male UK champion in 1980. In the early 1980s, Jackie Ransom bought two more bitches, Leijazulip Jacqueline of Tresilva and Pengorse Felicity of Tresilva, and campaigned them to their titles with the help of her sister-in-law Marjorie. But it wasn't until 1990 that the Tresilva kennel teamed up with Joan Gadd-Davies of the Suanalu affix. With Joan's talent for beautiful presentation and her enthusiasm for campaigning the Tresilva dogs, the two kennels have together become a significant force. With the help of Geoff Corish and Michael Coad, their Tresilva Toby of Suanalu was crowned and, since then they have produced a further four champions: Tresilva Minuette of Honeylyn, Tresilva Little Madam at Suanalu, Tresilva Snowden at Suanalu and, their latest girl, Ch. Tresilva Bright Spark at Suanalu.

Jackie is one of the country's top all-rounder judges. She also writes for *Dog World* newspaper as a breed-note correspondent, and is well known for her thought-provoking articles. Her greatest contribution to the Tresilva/Suanalu team is made behind the scenes as breeder and enthusiastic promoter of her lines, leaving Joan to take the spotlight in the ring, which she certainly did at Crufts 1998 when she took Best of Breed with Bright Spark.

Jackie has been responsible for much of the advancement of the breed. Her book *The Bichon Frise* was first published in 1978, only four years after the breed was introduced to the UK; now out of print, it is a sought-after collector's item. Her second book on the breed *The Bichon Frise Pedigree Book*, is essential reading for anyone who wants to trace the ancestry of a particular Bichon right back to the early imports and beyond. Jackie is a great character, whose long-standing passion for the breed has made her name synonymous with it.

## Twinley

The late Pauline Block was the secretary of the Bichon Club of Great Britain when I started out in the breed. She was a tremendous enthusiast for all dogs, as well as her Bichons (some of whom she sent abroad), and she made up champions in Tibetan Spaniels, Chihuahuas and Pharaoh Hounds. In Bichons, a UK title eluded her, although Chris Belcher and Richard Blackwell almost succeeded for her when they campaigned Twinley Pantomime Prince at Melsel to two CCs. His career was abruptly brought to an end when his tail was cut in suspicious circumstances and he became nervous and uneasy with strangers.

Pauline sent some of her dogs abroad, and was one of the first people to import a Bichon: Astir de Chaponay of Twinley, bred in Belgium by Mme A. Berben, was exhibited at the first Bichon Frise Club show in 1978. There were eight other Bichons shown that day, all bred by Pauline – such was her influence in those important early days.

## Vythea

Ivy Colvin and her daughter Anthea have been responsible for a large number of lovely dogs, many of them CC winners and gaining their titles. Anthea started showing as a junior and won the highly acclaimed Junior Handler of the Year, but with a Shih Tzu not a Bichon. Her first claim to fame within the breed was with Gosmore Tresilva Crystal (a bitch born in 1978 out of Zena De Chaponay of Tresilva and by Zethus De Chaponay of Tresilva), whom she handled at the first Crufts when the first set of CCs were awarded. Crystal won the Reserve CC. They also had much success with Vythea the Page Boy, a Ch. Leijazulip Jazz son, and then Vythea Thistledown (by Ch. Kynismar Boogaloo), who won the bitch CC at the East of England show under judge Ferelith Somerfield. But it wasn't until they used another of Myra's dogs, Ch. Kynismar Boogie's Boy, that they had a champion, Vythea Jumpin' Jack Flash, who also won the toy group at Richmond Championship Show in 1991. Their next champion was a bitch, Snow

White Pippah at Vythea, and the next Vythea Jack's The Lad at Melsel, a dog owned by Chris Belcher and Richard Blackwell.

Anthea now has children of her own, but this doesn't prevent her from still continuing to breed and campaign some lovely dogs that are always immaculately presented and handled. Ivy had been on the committee of the Bichon Frise Club of Great Britain for many years and took over the role as chairman when Pauline Block became ill. Anthea also worked on the committee and was the treasurer until her son was born. Her latest boy (a Bichon), Vythea Columbus, is already on his way to his title.

## *Warmingham*

This kennel, owned by Ann and Lawrence Lee, is quite a success story, most notably in the last few years. In a career in dogs spanning three decades, more than half of it in Bichons, it wasn't until 1994 that they made up their first champion, Warmingham Hobson's Choice. They had decided to use a different dog on their bitches, and they chose Ch. Rusmar Magic Rainbow for the task. The combination of their closely bred bitches and this dog certainly worked some magic. From repeat matings. they bred four champions in less than two years. The girl who really stole the limelight was Ch. Warmingham Scarlet O'Hara who won not only the top Bichon award for 1997 but the Top Toy event at Stafford in February 1998 – a remarkable achievement for any kennel. The Lees have also been the breed's top breeders for 1994, 1996 and 1997.

*Ch. Warmingham Crack of Dawn.*

## *Zudiki*

Jo Emmerson (née Brown) was already a very successful breeder of Afghan Hounds when she made up Ch. Leijazulip Jazz of Zudiki, who became the first champion to win a group. Jazz's fame is world wide, and his success as a sire is well recorded. He and his brother Kipling were the two most important and influential early dogs. Because of her personal circumstances, Jo had to sell Jazz, early in his career, to John and Wendy Hutchinson in Australia, with whom he continued to enjoy great success.

Jo later had a Jazz son, Monjoie Pride of Zudiki, sent back from Australia. He sired many prominent dogs for other people as well as Jo. He could offer British breeders the benefit of his dam's Austral. Ch. Azara Ma Belle Ami lines, as well as Jazz's. Ch. Avana Madam I'm Adam was a first for Jayne Smith. He is also behind Margaret Hoad's Ch. Mahendi Miss Bliss. Jo no longer exhibits Bichons but she still judges and awards CCs in both Bichons and Afghan Hounds.

# USA

### (by Ann Hearn)

The early Bichons that were imported into the United States came from various bloodlines, including de Steren Vor and de Warnarby from France, and Milton, Villa Sainval, Chaponay, and de la Buthiere from Belgium. From France came the whiter coats and the finer, more delicate toy-like structure, and from Belgium came the heavier-bodied, more 'up on leg' dogs that had creamier, but profuse, coats.

Official American Kennel Club recognition of the Bichon Frise came in 1963, and those of us who had been entering our Bichons in Miscellaneous classes – a sort of introductory and proving class for new breeds – were delighted when we were finally able to show and finish our early breeding stock. One of the first American Bichons to become a champion was Ch. Jalwyre Veni Vidi Vici, a bitch from a mating that I helped to plan for some local breeders.

It is often said that Americans want 'bigger and better'. While 'better' is certainly in the eye of the beholder, bigger we have achieved. Upon recognition of the breed, the American Kennel Club required us to decide whether the Bichon Frise should be classified in the Toy or Non-Sporting Group. We felt that although we were basing our Breed

Standard on the original French – and had found the dogs from France to be more petite – we did not want the Bichon to be classified as a toy dog. Rather, we wanted him to be of sufficient height to encapsulate elegance, and with enough length of leg to provide the movement and stride befitting an active, playful 'circus' dog. So after a great deal of discussion among the members of the Bichon Frise Club of America, it was voted that the Bichon should be put into the Non-Sporting Group to compete against breeds as large as the Dalmatian, as hefty as the Bulldog, and as diminutive as the Schipperke.

Eddie de Steren Vor, Etoile de Steren Vor, Gipsie de Warnarby and Gigi de Hoop from France were some of the first Bichons imported to the States. They were purchased and brought over by the Picaults, and eventually owned by Gertrude Fournier. This was fortunate for the breed as Mrs Fournier had many friends already involved in breeding and exhibiting dogs, which meant that the Bichon's introduction to the enthusiastic Americans was a speedy one. Barbara Stubbs's book, *The Complete Bichon Frise* (*see* Bibliography) can provide you with a history of the early American Bichon, including the French, Belgian and English imports. However there are three or four dogs from the UK that have done so much for the breed that I feel they must be mentioned here. When Wendy Streatfield introduced some American bloodlines to her English stock she

*Am. Ch. Leander Snow Star (UK imp.).*

221

produced Leander Snow Star. Laura Purnell, of the highly successful Stillwell kennels in Kansas, bought Snow Star and introduced him to the US show scene at the prestigious Westminster Show in New York. Everyone agreed that he was exactly what we had been looking for. We already had sound, good-bodied (but longish), pretty-faced, excellent-coated Bichons; what we did not have was elegance, style and presence. We also needed a bit more leg to provide the propulsion to create the 'wind-blowing-from-behind' look. Eureka! Laura had found it. From Snow Star there were thirty-four champions who formed the foundation stock of many breeders throughout the States. Quite a few bitches from various bloodlines were brought to this dog. I have had several champions out of my bitches when bred to Snow Star.

Den Thomas, an English handler and Bichon breeder of renown, brought a small but typey dog over and made a US champion of him: Roushka's Solo Dancer went on to produce fourteen champions bred to different bitches. But the pinnacle of English bloodlines introduced to the US came from the vision of Roy Copelin of the Sumarco kennel. I had known Roy and his family since he first got into dogs while he was in my hometown of Atlanta, Georgia. From the start Roy's goal was to have a top-producing male that would do for Bichons what the Dalmatian Ch. Fireman's Freckled Friend had done for the Dalmatian community. (Freckled Friend still holds the record of top-producing dog of all breeds in the US.) His business frequently sent him to England where he met Mrs Pauline Gibbs of the Montravia kennel; she finally succumbed to Roy's enthusiasm and sold him the dog that was to become Am. Ch. Montravia Jazz M Tazz. This dog produced twenty-seven champions – a fairly impressive record in itself. But the proof of a superlative dog is in what follows that first generation. Jazz M Tazz produced a dog that Roy named Ch. Sumarco's Top Gun who produced twenty-six champions, as well as a gorgeous bitch bred by Doris Hyde of Fairfield, Connecticut, named Ch. Dove Cotes Poise N Ivory who has produced fourteen champions all by one sire, Ch. Dove Cotes Mister Magoo. The saddest part of this story is that our creative genius, Roy Copelin, died of a heart attack without fully realizing the gift he had given his fellow breeder friends.

The American breeding programme would certainly have progressed without the established bloodlines from England – which must also include Kynismar (Myra Atkins) and Sulyka (Sue and Roger Dunger) – but not with the speed that it has. Indeed, the Bichon Frise is most fortunate in that its breeders communicate internationally, enjoy mutual support and encouragement, and ultimately appreciate each other's contribution to the development of the breed.

222

# Bibliography

Eerden, P.J. *Teyde a Bichon Frise*, Padache Desktop Publishing, Australia (1995).

Horner, Tom, *Take Them Round, Please: The Art of Judging Dogs,* David & Charles (1975).

Ransom, E. Jackie, *The Bichon Frise,* H.F. & G. Witherby Ltd (1990).

Ransom, E. Jackie, *The Dog Directory Guide to The Bichon Frise,* Dog Directory (1978, out of print).

Stubbs, Barbara B. *The Complete Bichon Frise,* Howell Book House (1990).

# Index

affix, 59, 60
afterbirth, 150, 151
    retained, 151

bathing, 81, 81–4, 145, 157
bedding, 62
bite, 54–5
bladder stones, 159–60
breed clubs, 23–6
breeding, 133–46
breeding terms, 59
breed standard,
        American, 30–3
        first, 33–5
        UK, 27–30
        understanding the, 36–47
brood-bitch, assessing the,
        142–3
        nursing, 154, 155–6
        pregnant, 147–8
        see also whelping

Challenge Certificates, 107,
        116–18
champion, making, a 116–20
critique writing, 132
Crufts, 107, 108
coprophagy, 160

defects, hereditary, 54–7,
        139–41, 164–8
dew-claws, 101
diarrhoea, 160–1
diet, 61, 66–71, 77
        adult, 68–71
        brood-bitch, 147–8, 154
        elderly dog, 79
        puppy, 66-8, 158

ears, care of, 100
eclampsia, 155–6
endorsements, 57–9, 62
euthanasia, 79
exercise, 77–8, 79, 110

faeces, eating, 160
feeding, see diet
fussy eaters, 71
fault-judging, 127–8
faults, conformational, 45–7,
        90–3
        see also defects
fontanelle, open, 165

genetics, 137–41
grooming, 80–103
        equipment, 81–2
        workshops, 84
        see also trimming

handling, junior, 120–3
        see also ring procedure
hip dysplasia, 164
hot spots, 161
hypothermia, 161–2
identification, 78
inbreeding, 134
inertia, uterine, 152
judging, 111–14, 124–32

kennel cough, 162

line-breeding, 134

mastitis, 156
mating, 144–6

obedience, 75–6
oestrus, 145
outcrossing, 134–7

parasites, 163–4
patella, luxating, 166–7
pedigrees, 61
Perthes disease, 167–8
pigment, 40, 45, 56–7, 112–13
postnatal problems, 155–6
pregnancy, phantom, 147
puppies, assessing, 52–7

feeding, 66–8, 155, 157
postnatal development of,
        157
        see also whelping

registration, 59
rescue, 51–2
ring procedure, 111–15

season, see oestrus
show, choosing a puppy for,
        49–50, 52, 54–7
        entering a, 108-9
        preparing for, 109–10
        training for, 74, 104
        trimming for, 84–100
        types of, 106–8
        see also handling
showing, 104–23
        equipment for, 110
        reasons for, 104–6
soft palate, spasm of the, 168
staining, 81, 98, 99, 109
stewarding, 125–6
stifle, slipping, see patella
stud-dog, choosing a, 143–4
Super Match, 26

teeth, care of, 102–3
tie, 146
training, 71–7
travel sickness, 162–3
trimming, 84–100
        equipment, 88
        for balance, 89–99
        nails, 101–2
        the pet Bichon, 103

vaccination, 61, 64–5

whelping, 148–53
        complications in, 152–3
        signs of imminent, 149
worming, 61, 163